ECONOMIC POLICY
IN SOCIALIST YUGOSLAVIA

Soviet and East European Studies

Editorial Board

T0318175

ECONOMIC POLICY IN
SOCIALIST YUGOSLAVIA

RUDOLF BIĆANIĆ

CAMBRIDGE
AT THE UNIVERSITY PRESS
1973

CAMBRIDGE UNIVERSITY PRESS
Cambridge, New York, Melbourne, Madrid, Cape Town, Singapore,
São Paulo, Delhi, Dubai, Tokyo, Mexico City

Cambridge University Press
The Edinburgh Building, Cambridge CB2 8RU, UK

Published in the United States of America by Cambridge University Press, New York

www.cambridge.org
Information on this title: www.cambridge.org/9780521153300

First published 1973
First paperback printing 2010

A catalogue record for this publication is available from the British Library

Library of Congress Catalogue Card Number: 72–80588

ISBN 978-0-521-08631-8 Hardback
ISBN 978-0-521-15330-0 Paperback

Contents

Contents

Foreword

Rudolf Bićanić was to the study of Yugoslav economic conditions and policy as Pigou was to Marshallian economics: he infused it with a social consciousness generated by his innate humanitarianism, and fostered by his early experiences.

Born in 1905 in Bjelovar (Croatia), he was initiated into the harsher realities of economics with the world depression: after completing law studies in Zagreb and Paris he sold his not inconsiderable collection of books in a vain effort to staunch his father's bankruptcy. From that time on, he became active in the Croat Peasant Party, but incurred a term of imprisonment (1932–5) when found in possession of a stock of pamphlets condemning King Alexander's personal rule. He described that goal as his most formative influence, collaborating there with his fellow-prisoner, the Croat leader Macek, on a new economic and social programme for the Peasant Party. Released after the king's assassination, Bićanić devoted his time as political activist and journalist to the study of the poorest rural regions of the country: travelling mostly on foot, he crossed the Dinaric Alps from Split, and from intimate knowledge of the villages of Dalmatinska Zagora could entitle his first book *Kako živi narod* (How the People Live) in 1936. His next study, *Ekonomska podloga Hrvatskog pitanja* (The Economic Foundation of the Croatian Question) of 1938, which went to the heart of the economic and political duality of Yugoslav development and which was forthwith banned, was among the influences conducing to the admission of the Peasant Party to the government in the following year. Under that coalition, Bićanić became director of the Yugoslav Board for Foreign Trade; the negotiations he undertook included a mission to the Soviet Union and a meeting with Mikoyan. When the German invasion forced the government to take refuge in London, he accompanied it as deputy governor of the National Bank but declared against the Royalist faction and for the Partisans in 1942. He thus held office in the Tito-Šubašić administration in liberated Belgrade but soon preferred the new Chair of Economic Policy in the Law Faculty of Zagreb, which he occupied from 1946 until his death in 1968. Again, though under a radically different government, his research incurred official disapproval and, unable to publish his studies of contemporary economic policy, he turned to economic history. *Doba manufakture u Hrvatskoj* (The Early Factory Period in Croatia) was criticized on its appearance in 1951 for being insufficiently marxist, but he maintained his interpretation for the drafts, never completed, of two further volumes, devoted respectively to the industrial revolution and to nineteenth-century economic thought in Croatia.

The change in the intellectual climate of the mid-fifties found him more anxious to re-enter the contemporary field than to devote himself to history; articles in local, European and American journals made him the most internationally known of Yugoslav economists. In 1962 his book *Ekonomska politika FNRJ* (Economic Policy of the Yugoslav Federation) confirmed that reputation in his own country. Two sabbatical years in the United States (University of Texas at Austin, and Center for Advanced Studies in Behavioral Sciences at Palo Alto), and lectures and conferences from Oxford to Melbourne and from Tokyo to Caracas, brought his wisdom and warmth to countless audiences in economics faculties and their students, but he made ample time both for his own pupils at Zagreb, many of whom now hold senior posts in Yugoslav ministries and universities, and for two further books, published in English – *Planning, East and West* (1966) and *Turning Points in Economic Development* (posthumous, 1972). His last article, published after his death with its conclusions only as abbreviated notes, was characteristically on 'The Unity of the Yugoslav Economy', and he wrote all but two of the chapters of the present book, which was completed by his colleague of a quarter-century, Marijan Hanzeković, Professor of Economics at Zagreb University, and edited by Dubravko Matko of the Institute of Soviet and East European Studies, University of Glasgow. The contribution of his English-born wife, Sonia, docent in the Faculty of Philosophy at Zagreb University, was as important in giving this book its final form as was her intellectual and moral encouragement throughout the vicissitudes of the postwar years.

St Antony's College, Oxford   MICHAEL KASER

I

The economics of the creation of Yugoslavia

The political changes of 1918, when Yugoslavia was created, meant the creation of a new economic entity different in both size and structure from previous political formations. It was more than merely a question of a new economic entity in a quantitative sense (size of population, territory, national income and wealth, etc.). There was a qualitative change too, i.e. a new socio-economic structure appeared with its own special characteristics. Instead of the more or less liberal industrial capitalism of pre-war Austro-Hungary, the stage was set for the creation of a new monopoly capitalism. But monopoly capitalism in Yugoslavia had only a small and rather poorly-developed area in which to operate, although it tried to conceal this by resounding slogans about the formation of national capital in a national state. In point of fact the capital was to a large extent foreign dominated and the state was multinational.

The new economic unit

The formation in 1918 of the new political unit of Yugoslavia meant a change in the size and structure of the market. This was the first fundamental fact. Secondly, the new customs frontiers put the constituent parts of the national economy in a fresh situation *vis-à-vis* the international set-up. Within the new political territory itself great changes had to take place: first there was a disintegration of the old economic territorial units (the Kingdoms of Serbia and Montenegro, the Yugoslav parts of the Hapsburg[1] and Ottoman Empires), then a period of adaptation

---

[1] Some of these were autonomous, like the Kingdom of Croatia, others were administrative units with their local diets and governors (Dalmatia, Istria, Carynthia, Bosnia and Hercegovina). Still others were parts of other provinces with centres outside present-day Yugoslavia (parts of Styria, Hungary, Bulgaria).

followed by gradual integration into a new economic system. These processes were neither easy nor painless, and were concealed by the threefold screen of political conflict, the aftermath of the war and inflation.

Without an analysis of these economic changes it is not possible to understand the great political movements which attracted the dissatisfied masses after the First World War, the ultimate breakdown of the Kingdom of Yugoslavia or present-day economic problems such as the economic reform.

Drawing the new political frontiers

For most of the people who found themselves citizens of the new state, the formation of Yugoslavia meant an absolute reduction in the size of the domestic market. Those areas which had been part of the economic and political formation of Austro-Hungary, with a population of 59 million, now found themselves within the frontiers of Yugoslavia which numbered 12 million people. A market of 677,000 square kilometres was for them reduced to a unit with no more than 248,000 square kilometres. For pre-war Serbia the process was the other way round; the new state meant an increase from an economy embracing 2.9 million people to a market with four times that number. Thus in Serbia a feeling of national pride was created by the number of things one could now buy on the domestic market, while in Slovenia, Croatia, Vojvodina and Bosnia people were surprised to find how little the domestic market had to offer. This was also partly true of Macedonia, formerly part of the Turkish Empire, which gravitated economically towards the south. It was not so with the remote inland areas of Sandjak and the Kingdom of Montenegro which gravitated largely to the Adriatic coast.

Self-congratulation on one side and disappointment on the other were to be at the root of many tensions in the future between those who considered it their sacred mission to consolidate their war gains and build up a self-contained (autarchic) National State, and those who felt more or less clearly that the development of the country's economy required larger markets and a wider extension of economic forces than the Yugoslav frontiers permitted. The former developed a sense of economic xenophobia, originating in an inferiority complex about under-development and an insecurity caused by fear of foreign com-petition. The latter considered themselves able to meet foreign competition on an equal footing in specialized fields of produc-tion, as had been the case before 1914, and they favoured an open economy which would trade with foreign countries on a wide scale. This struggle between two conceptions continued through the inter-war period and even after the socialist revolu-tion. Not until the mid-sixties did it become clear to the majority of people that even if the area of Yugoslavia were ten times larger and her income per head four times bigger this would still not provide a basis for a successful autarchic policy.

Not only was the new market smaller in size in the absolute sense, its productive capacity was also smaller and the pur-chasing power of the population smaller still. The national income per head in the Austrian part of Austro-Hungary was 5,200 dinars (at 1938 values) and in the Hungarian part 4,400 dinars per head. The average income per head of the new state of Yugoslavia was some 3,000 dinars. The new Yugoslav con-sumer was a poorer one who could only afford poorer-quality goods and this affected both agrarian and industrial production unfavourably. Moreover, the fixed assets of Yugoslav national wealth fell between 1909–12 and 1919 by 8 per cent, or 241 milliard dinars, and the pre-war level was not reached again until 1925. Most of these losses occurred in Serbia and Mace-donia. The national income fell by 7 per cent as a result of the war, and regained the pre-war level only in 1923.[1]

The new area was also different with regard to sectors of production. In the industrial-agrarian Austro-Hungarian eco-nomic territory the agricultural products of Croatia, Vojvodina and Slovenia had found ample markets in the industrial parts of the state. Serbia was a homogeneous agrarian state which also exported agricultural products to the same market. The new economic territory of Yugoslavia was predominantly agricul-tural and so there was no longer a domestic market which could absorb the surpluses of agricultural production.

The economic position of some territories also underwent

[1] I. Vinski, '*Nacionalni dohodak i fiksni fondovi na području Jugoslavije*' (National income and fixed funds in the territory of Yugoslavia 1909–1959), *Ekonomski pregled*, no. 11–12 (1959).

relative changes. For example Croatia, which had been one of the least developed parts of Austro-Hungary, suddenly found itself one of the most developed parts of the new political entity. The size of this relative change for the economies of Croatia, Slovenia and Vojvodina may be shown by a few examples. Pre-1914 Croatia, Slavonia and Dalmatia, made up 23 per cent of the territory of the newly-created state of Yugoslavia in 1918 with 27 per cent of its population and 33 per cent of its industrial workers. Their trade amounted to 27 per cent of the total internal trade of Yugoslavia. The greatest change in concentration was manifest in the field of banking and financial capital. In 1912 the banks and credit institutions of Croatia had altogether only 5.4 per cent of the assets of the banking and credit institutions of Hungary, whereas in 1921 the capital concentrated in the banks of Croatia amounted to 50 per cent of the total bank capital of Yugoslavia.

In the new territory Zagreb became the strongest financial centre, as well as the biggest industrial and commercial centre, but it lost both its administrative position and its political power and could not reconcile itself to this. Political and military power were concentrated in Belgrade, which tried to compensate for its economic disadvantages by becoming the leading political centre.

The changing role of foreign trade

Because of the changes in frontiers after 1918, foreign trade in the new political territory became much more important and played a much more propulsive role than it had under the old political set-up. The volume of foreign trade grew faster than the national income. The bulk of the exchange of goods which beforehand had been a matter of domestic trade within Austro-Hungary or the Turkish Empire, now, because of the new customs frontiers, became international trade. This was especially true of the exchange of goods between agriculture and industry, which began to have a significant effect upon the balance of payments. It is also true that what had earlier been foreign trade between Serbia and Montenegro and the Austro-Hungarian and Ottoman Empires now became internal trade, but, in spite of increased inter-provincial exchange after the war, this amount cannot be compared with the former. It is surprising to see how little trade in industrial products there had been before the war between the various parts of Yugoslavia. For instance, in 1912 the larger factories in Croatia and Slavonia exported 31 per cent of their total products to Austria and 42 per cent to Hungary, while only 5.5 per cent went to Bosnia and Hercegovina and 6.7 per cent to Rijeka. Serbia bought only 0.4 per cent of Croatian industrial exports. On the import side, the total purchases by Croatian industry in Serbia amounted to 300,000 gold crowns (or 1 per cent) of a total value for imports of industrial products of 29 million crowns.[1] Macedonian trade showed similar tendencies, being directed mainly south, towards Salonika.

The separation in 1914 by political and customs frontiers of producers from their traditional markets meant a great change in the whole structure of the economy. In 1910, livestock and livestock products were exported from the present territory of Yugoslavia to an annual value of 3.5 milliard dinars, while on an average between 1921 and 1927 the whole of Yugoslavia exported only 1.9 milliard dinars per annum of livestock and livestock products – little more than half the pre-war value.[2] It is true that livestock suffered from the effects of the First World War, and also that the volume of exports fell in the first years after the land reform. But there is no doubt that commercial policy played a great role in the reduction of exports and caused important losses to the most advanced regions in Yugoslavia.[3]

Wine was bought and sold internally all over Austro-Hungary before the First World War and was not subject to customs duties. So Dalmatian wine could be bought duty-free in Vienna, Prague, Lwow, Cracow, etc. Exports of wine, which before the war amounted to 48 million gold crowns (or 770 million post-war dinars) annually, fell to between 7 and 14 million dinars a

[1] *Statistički atlas Kraljevine Hrvatske i Slavonije* (Statistical atlas of the Kingdom of Croatia and Slavonija) (Zagreb, 1915).
[2] V. Stipetić, *Kretanje i tendencije u razvitku poljoprivredne proizvodnje na području NR Hrvatske* (Trends and tendencies in the development of agricultural production on the territory of the People's Republic of Croatia) (Zagreb, 1959), pp. 97, 174.
[3] The export of cattle from Croatia amounted in 1910 to 71 million gold crowns; from Bosnia and Hercegovina 8 million; from Vojvodina (Srijem excluded) 85 million; from Serbia 18 million (in 1911 this increased to 38 million gold dinars); and from Slovenia 17 million gold crowns.

year in 1921–7. This affected especially badly the wine-growing areas of Croatia, Vojvodina and Eastern Serbia.

The food-processing industry was also affected. In pre-war times it was specially favoured by the Hungarian Government, which gave state premiums for exports of flour, sugar and alcohol. After the war these exports were considerably less, causing the biggest losses to Vojvodina and Croatia. When the first post-war hunger in Central Europe had been satisfied, the flour mills in Yugoslavia were greatly affected by the loss of markets. Exports of flour in 1923 still amounted to 239 million dinars, but in 1927 they had already fallen to 89 million, and in 1928 to a bare 8 million dinars a year.

The alcohol distilleries reduced their total production to one-tenth of their capacity and their export in 1923 amounted to only 1 per cent of their productive capacity. The fish-canning industry on the Adriatic was heavily hit. The 23 factories on the coast used to supply the whole Austro-Hungarian market but for the new and poorer territory of Yugoslavia their products were too expensive and their capacity too large and they were therefore only able to work at 25 per cent of capacity.

The autarchic industrialization policy

Industrial development presented the other side of the picture. A vacuum in the supply of industrial products was felt as a result of the creation of the new customs and political frontiers. The old suppliers of industrial products in Central Europe (Czechoslovakia, Austria, Hungary) were now cut off and frontiers prevented the free flow of goods from abroad. The first consequence was that some branches of industry within Yugoslavia started to expand very fast. In 1919, 109 factories were opened in Yugoslavia, in 1920, 144 and in 1922, 170 – the largest number started up in any one year between the two wars.

The policy of industrialization also affected the structure of fixed capital. Taking 1919 as 100, total fixed capital increased to 119 by 1929. Industrial fixed assets rose to 183, while fixed assets in agriculture remained at only 117, and in transport grew even more slowly (107). This shows to what extent the new situation favoured industrial capital formation, and how neglected and exploited agriculture was, in spite of the fact that

77 per cent of the active population made their living from agriculture. On the other hand, fixed assets in housing increased considerably, because of growing urbanization.[1] The following government measures were taken to control industrialization: increased customs duties; considerable but one-sided credits for industrial development, given by the National Bank and the State Mortgage Bank; opening of state mines; granting of mining concessions; developments of transport by the use of public funds and subsidies for industries.

Customs duties were mainly determined from the outset by the policy of creating domestic industries. This had already been evident in the pre-war Serbian customs tariff of 1903 which was now extended to Yugoslavia as a whole. The new customs tariff of 1925 increased protection still more.

The customs import duties of 1925 amounted, for specific groups of commodities such as ceramics and glass, to 50–100 per cent, for agricultural products and food to 20–100 per cent, alcohol and beverages 300 per cent, metal industries 20–50 per cent, machines 5–15 per cent, textiles and hides 10–30 per cent, and some chemical industries 50–100 per cent. Besides import duties there were also at this time quite heavy export duties introduced especially for the export of certain foods and live-stock, raw materials such as hides, linseeds, oil seeds, scrap metal, rags, timber, etc.[2] For instance, imports of raw cotton amounted in 1923 to 20.5 per cent of the total weight of imported cotton and cotton fabrics and in 1930 increased to 40.8 per cent. The general tendency was to reduce imports of fabricated products and to increase imports of raw materials and semi-finished products. Imports of finished cotton fabrics fell from 57.6 per cent to 30.9 per cent of the total imports of cotton. Imports of woollen fabrics were reduced between 1923 and 1930 from 60 to 29 per cent of total wool imports and imports of raw wool increased from 23 to 47 per cent. (These figures are related to the total weight of wool and woollen products.) A similar tendency is seen in iron imports. Imports of pig iron increased from 29 to 36 per cent, while imports of iron products fell from 71 to 64 per cent.

[1] Vinski, *Ekonomski pregled*, no. 11–12 (1959).
[2] M. Savić, *Industrija i carinska tarifa* (Industry and customs duties) (Belgrade, 1929), pp. 23–4, 37.

Before 1925 this protection was 23 per cent of the value of imported industrial products, and after 1925 it amounted to 32 per cent. In 1931, during the great crisis, customs protection increased to an average of 46 per cent. A similar policy of domestic autarchy was also practised by other countries in Eastern and Southern Europe (Austria, Czechoslovakia and Italy on the industrial side, and on the agricultural Hungary, Poland, Romania and Bulgaria). Agrarian countries protected their industries by customs duties and industrial countries protected their agricultural production. In this way the volume of their mutual trade declined, and they all became more vulnerable to crises.

Customs protection in Yugoslavia particularly favoured textiles, leather, hides, metal and other general consumer foods industries (Table 1).

This policy then was one of highly-protected industrialization at the expense of the domestic consumer. The agricultural producer was cut off from his external market and left to the mercy of 'national' dealers, who were in fact very often middlemen or agents of foreign firms. There was a general fall in the standard of living and that the great mass of peasant producers were enormously worse off can be seen by the wide opening of the price scissors in favour of industrial over agricultural prices. This was still more emphasized by the monetary policy of deflation after January 1923, which imitated the monetary policy dictated after the Genoa Conference in 1922 by international financial capital. Table 1 shows the disparity between prices of agricultural and industrial products in Croatia, which can, by and large, be taken to be representative for the whole of Yugoslavia. In constant prices, expressed in gold, the 1926 prices show the following increases compared to those of 1913: a man's shirt which before the war cost 1.2 gold crowns was sold after the war at 4.27 gold crowns (index 356); woollen fabric after the war was at index 273, coffee 242, salt 129, and sugar 151 (taking the pre-war prices in gold equivalent as 100).

Other manufactured articles of general consumption showed still greater differences. For instance paraffin (*kerosene*) had an index of 211, soap 272, matches 454. In 1928 the indices of retail prices (1914 = 100) were 145 for food, 190 for textiles and 177 for all other consumption goods. The general index of

TABLE I

Price disparity between agricultural and industrial goods in Croatia

	Quantity	Price in gold		
		1913 crowns	1926 dinars	1913 = 100
Arable land	1 ha	1,670	1,273	76
Wheat	1 q	22	24.09	109
Sugar beet	1 q	2.60	2.18	84
Maize	1 q	16.50	16.80	102
Wine	1 hl	46	45.50	99
Fattened oxen	1 kg	0.65	0.68	105
Fattened pigs	1 kg	1.12	1.13	101
Superphosphate	1 mtc	7.76	8.45	109
Copper sulphate	1 kg	0.65	0.91	140
Saltpetre	1 kg	28.0	47.30	169
Bricks	1,000	28	54.50	195
Plough	1	58	91	157
Cart	1	160	364	227
Scythe	1	2	3.2	160
Maize drill	1	55	77.3	140
Man's cotton shirt	1	1.2	4.27	356
Woollen cloth	1 m	3	8.20	273
Sandals	1 pair	3	11.82	394
Hat	1	2.40	10.9	454
Salt	1 kg	0.28	0.36	129
Sugar	1 kg	0.96	1.45	151
Coffee	1 kg	3	7.27	242
Matches	100 boxes	2	9.08	454
Paraffin	1 lt	0.28	0.59	211
Soap	1 kg	0.60	1.63	272
Yeast	1 kg	1	2.54	254

SOURCE: S. Poštić, *Istraživanje o realnosti reformiranog katastra zemljišta* (Research into the rationality of reformed land cadastral) (Zagreb, 1935), Table 7.

consumer goods, again taking 1914 as the base year, rose as high as 168. In more concrete terms,[1] before the war 1 quintal of maize would buy one suit for a peasant, or one pair of good boots. After the war 2½ quintals of maize were necessary to buy a pair of boots, and a suit would cost the equivalent of 4 quintals of maize.

In 1913 for the equivalent of one pair of average oxen a peasant could buy 20 ploughs. After the war they would bring him only 10 ploughs. For the same price in oxen before the war he could buy 2 drills or 4 new carts, but after the war only 2 carts or half a drill could be bought. One quintal of hay was equivalent before the war to a can of kerosene or 3 packets of nails. After the war a can of kerosene cost 3 to 5 quintals of hay, and 3 packets of iron nails 2 to 3 quintals.

The decline of real wages

The policy of monopolistic industrialization and excessive protection also caused a decline in real wages of workers, government servants and other employees.[2] If we take as our measure a theoretical minimum list of necessary expenses, then only 64 per cent of the cost of living for a family of 4 could be met in 1914 out of an average worker's wage, and in 1930 only 58 per cent (Table 2). Employees (white-collar clerks) in the business sector could cover up to 113 per cent of such a minimal list with their average salaries, and government servants 204. They thus had incomes above the theoretical subsistence level. By contrast, agricultural workers could cover only 44 per cent of the minimal list in 1914. By 1930 the real wages of workers declined by 9 per cent, as compared to 1914, being 32 per cent below the theoretical minimum level; over the same period, the real incomes of white-collar workers fell by 15 per cent and those of government servants by 44.6 per cent. Agricultural workers had their real wages reduced to 30 per cent, i.e. they were 70 per cent below the theoretical minimum.

This means that, in spite of considerably increased demand

[1] O. Frangeš, *Koje se granice postavljaju poljoprivrednoj proizvodnji u Kraljevini Srba, Hrvata i Slovenaca?* (What are the limits set to agricultural production in the Kingdom of Serbs, Croats and Slovenes?) (Zagreb, 1920), pp. 10, 11.
[2] 'Indeks', *Socio-Political Review*, xi, no. 2 (1939).

TABLE 2

Real wages and minimum of existence

	Real wages as % of existence minimum			Indices		
	1914	1930	1938	1914	1930	1938
Agricultural labourers	44.2	30.3	30.1	100	68.6	68.1
Other workers	63.6	57.9	53.3	100	91.0	83.8
White-collar workers	113.2	96.2	89.5	100	85.0	79.1
Government employees	204	112.8	111.4	100	55.4	59.7

SOURCE: 'Indeks', *Socio-Political Review*, XI, no. 2 (1939).

for industrial workers, their real wages not only did not increase but actually deteriorated. This was even more true of agricultural workers. Squeezed by the threefold pressure of a reduced demand for their services because of the land reform, an increased supply of labour because of proletarianization of those peasants below subsistence level and the closing of emigration outlets to America, their wages were seriously reduced, despite the fact that even before the war they had been well below the theoretical subsistence level. There was increased pressure from agricultural workers on the labour market and they had to augment their incomes from sources other than employment, i.e. produce from small family holdings and the earnings of more than one member of each family, including women and children. Thus the increased demand for industrial workers was to a large extent met by the pressure of the exodus from agriculture, and the fact that many peasants who had fought in the war did not want to return to agriculture and a rural way of life.

Changes in agriculture

Compared with the twenty-two years of protracted crisis (1873–95) which had earlier shaken European agriculture,[1] the years immediately before the First World War were a period of

[1] For its effect in Croatia, see R. Bićanić, 'Agrarna kriza u Hrvatskoj 1873–1895' (The agrarian crisis in Croatia 1873–1895), *Ekonomist*, no. 3–5 (1937).

recovery and prosperity. The war actually strengthened this tendency. Agricultural prices went up in spite of price control and government requisitioning. The increased demand for agricultural products percolated to the small peasant producer by way of a black market. Inflation freed the peasants from their debts and eased the burden of taxation. Nevertheless, agricultural production was shifted from the shoulders of the men, who had to go to war, to their women. This meant a deterioration in the quality of labour in intensive agriculture, but led to greater emancipation of women. For the first time in history the peasant was not short of money. Easier access to money on one hand and shortage of free time on the other changed consumption habits and opened the minds of people to new products and new ways of working in agriculture. The impact of war changed the traditional relations between town and country.

The authority of the state was badly shaken by the war and its incapacity to satisfy the basic needs of the population. This led to an ever-growing revolutionary situation, as the burden of war began to be more heavily felt.

Thus the end of the war found a very different rural population, more mobile and more emancipated, more used to money calculations, less frightened of the government and more self-confident than before the war, and thinking in terms of new methods of production, marketing and consumption. Dissatisfaction with pre-war conditions of peasant exploitation found expression in post-war peasant unrest, which later crystallized into political and social peasant movements, most clearly expressed and best organized in Croatia.

The high prices of agricultural products during the war and in its aftermath made possible changes in production. Fallow land was disappearing fast. Livestock, decimated during the war, was found to be the most profitable branch of agriculture and gains from it increased, despite the existence of a large number of middlemen and cattle dealers, who spread extremely quickly and made large profits. Iron ploughs replaced old wooden ones to an increasing extent. The demand for land increased, as did the area under cultivation. But this boom in agricultural production had an adverse effect on the quality of products, which had rapidly improved at the beginning of the century. During the war, as everything that could be grown could be sold, less care was given to quality. This happened in the fertile and technically advanced agricultural areas of the north. A different situation developed in the mountainous areas, where there was large-scale agricultural overpopulation. During the war hunger reigned in the greater part of Southern Croatia, particularly in Lika, Istria and Dalmatia, in Bosnia, Hercegovina, parts of Serbia, Macedonia, and Montenegro. Most of these were areas with few resources and small local markets whose economy was based mainly on a meagre subsistence agriculture and one or two commercial crops (wine, tobacco, etc.) dependent on very intensive labour. Shortage of men adversely affected this type of agriculture. The position of agriculture in Serbia was particularly unhappy. Its population was poorly supplied with agricultural and industrial products, being under enemy occupation and in addition to this the whole of Serbia and Macedonia were twice flattened by the effects of the war. As a result, Serbian agriculture was severely damaged, particularly because it was based on livestock, which is the first victim of every war. The smallness of agricultural production for the market did not allow the peasants to increase their cash earnings much.

We have already mentioned the adverse effects of the widening gap between agricultural and industrial prices all over Yugoslavia. This was affected by the great shortage during the war of both industrial products and the means of production caused by the fact that much of the production capacity was taken over for war purposes. There was also a great shortage of raw materials for textiles, especially cotton and wool. This was made worse by the increased demand of the peasants who no longer had a labour force available to produce home-made clothing and tools in their own homes, and, in any case, possessed more money to buy these things. The price scissors, encouraged by the policy developed after the war, increased the gap further and caused great distress among the peasants, so that by 1926 a structural agricultural crisis was in full swing.

The adverse situation that developed in the new state immediately after the war can be observed in three different fields. While there was still a great shortage of agricultural products everywhere, and hunger reigned in Central Europe, prices of agricultural products were high. The peasants hoped that this situation would last, and the fallacies of inflation encouraged their belief. Therefore the peasants returning home from the war started to re-equip their family holdings, to invest in means of production (iron ploughs, machinery and live-stock) and to buy land. The price of land rose to a very high level and land was often bought on credit from moneylenders and small local banks (which were not much better than the former), even by small peasants who wanted to increase their means of subsistence. Better and more comfortable houses were built in villages. Soon a deflationary policy was introduced in order to stabilize the dinar (January 1923) and this established some stability in the value of money, but it was deliberately stabilized at a level which was some 50 per cent above the actual domestic purchasing power of the dinar. Thus a person who before 1923 contracted a debt for 100 dinars (then equiva-lent to 6 Swiss francs) in 1925 had to repay this debt with the equivalent of 9.13 Swiss francs in real terms. The price of arable land, which increased considerably immediately after the war, suddenly fell in the mid-twenties to one-half or one-third of its pre-war value in real terms. This policy (inaugurated by M. Stojadinović as minister of finance) was in the interests of financial capital (bankers, creditors and moneylenders), but it was disastrous for the peasants, particularly the most advanced peasants who had entered into debt in order to improve their holdings. The indebted peasants were exploited and the burden of their debt increased in real terms by half, without the sanc-tity of existing contracts and civil law being affected. Private moneylending at high rates of interest found plenty of oppor-tunities to exploit this government policy of deflation.

The second field which reflected the worsened situation was that of taxation policy. During inflation taxation was eased, but after the war the burden of taxes increased out of all proportion. Expressed in terms of wheat, one hectare of arable land in Croatia in 1912–13 paid in taxes the equivalent of 10.2 kilo-grams of wheat. In 1919–20 this tax was only 1.47 kilograms, but by 1924–5 the burden of taxation had already increased to 8.15 kilograms of wheat, because of the increased rate of taxa-tion and the decline in prices of agricultural products. These figures relate only to direct taxation. If we take into account all direct and, especially, indirect taxes, including a progressive income tax introduced during the war, excise and communal taxes, etc., then, for example, one household of 22 hectares in Croatia, which in 1913 paid total taxes to the value of 319 kilograms of wheat, in 1924 had to pay taxes worth 8.495 kilograms of wheat.[1]

The third field in which there was rapid deterioration was that of foreign trade and exports of agricultural products. Yugoslavia's links with the world market were stronger in 1914 than they ever were later. At that time Zagreb bought, duty free, not only Czech linen and Austrian woollens, wheat from Banat and potatoes from the sub-Carpathian hills, but also ploughs from upper Styria and salt from Slovakia. All production, particularly agricultural, was linked to the world market and one agricultural economist[2] in 1920 was already warning the cooperative producers of Yugoslavia that they should not forget the effects of this link. Wheat and maize, wine, wool and livestock, all had their prices determined by the world market and not by the costs of domestic producers. Before the First World War Zagreb consumed a large amount of butter from Denmark and Siberia. Bosnia, the homeland of prunes, was purchasing prunes from California at the time of Sarajevo, and Dubrovnik consumed condensed milk from Switzerland. The export prices of cattle to European markets were determined by the prices of frozen and tinned meat, and prices of exported wine were determined by Italian competition.

Competition under world market conditions had a favourable effect on agricultural exports in the long run. We have already seen that in this period exports of cattle were twice as large as after the war, when an autarchic policy was inaugurated. Wine exports were almost twenty times larger than after the war. Export of alcohol was just 1 per cent of the productive capacity of distilleries, and sales of Adriatic sardines amounted to 25 per cent of pre-war capacity. The same was true of exports of flour, cattle, etc., as we have already seen.

The increased political restlessness of the peasants at the end of the war and the Serbian Government's promise of land to the Yugoslav volunteers who had joined the army during the war

[1] S. Poštić, *Poresko opterećenje privrede i poreska reforma* (The tax burden on the economy and tax reform) (Zagreb, 1926), pp. 55–7.
[2] Frangeš, *Koje se granice postavljaju poljoprivrednoj proizvodnji*, pp. 11, 12, 13.

led to an extensive land reform after 1918. This reform distributed great areas of land to the landless and small peasants, to
peasants from overpopulated mountainous areas who went as
colonists to the Danubian plain, and to war volunteers. As most
of the land so distributed came from estates belonging to the
aristocracy of various nationalities living in the Austro-Hungarian monarchy, this was also considered as an act of 'nationalization', bringing land into the hands of the peasants in
Yugoslavia. Nevertheless there were some serious distortions, so
that the land reform also unfortunately had some adverse
effects. One use to which it was put was to infiltrate Serbian
settlers into territories in Croatia and Macedonia, in order to
create local Serbian majorities. Agricultural proletarians of
Hungarian nationality in the Vojvodina got no land at all
from divided estates.

In the area south of the River Sava peasants who were
liberated from serfdom were granted ownership of the land they
farmed and ceased to pay feudal rent to the landowners, who
were compensated by the state.

The land reform did not solve the problems of landless
peasants for several reasons, the main reason being that there
was too little land to be distributed. When landless peasants
were given land they were allocated barren soil without houses,
tools or livestock for agricultural production; the large estates
were often distributed in an irregular manner and no systematic
agricultural policy was subsequently put into operation. The
whole move was conceived more as a reward to the peasants for
their war effort and as a political act than as a sound economic
proposition, which it could have been if carried out properly.
The immediate consequence of this land reform was that the
value of agricultural production in the areas where it was carried
out fell by 20 per cent, as a result of declines in both quantity
and quality. Food-processing industries which had been set up
on the basis of large agricultural estates suffered severe decline
because of lack of raw materials. In noting this initial adverse
effect a more important fact must not be forgotten, i.e. that the
distribution of land was a political and social necessity of the
first order, which in fact did help a great number of poor
peasants and landless labourers and their families to find a means
of existence. If the market sector of agricultural production was

adversely affected there is no doubt that there was a considerable increase in the subsistence part of the peasant economy;
many more people were able to make their living from agriculture, and to live better than earlier, when no other opportunities were available. After some five years the loss incurred was
made good and the pre-war level of agricultural production
regained.

The formation of national capital

The main aim of post-war economic policy was the creation of a
national market and the formation of national capital. From
the very start two different lines of policy were advocated to
attain this objective, held sacred by all bourgeois political
parties and governments. One trend of thought was clearly set
out in the first annual report of the newly-created Zagreb
Stock Exchange, the mouthpiece of Croatian financial circles.
This report, issued in 1920, first underlined the importance of the
fact that Yugoslavia was surrounded by capitalist countries and
must follow the same policy as they did. Doubt was expressed
about the efficiency of state machinery which, it said, would
have to be built up over many years. Then the report added:

> We have a rich country endowed with natural wealth, we
> have a very favourable geographic position, we can rely on an
> able people, and we must use all these factors in order to set
> up the economic organization of our state as quickly as
> possible...We cannot do this in any other way but by
> organizing capital and giving full play to private initiative
> wherever it appears...We must give our domestic capital by
> all possible means the maximum security of action so that it
> can exploit all the wealth of the subsoil in our state. Other-
> wise there is no doubt that foreign capital will flood over us,
> exploit our riches in its own interests, and economically
> enslave us.[1]

This capitalist accumulation expressing monopolistic tendencies
was meant to be carried out predominantly by the instruments
of capitalism, i.e. concentration of capital in large private
banks, creation of banking concerns, links with world monopoly

[1] *Izvještaj o poslovanju Zagrebačke burze...1920* (Report on the activity of the Zagreb
Stock Exchange for 1920) (Zagreb, 1921), pp. 12 and 13.

capitalism, etc. The main sponsors of this capitalism were the big banks and industrialists.

The other tendency was particularly developed in Serbia, where those in power or close to power had greater opportunities for using the state machinery under their control for their own benefit.[1] Here the demands for the strengthening of national capital came mainly from the domestic dealers in agricultural trade, small local banks and moneylenders who were linked to political parties. State policy was predominantly in the hands of people whose outlook had not developed beyond the mentality of what Marx called primitive accumulation and who considered the state apparatus and state economic policy not as instruments with which to build modern capitalism, but as means for private accumulation by extra-economic means, i.e. using the state machinery and the state budget instead of capitalist economic machinery.[2]

One of the men who put into operation this economic policy of nationalistic protectionism, and who was in charge of industrial policy for several years, despite changes of government, formulated the objectives of the policy of state monopoly capitalism in the following way: increase of total national production; building of a complete national defence industry; development of the production of all necessary articles. The purpose of

[1] The programme of the most powerful political party in Serbia, the Serbian Radical Party, demanded that 'the natural wealth of our country be well preserved and exploited for our people'. The programme thus declared itself against a policy of alienation of large national riches and wealth, be it mines, forests, water-power, etc., but it was not against the participation of foreign capital in the exploitation if domestic capital could not be found.

'It is the duty of the State to preserve all national industries which use domestic raw materials for building the State, wherever it is possible, even with the aid of exceptional monetary and credit means...The necessity is underlined for the ever-increasing influence of the state and state policy on the administration of the National Bank...There are complaints against the National Bank which, people say, has distributed large credits to private banks and financial institutions at a rate of interest of 6%, which institutions lend this same national money at a rate of 20–30% interest.' Lazar Marković, *Ekonomsko-financijski program narodne radikalne stranke* (Economic-financial programme of the National Radical Party) (Belgrade, 1925), p. 16.

[2] Monopolistic tendencies of state capitalism were already strong in Yugoslavia, especially in Serbia where there were several state factories (e.g. sugar refineries, defence in Austria) and the state monopoly of sales of matches, salt, tobacco, cigarette paper and kerosene, which were given as securities to foreign creditors when contracting state loans. The State Mortgage Fund and the National Bank which were given important privileges by the state, also wielded great influence.

this economic programme was to supply national needs and to assure the export of industrial products.[1] One of the leading members of the ruling Serbian Radical Party, Lazar Marković, formulated the programme of this party as follows:

> The main and important reform was the emancipation of our foreign trade from the Austrian markets, penetration of the world market and an attempt to export our main commodities, as far as possible in a semi-finished state...The struggle with Austria in the economic and commercial field increasingly strengthened the national spirit in Serbia and it can be considered a constituent part of Serbia's national policy directed towards the liberation and unification of the whole Serbo-Croato-Slovene nation.[2]

Agriculture was left to find its own consumers in the country.

The economic policy in the newly-formed state of Yugoslavia immediately after the war purported to integrate its constituent parts into one economic system dominated by the monopoly of national capital. From the foregoing account of the various changes brought about in 1918, four particular points of emphasis arise which still have relevance today.

(1) The experience of large markets, almost forgotten in Yugoslavia. We have seen that before an autarchic policy was followed, in spite of large imports, including certain agricultural products, there had been even larger exports, also including agricultural commodities. Yet there were until very recently, and in some circles still are, people who retain the autarchic spirit and its value judgements. Indeed an attitude of reserve towards foreign markets was dominant in Yugoslavia until the reform of 1965 accepted the principle of joining the world market. This is not to suggest that the Austro-Hungarian monarchy was a good thing, or that any of its economic substitutes, such as a Central European Zone or a South-eastern European Common Market would be workable or preferable today. The time for such small regional units has passed; the techniques of the mid-twentieth century have greatly outstripped them and require wider solutions.

---

[1] M. Savić, *Što da se radi u ovo ekonomski teško doba?* (What to do in these economically difficult times?) (Belgrade, 1929).

[2] Marković, *Ekonomsko-financijski program narodne radikalne stranke*, pp. 8–9.

(2) In 1918 a nationalistic attitude was accepted by the rulers of Yugoslavia as a guide in economic policy. It was considered that what is national must be good, and national capital formation was thought from the outset to be the supreme goal of economic policy. As Yugoslavia consisted of several nations, the best way to maximize the benefit was to recognize only one nation. We have seen how this policy led simultaneously to a high rate of accumulation of capital and high prices of industrial goods, which were nevertheless dearly paid for by a declining rate of growth. Yet the attitude that the creation of a national market led by national enterprises and national capital formation must be the supreme aim of economic policy has remained dominant in some circles even under socialism. Such an attitude in a small multinational state is bound to lead to many distortions.

(3) The policy of autarchic industrialization perpetuated the imbalance between agricultural and industrial prices created during the First World War, and opened up a gap between the prices of manufactured and agricultural products which was a long-run phenomenon. How to balance imports of clothing and of capital goods with exports of food and products of the extractive industries remained the basic problem of Yugoslav foreign trade up to 1957, or, more accurately, up to the reform of 1965,[1] which had different effects on various sectors of the economy.

(4) The different parts of Yugoslavia entered the process of creating the economy of the new state at different levels of development and their attitude towards this integration varied correspondingly.[2] This had two consequences:

(a) that those who found themselves part of a greatly increased market became autarchic centralists and conservative in their policies as the 'guardians of the State', while those who had earlier been part of a larger market wanted the new

---

[1] Clothing had a high income elasticity of demand in Yugoslavia, like luxury goods in other countries.

[2] Some economists still try to explain the problem of underdeveloped areas in Yugoslavia today by historical reasons, comparing the favourable position of those parts that had been part of Austro-Hungary with those that had been part of the Turkish Empire. When applying this argument, however, it must be remembered that Austro-Hungary and Turkey ceased to rule Yugoslav territories between 50 and 100 years ago.

national market to expand and advocated a democratic, federalist and liberal policy;

(b) that those at the centre of political power used their influence to redistribute national income by extra-economic means in order to create a counterweight against those areas which were more developed. These dilemmas of policy which began in 1918 are still felt in Yugoslavia today and lie behind two different concepts of economic development, as we shall see later.

2

The formation of the socialist sector

Changes in property relations

The formation of socialist-owned property was considered to be the most significant act in the policy of building socialism in Yugoslavia after the Communist Party seized power in 1945. It should be stressed from the beginning that since 1950 a special characteristic of socialism in Yugoslavia has been the essential importance given to the question of who controls social property, i.e. the problem of workers' management as opposed to state ownership.

We shall here consider the way in which socialist ownership was brought into being, i.e. how property that already existed was transferred from the private sector or the publicly-owned sector into the state sector.[1]

Rationalization of nationalization

The plan of action for nationalization was worked out during the liberation struggle before the end of the war, but its roots reach more deeply into the very doctrine of socialism. In the programme of the Communist Party of Yugoslavia, as in the programmes of other communist parties, transfer of property was considered to be the main factor in building socialism. Thus transfer of property was ideologically motivated and was more often conceived as a long-term ideological postulate of the socialist revolution than as a short-term economic proposition addressed to the problem of how the war-shattered economy of Yugoslavia could best be organized. The demonstration effect of the USSR played a very important role, and the less people knew about its practical implications in that country the more attractive were its principles.

[1] How the originating source of socialist property, i.e. the socialist sector, developed through its own resources will be discussed in Chapter 7.

The emotional reaction of the revolutionary workers, after the social revolution had been won, was understandably directed by their pride in becoming masters of the means of production with which they worked. There was revolutionary zeal in carrying out the 'expropriation of the expropriators' as Marx called it. Transfer of property was made easier in Yugoslavia in that it was also, at least in part, a form of retaliation against those who had collaborated with the enemy during the Second World War, and in part it was a re-expropriation of property which the enemy had already expropriated from the previous owners (e.g. the Jews).

The emotional factors explain some exaggerations and unnecessary victimization in a process which could perhaps have been carried out less painfully. Perhaps a feeling of insecurity among the new rulers, inexperience in government and a lack of rational behaviour, especially among the lower revolutionary echelons, can account for at least some occurrences. There was, however, a rational element in the nationalization action, perhaps not very obvious to all concerned, but nevertheless there. Some cool heads must have been behind the revolutionary action of the transfer of property.

Property was transferred from the private and capitalist sectors into the state sector of the communist-controlled state (which later was transformed into the socialist sector) according to the well-defined socialist principle that indivisible means of production, which require a considerable number of hands to work collectively, should be socially owned – which at that time implied state ownership. The rule followed was that financial capital should be expropriated first, since it had an abstract common denominator and was therefore the most homogeneous among economic activities. Next on the list came those means of production most specific in physical terms, i.e. needing special managerial skill in their running. Thus banks and financial institutions, such as insurance companies, were nationalized first and after them big industrial and mining enterprises, followed by means of transport, commercial services and, last of all, agriculture.

A second rule which can be reconstructed from practical action was that the most concentrated units, requiring the smallest number of decisions in their running, should be transferred to social ownership first and the more decentralized ones, requiring replacement of a greater number of managers or decision-makers, should come afterwards. Thus the expropriative transfer of property took place in the following way.

All banks (private and limited companies) were simply closed after the expulsion of the enemy forces, or were not reopened but sequestered. The liquidation of their affairs was a long process, some details of which are still being settled (after 25 years) under the control of the National Bank of Yugoslavia.

Rail transport was already state owned before the socialist revolution and even before the war was run by a minister of state, as was a large part of river shipping, which during the war was in any case under enemy government control. There was therefore no great problem in incorporating these into the state sector. The question of the merchant fleet, most of which was at sea and chartered to the allies, was not so simple.

Basic industries whose output depended on continuous mechanized production, and also mining and highly concentrated manufacturing industries, were next in order to be nationalized. They were taken over in 1946. Scattered, local and small industries came later (1948). Small craftsmen were left in the private sector where they are still today.

Although commercial firms were privately owned they had been under the control of the war-time economy, with general food, clothing and footwear rationing through administrative supply centres. Their nationalization took place formally after a period of three years (in 1948).

Lagging behind came agriculture. The 2.6 million small, private, family holdings, where hundreds of varied decisions have to be made daily on every farm, were hardly touched up to 1949. Moreover, two land reforms (in 1945 and 1953) redistributed land and set the maximum size for family holdings at 10 hectares, which further increased the number of small landowners. The land reform of 1945 transferred great areas of forest to state ownership, along with quite large areas of agricultural land (altogether 1.5 million hectares). Village shops and inns were confiscated and replaced in 1948 by cooperatives and state commercial enterprises. This was more for political than for economic reasons, as the village shops and inns were considered as meeting places from which political control over the peasants might be exercised by adversaries of the new regime.

Residential apartment houses were last to be nationalized. It was not until 1959 that all houses with more than two large or three small apartments and all building sites in urban and tourist centres were nationalized.

The inheritance of the past

A reasonably strong public-property sector had existed before the war in Yugoslavia. There had been state ownership of railways and roads, great areas of forests, two sugar refineries, the defence industry and eleven coal mines. The state was also the largest banker, controlling the five biggest state or privileged banks (the National Bank as the bank of issue, the State Mortgage Bank, the Post Office Savings Bank and the privileged agricultural and artisan banks). There had been a state monopoly of some items of wholesale and retail trade, including salt, tobacco, matches and petrol. The export of wheat and some other cereals was entirely in the hands of state commercial corporations. This former state property was the first to be incorporated into the state sector.

Local government bodies, provincial and municipal, had before the war been owners of considerable property which was transferred to overall state ownership, as were public corporations, such as social insurance, and state and government agencies. Village forests and pastures were also made part of the new state sector.

Forms of property transfer

The forms by which transfer of private property to the state sector took place were: sequestration, land reform, nationalization, confiscation, expropriation and gifts.

Sequestration. As certain areas were liberated from the enemy most of the firms in them were sequestrated and provisional trustees, having the confidence of the new regime, were appointed by the new government to be responsible for current operations. This temporary solution was later followed by other, more permanent, measures.

Two *land reforms* were carried out by federal laws providing the framework for subsequent laws in the republics, which worked out land distribution in detail. The first land reform law was passed by the provisional federal assembly in 1945, even before the constitution of the country had been approved. The second law was passed in 1953.

Nationalization. There were two nationalization laws. The first was voted by the federal parliament in December 1946 and nationalized banks, industries of federal and republic importance (not those of local importance), wholesale trade, etc. The 1948 nationalization act covered industrial enterprises, including local manufacturing industries, transport, the retail and catering trades, etc.

There was a difference between the first and the second nationalization law. While the first nationalized property used for a certain activity in a functional sense, the second nationalized property belonging to enterprises as such in an institutional sense.

In 1959 housing and building sites were nationalized by federal law.

Confiscation of property involved a transfer of property from the private to the state sector by a ruling of the courts. The property chiefly affected was that of people sentenced in court – for war crimes, or for economic or political collaboration. There is little doubt that some of these confiscations were less proper legal acts than they were instruments of revolutionary retaliation. The term collaboration was often loosely interpreted, according to the size of the property in question.

Expropriation in a legal sense denoted administrative acts of the government transferring private property to the state for reasons of public interest. This again was subject to wide interpretation and in many cases it took a long time before a proper legal procedure was consolidated.

Gifts. Many persons after the war made gifts of their private property to the state. Some did it from revolutionary conviction, but many gave their property under pressure or from fear of being persecuted for their class position or activities during the war. Some struck a deal with the government and in exchange were given employment in their old firm, a pension or some other compensation.

Another set of sources from which the state sector was formed was connected with the *settlement at the end of the war*. There was the property of enemy nationals, such as citizens of the German Reich (but not Italians or Hungarians), and of members of the German national minority settled in Yugoslavia, except those who had cooperated with the People's Liberation Forces. Under this heading is also included restoration and restitution of property taken by the enemy.

Of particular importance were the reparations for war damage caused by enemy action[1] and allied help, especially that of the United Nations Relief and Rehabilitation Administration (UNRRA). Most goods provided under this last were consumer goods, but such capital goods as there were were incorporated into the state sector, since UNRRA aid was aid given to governments.

Property of persons lost or missing after the war also went to the state. Special treatment was accorded to Yugoslav nationals who were Jewish. Their property had been confiscated by the enemy and most of them succumbed tragically, though a number escaped and joined the People's Liberation Forces or went abroad, some to return later, others to stay. Those Jews who emigrated to Israel after the war were allowed to take a large part of their property with them.

Special treatment was also required for property owned by foreigners. During the war changes were made by the forces of occupation and local quisling governments, such as mergers, replacements, destruction and some innovations and transfers of property. It was therefore often difficult to establish the origin and amount of change in property. Foreign enterprises were nationalized by law in the same manner as domestic ones. This created some difficult problems in relations with allied or neutral foreign governments, which demanded compensation for the property of their citizens which had been nationalized by Yugoslavia. After a time a longer-term view began to be taken by the Yugoslav Government of its interest in promoting economic relations with foreign countries, and foreign owners reconciled themselves to the permanence of the new socialist government and of its settlements. In this way agreements were

[1] Reparations were paid by Germany, Italy and Hungary. Yugoslavia unilaterally freed Bulgaria from payment of reparations and did not ask for any from Romania.

reached with many governments and compensation for nationalized foreign property was paid by Yugoslavia. The government had to put on one side of the balance its interest in entering into regular trade agreements with important foreign countries, and weigh these against demands for gradual repayment of the confiscated property of foreign nationals. The desire to develop current trade and the prospects for commercial and other credits and aid were considered as worthy returns for payment of compensation. To this one must add the arguments of international law and the desire to become a respectable member of the international community and to play an active role in world politics.

The process of legalization

In January 1946 the first Yugoslav constitution after the Second World War laid down that the economy should consist of three sectors, based on property relations:

> The means of production in the Federative People's Republic of Yugoslavia are the property of the entire people, i.e. property in the hands of the State, property of the people's cooperative organizations, or property of private persons or legal entities. All mineral and other wealth underground, the waters, including mineral and medicinal waters, the sources of natural power, the means of rail and air transport, the post, telegraph, telephone and broadcasting are national property.[1]

Thus the constitution of 1946 recognized three kinds of property with a decreasing degree of government support: state property, cooperative property and private property. The first was termed in the constitution (Article 16) 'the mainstay of the State in the development of the National economy', and was identified as the property of the entire people 'under the special protection of the State'. It included all property used by state enterprises, property which enabled government agencies, from local to federal level, to operate, and all the other forms of state property which we have already mentioned.

Cooperative property was, by the terms of the constitution (Article 17), given 'special attention' by the state, and offered

[1] *Constitution of the Federative People's Republic of Yugoslavia* (1946), Article 14.

'assistance and facilities'. This sector included consumer co-operatives, and agricultural and some other small producers' cooperatives.

For the private sector the constitution (Article 18) found the formula that it was 'guaranteed by the state'. This sector consisted of privately-owned property such as housing, agricultural holdings of limited size, the tools of private handicraftsmen, etc.

The main purpose in forming the state sector, which brought property under the control of federal, republic and local authorities, was to centralize the means of production in the hands of the organs of state authority, so that a controlling position could be secured from which to change production relations and reorganize the national economy, transforming it from a capitalist system into a socialist one.

The private sector was presented with two kinds of negative prescription. The constitution prohibited all types of private monopolistic organizations such as cartels, trusts, etc. It omitted to say anything about state monopolistic organizations, and this problem was later to emerge as one of the main obstacles to creating socialist social relations in the 1960s, as we shall see. Large agricultural estates in private hands were prohibited. The constitution also laid down the general rule that nobody could use private property to the detriment of the social community.

The positive rules of the constitution regarding the private sector stated that 'everybody has the duty to work'. Nothing was said at that time about the right to work, which was introduced in the 1953 Constitutional Law. (Later laws introduced other limitations to the private sector.) It was also stated in the 1946 constitution that the land should belong to those (in the plural) who tilled it. The statement made in the plural presupposed the existence of individual, family and collective owners of land.

Some comparisons of the growth of the socialist sector in Yugoslavia with that in the USSR and some other socialist countries

The socialist sector in Yugoslavia was formed under different conditions from those in the Soviet Union and other East European socialist countries. These differences, which had great consequences in later development, were the following.

(1) The socialist sector was largely created concurrently with the confiscation of enemy property in the war. Thus the socialist revolution to a large extent took place under the mantle of action against a national enemy.

(2) There was no blockade of Yugoslavia by the capitalist countries and no civil war after the revolution, as there had been in the USSR. On the contrary, Yugoslavia was given aid by the United Nations and by Allied countries of the West. The economic blockade was the work of socialist countries.

(3) The formation of the state sector developed much faster than in the Soviet Union and the process was comparatively less costly in human lives. In 1946, i.e. just one year after the revolution, 82 per cent of industry, including mining, was in the hands of the state, while it took the Soviet Union eight years to reach this percentage (in 1925). After the second Nationalization Act in 1948 industry was 100 per cent state-owned, a situation which was not reached in the USSR until 1929. Nationalization was completed after three years in Yugoslavia and after twelve years in the Soviet Union. Eighty-eight per cent of the turnover in retail trade in Yugoslavia was in the hands of state enterprises two years after the revolution; in the Soviet Union this took ten years to achieve. This, of course, had a great bearing on the whole development of socialism in Yugoslavia.

Before the 1946 Nationalization Act, 55 per cent of all industry was already in state hands, and 27 per cent under sequestration. This meant that only 18 per cent of industry was in private hands. After the first Nationalization Act of 1946 all industries of significance at the federal and republic levels were in the hands of the state, as was 70 per cent of local industry, while 30 per cent of local industry was still privately owned. In 1946, 4.5 per cent of the shops, handling 19 per cent of the retail trade, were in the state sector; by 1947 the figure was 48 per cent, handling 59 per cent of the retail trade. In 1946 40,146 shops, i.e. 75 per cent of the total number, and 49 per cent of turnover were in the private sector. By 1949 there were only 433 private shops, that is 1 per cent of the total, dealing with 0.7 per cent of the turnover (greengrocers' and pastry shops).

Agricultural land was distributed as follows: in 1947 the state sector had 1.2 per cent, 0.9 per cent was in the cooperative sector and 98 per cent of all agricultural land was privately owned by small peasants. By 1951 land in the state sector had increased to 5 per cent and in the cooperative sector (this was the period of forced collectivization) to 15 per cent, while 80 per cent still remained private. In 1955 the state sector reached 5.7 per cent and the cooperative fell to 11.3, leaving 91.2 per cent of land in private hands; by 1959 this was slightly reduced to 89.4 per cent.

The transformation of the state sector into the socialist sector

The original, rather rigid, distinction between three normative sectors underwent many changes. By the middle of 1946 there was already a distinction made between private property in the hands of those who worked it and those who did not. In 1950 workers' management was introduced into state enterprises which meant that control of management was taken away from the state bureaucracy. This was an important step towards transforming the state sector into a socialist sector.

The state sector had increased considerably in size during the same period, so that the situation was ripening for legal recognition of a change in the quality of social relations, which came about in 1953. The Constitutional Law of 1953 recognized only two sectors, called the social sector and the non-social sector. The main reasons for the change were the introduction of workers' management in socialist business organizations and the fact that these organizations had to a great extent freed themselves from state interference in their current affairs (the state administration maintained its organizing and regulative jurisdiction but ceased to use it). Also, state property changed its legal character and became general social property. The whole of what had been the cooperative sector now became part of the socialist sector and the cooperatives to a large extent lost their distinguishing characteristics and were made almost equal in rights and duties with the socialist enterprises. In 1953, the 5,200 cooperatives had some 1,370,000 cooperative members and employed 86,500 permanent personnel. By 1958 socialist production run by direct producers working with general social property organized by workers' management covered 11,631 enterprises employing 1.9 million workers.

A small part of the socialist sector still consisted of property administered by government agencies and institutions under the hierarchical control of the general government administration. There were also still some socialist enterprises which remained under limited workers' management (i.e. the national defence enterprises). Social management of a different type was introduced in such enterprises.

A new sub-sector called the social organization sector, was added at this time to cover types of organization which dealt with non-productive occupations and services, such as cultural, political and sports organizations and labour unions. The overall state administration (general government) covered cultural and educational services and also health and other public services. It employed 452,000 people in 1953.

Thus from 1953 onwards in Yugoslavia one can no longer speak of the state sector, state enterprises or state farms. In the first place, as we have already said, the enterprises are neither owned nor run by the state, i.e. the government bureaucracy, nor is the property owned by the state. The legal term used in the property register is *opća narodna imovina* (general social property) managed by enterprise X and this enterprise is run by workers' management.

In 1958, the *non-socialist* sector was rather heterogeneous and various forms of production relations and ownership were found in it. It included 2.2 million peasant and family agricultural holdings (10 million people) and 147,000 private artisans, of which only 16,000 employed hired labour.

Problems of socialist property in the period of the reform

The period of the reform started with the new constitution of 1963. It was considered that the 'expropriation of the expropriators' was now over and therefore all provisions regarding nationalization were purposely omitted from the new constitution, which guaranteed the right of existing property relations.[1]

[1] In June 1967 the Federal Constitutional Court was approached by the Constitutional Court of Slovenia, several regular courts and many private individuals, complaining about the laws of the Republics of Slovenia, Bosnia and Hercegovina and their regulation of compensation for nationalized land, i.e. building sites and houses. It was claimed that the constitution did not ensure that this compensation was adequate. There were also general complaints relating to nationalized building sites in the tourist areas of Croatia and Montenegro. These complaints were made on the ground that in general the 1963 constitution did not contain any provision about nationalization, and that in the discussions in the Federal Parliament it was stated that the period of nationalization was now over and

Some problems in connection with the formation of social ownership now under discussion are often misinterpreted abroad. The two most important of these are:

Landownership. As we have seen, land can be owned, by private persons whose occupation is agriculture. There is a limit here. No agricultural household can own more than 10 hectares of cultivable land, i.e. excluding forests and pastures. In some areas where there are large joint families with ten or more members this maximum can be somewhat increased. The number of livestock is not limited, but peasants could not own large agricultural machines until 1967. There were in fact 5,000 privately-owned tractors in 1965, but these were mainly old and had been discarded by the socialist holdings. In the same year there were 40,000 tractors in the socialist sector. Since 1967 privately-owned agricultural machines can be used on the fields of the owner, and can be hired out for services to other agricultural holdings on condition that they are operated by the owner himself or a member of his family and not by hired labour.

After the forcible collectivization of land had failed (1949–52) any increase in the amount of land in the socialist sector could be achieved only through the purchase of land by agricultural estates or communes from private owners (i.e. small peasants). The Agricultural and Cooperative Bank made considerable sums available for this purpose. Another way by which socialist land is increased is by the socialist estates paying retirement compensation to old peasants who have no successors to till their family land and are therefore willing to leave it to the socialist estate in exchange for old age benefits.

existing private property relations, after 20 years of revolutionary change, had to be stabilized and guaranteed by the constitution. The only procedure kept was that of legal expropriation for reasons of public interest, and for that purpose full compensation had to be paid by the authorities. The state's case against these claims did not contest the clear text of the constitution but interpreted nationalization as another form of administrative expropriation. The state also petitioned that on nationalized private land, e.g. in Croatia, tourist centres of the socialist sector had been built to the value of 950 million dinars, which the Federal Constitutional Court should take into account. Moreover, the representatives of the Federal Government stated that a new law was being drafted to regulate the indemnity problem but that no agreement had been reached (June 1967) regarding the fundamental issues. The Federal Constitutional Court decided that compensation had to be paid in full, and that if the federation did not pass a new law within 6 months, the existing laws on compensation would be considered operative and valid.

Small-scale private crafts. Between 1959 and 1964 the number of small craftsmen decreased by 17,000. A large number (118,000) of these craftsmen left the private sector and joined craft cooperatives where they were not under pressure from the communes for taxes and did not have to pay high rents for their premises. The work of craftsmen is limited by law. They cannot employ more than five workers and therefore it is inaccurate to call such people (in 1964 118,200 of them altogether employing 42,000 helpers and apprentices in their workshops) private capitalists, as some Chinese sources do.

In view of the great demands of the growing urban population and the spread of the urban way of life to the villages, and because of the general mechanization of the country, increased house building and widespread expansion of household appliances, there is a widespread and increasing need for craftsmen, whose services are becoming more and more expensive. Recently a policy has been adopted of encouraging private craftsmen all over the country, but this government policy is counteracted by the local authorities who find such people a convenient source of taxation. Such a development, however, could help to reduce unemployment.

The spectacular increase in the tourist trade and the expansion of car ownership has brought about an increased demand for catering services, which the socialist enterprises cannot fully meet. Therefore private inns and restaurants, run by the innkeeper and his family and a small number of hired people, have been allowed to open.

The great shortage of housing and the inability of the socialist sector to meet the urgent demand for more apartments has left the field open to private builders of small family houses with one or two apartments. For such houses, sometimes built by private builders, sometimes by the workers themselves, credits can be obtained from the socialist banks.

Some more recent problems concerning the socialist sector

So far we have described nationalization as a process by which socialist property was formed. In the early days the formation of the socialist sector by nationalization was considered to be identical with the creation of socialism. The socialist sector had to be built up as fast as possible and made as all-embracing as it could be. Complete nationalization was considered to be the way of bringing about socialism, and to be identical with the abolition of exploitation of man by man.

In this drive to create a socialist sector sufficient consideration was not always given to the special nature of each kind of production, its social character and the level of development of production forces. As a result, particularly in 1948, very small industries were nationalized, as were services, which were not developed in a way which could be described as the socialized development of production forces.

With regard to the socialist sector in agriculture the error was soon recognized and in 1953 small peasant farms, which had been too hurriedly rushed into collectives, were decollectivized, but in other sectors of production nationalization went on. One reason for overlooking the fact that there was a limit to the extent to which production forces could be developed through socialization was the sense of political insecurity felt by the new regime. However, it also believed that the nationalization movement was so strong that it would be able to absorb those sections of production which were inadequately developed, regardless of the actual state of development of the productive forces concerned.

But the maximization of nationalization soon encountered obstacles which had not been foreseen.

The first awakening came at the country's national frontiers. It was soon discovered that the inter-relationship among socialist countries was not based on socialist principles, but on a method which in Yugoslavia was called the exploitation of one socialist country by another. It was this that lay behind the conflict with the Soviet Union and other socialist countries in 1948. Thus the limits set by national frontiers became the limits of nationalization. All dreams of crossing national frontiers and building one socialist system which would embrace all socialist countries were very quickly shattered.

A second objective limitation to the size of the nationalized economy was the discovery, soon made, that in the struggle to run a socialist enterprise effectively it was not enough to achieve state ownership of the means of production. This was because the state bureaucracy of the government in running the production of the nationalized industries showed an increasing

tendency towards exploitation. The number of restrictions imposed on socialist enterprises grew larger and larger and soon 66
per cent of the national income was distributed by the state
administration. It was in order to counteract this exploitation of
labour by the state bureaucracy, which developed through the
nationalized ownership of the means of production, that workers'
management was introduced. Nationalization had clearly not
solved the problems of exploitation and it was hoped that
workers' management would do so.

As workers' management developed, other aspects of the
problem became apparent. First there was a tendency for self-
managed socialist enterprises to work themselves into a monopoly situation, and, despite the existence of social property and
workers' management, the exploitation of workers by other
workers and of consumers by such workers began to develop. It
was found necessary to put some limit on workers' management
by administrative methods.

The first form taken by this limitation affected prices, which
were largely frozen in 1965. The second limitation was on
capital investment and credit, and was imposed in order to
check inflation, caused by investment. The third began to be
apparent in 1967, when a demand began to be heard for the
limitation of income distribution and of personal income of
workers. The next field was that of workers' employment. The
number of unemployed in the country increased and then pressure was put on the enterprises not to employ new workers to
any great extent, but at the same time not to fire them either, in
an attempt to solve the problem of unemployment within the
enterprise. Finally pressure had to be put on enterprises, in
spite of nationalization, or perhaps because of it, to limit the
extent of integration on both vertical and horizontal lines.

Another hindrance to the complete nationalization of industry concerned credit among socialist enterprises. Each working unit had its own accounting system within which exchanges
of finance took place, thus enabling several groups and units to
work temporarily with the financial means of other units, all
within the enterprise. Moreover large enterprises had internal
banks, which acted as sources of supply and means of transfer of
such funds. It was not difficult to take the step from this line of
development, which was quite spontaneous, to another, which

involved lending or investing the funds of one enterprise in another enterprise, in order to gain a profit and thus an increase in the invested funds. Thus one socialist enterprise could invest money in another and achieve gains from this investment of social capital. This activity did not overstep the limits of the system, in which socially-owned capital managed by one enterprise could be transferred from it to another. But it was a new principle, which in appearance contradicted the principle of 'to each according to his work' because it introduced gains from capital investment. Previously, the granting of credit to socialist enterprises had been limited to the banks, in exchange for interest paid and not participation. A new element was being introduced, and enterprises taking funds from one another had to weigh carefully all their interests and the risks involved.

It was found possible to extend this principle to the investment of foreign capital in Yugoslavia. Another argument for such investment, as we shall see later, was that gains can be achieved from invested capital while yet preserving the principles of workers' management and the competence of the workers' council. Arrangements between foreign investors and socialist enterprises in Yugoslavia have to be arranged by special contract. How to deal with these developments which were brought into the open by the reform is still an open question. Two trends have developed in policy. One school of thought has advocated a retreat from the self-management of socialist property and a return to the policy of the strong hand which meant in effect going back to central, authoritarian control of the economy, in effect from Belgrade. The strong hand, according to this reasoning, meant saving the country from chaos by reintroducing the earlier policy. The other line of reasoning was to extend workers' management and develop it into a new system. It was considered that workers' management had not in fact been fully introduced and that it should be freed from the need to submit to the state administration and fiscal considerations and from the pressure of political decision-makers, who were still very powerful, particularly in local affairs. Those advocating this line considered that a restructuring of the economy was necessary.

In fact the problem of ownership has turned into a problem of management. It is no longer considered sufficient to create social property and nationalize industries. After this has been done, problems arise over the running of the enterprises. It has been discovered that it is possible, within a completely nationalized economy, for there to develop not only the exploitation of one state by another but also that of one enterprise by another, and that this can even happen with a system of workers' management.

The private sector, or the sector of personal labour, has also been reappraised. With regard to the position of the private sector, discussions took place in 1967 about the fact that part of the private sector was based on the personal labour of individuals, independent of any form of socialist enterprise. The main problem was that of delimiting the socialist sector, and here we can distinguish five different approaches:

Some interpret the granting of unrestricted activity to individuals in business as a return to capitalism. The words of Lenin are recalled, that small-scale economic activity by independent producers will be continually breeding capitalism and that these enterprises will grow faster than the socialist sector. It follows that the socialist state should oppose small-scale private enterprise and should limit and ultimately prohibit all activity in the private sector, rather than allow it to expand.

A second view is that because of the problems of the economy and the economic recession the development of the private sector should be allowed as a temporary concession, which can later easily be withdrawn by the socialist state.

Another trend of thought considers that there is a permanent place for the activity of individual labour, even under socialism. It is felt that the workers concerned are operating a level of development of productive forces at which no socialist forms can develop. Therefore as long as they continue to exist and make their livelihood within the socialist society they should be allowed to go on existing and it should be recognized that they are not suited for socialist organization.

A fourth attitude is that the development of individual economic activity based on individual labour is just another step in socialist transformation, a further step towards self-management, in the sense that the private and the socialist sectors are not competitive but complementary. The activities of both sectors are complementary with relation to the economic activity of the country as a whole, in the following sense. The activity of the private sector is included in the socialist process of production, so that it either operates at the beginning of the economic process, providing natural products and raw materials for socialist industries, or at the other end, in further processing the semi-fabricated products provided by socialist industry, e.g. handicrafts, or providing services for the repair or utilization of products of the socialist sector.

Therefore, there is in fact cooperation between the socialist and private sectors, in which the private worker assumes the role which in earlier times was that of cottage industries, in which the worker operated at home with a small amount of fixed capital, often provided by large industry or by himself, and engaged in work with a large labour input of the kind which requires special care from the worker. This type of cooperation can be developed where economies of scale do not operate or are outweighed by more important considerations.

The fifth line of thought is a pragmatic one which considers that there are certain problems facing the Yugoslav economy today and that these should be tackled in all available ways, including by private labour if it provides the best available solution. This attitude does not take account of long-term effects, but is concerned only with the practical solution of existing day-to-day problems. It is said that when private sector services are no longer economically justified or socially necessary or when they become politically dangerous for socialism then the socialist state has the power to prohibit or curtail them.

The first approach is based on the idea that individual labour and the socialist sector are mutually exclusive, competitive and antagonistic – the principle of either/or. Behind these ideas is a fear that the socialist sector cannot compete favourably with the private sector and therefore needs to use political force in order to meet this competition. Economic strength is not enough. This feeling of insecurity and exploitation is difficult to understand in a country run by a socialist government.

The second concept is similar to the first, the main difference being that there is a greater feeling of security, so that it is felt that the socialist government can effectively control the private sector and can tolerate it. This reflects a belief that such economic operations can be run effectively by the socialist enterprise. This can continue temporarily, because the socialist sector is not able to organize or develop these functions economically.

The further attitude is that the competitiveness of the private and socialist sectors is so limited that the private sector cannot effectively threaten the existence of the socialist, with its much greater capital investment and concentration. Moreover, it is stated that economies of scale do exist and that there is an economic weakness underlying the fear of the socialist sector. Symbolically it has been stated thus. The owner of a heavy tractor of 150 h.p. does not feel that tractors of 10 or 15 h.p. compete with it, though the owner of a 40 h.p. tractor may; thus the competitiveness of the private sector depends on how far the socialist sector has developed its concentration of production and its acquisition of technological progress. If it is not sufficiently progressive, then of course it fears the competition of the private sector, but this competition will be to the benefit of consumers and workers as a whole. It is also believed that the competing capacity of the private sector should act as a corrective to any inefficiency or tendencies towards monopoly in public enterprises.

In fact when we examine the production process we can see that parts of it can be transferred from the socialist to the private sector and then back again after certain functions or operations have been performed. Examples are peasants getting seeds and fertilizer from the state in order to grow sugar beet which they then sell to the sugar refinery, or peasants getting eggs or small chicks or animals to be raised until they reach a certain weight and then sent back for the finishing process in the socialist sector.

3

Three models of planning in Yugoslavia

The first post-war constitution of 1946 gave Yugoslavia a planned economy. But the experience of the twenty years since has resulted in changes in planning, involving the people engaged, the ends aimed at, the means employed, and the environment in which it is carried out. It would be quite wrong to assume that these changes were made for purely ideological reasons or because of theoretical predilections for one type of economic planning rather than another. On the contrary, most of the changes in Yugoslavia have resulted from the pressure of events on preconceived ideas, and have meant a search to reconcile theory with changing conditions of development – political expediency with theoretical concepts. We have to bear in mind that the different areas of this country are very varied in their endowment of natural resources; that its parts have different historical inheritances and geographical situations; that it is a country of multinational composition; and that the levels of social and economic development of different areas are very different. This has brought to the fore much more quickly and clearly the weaknesses in a central planning mechanism on the Soviet pattern, which might have remained unrecognized for longer in a less complex country.

Planning experience in Yugoslavia can be summarized by using three models. We shall name them according to their main characteristics: the centralized model of planning (1947–51), the decentralized model (1952–64) and the polycentric model (1965).[1]

The centralized model of planning, a curious crossbreed of Marxist–Keynesian economics, is still considered in theory by

[1] A more general analysis of the development of the Yugoslav economy can be found in the author's article, 'Economics of socialism in a developed country', *Foreign Affairs* (July 1966).

41

some economists, mainly abroad, as the most rational planning pattern, even though some of its supporters do not agree with its political presuppositions. Centralization is taken as being almost equivalent to rationalization and optimization of the social interest.

Such a picture of centralized planning is overrationalized. One has to take into account that the limitations of this rationality have been demonstrated in all operating planning systems, even the most centralized ones. There are at least four such limitations.

Planning does not deal with a homogeneous environment, because the levels of development and the degree of socialization of different areas and sectors of the economy are so varied that it is not possible to bring them all under the same pattern in a homogeneous plan. The various resources and requirements cannot be balanced by a single method of planning, even under a macro-economic disguise. There must be – and always has been – a difference between planning international trade and planning domestic trade; between planning the banks and planning physical production, etc. This *de facto* heterogeneity is concealed in the uniformity of central planning.

The second limitation is that plans are presented in their final form as the unified and consistent, rational ('scientific') decision of the top planning decision-makers. The whole procedure by which these central decisions were reached, the norms which were applied, the sources of the initiative and the ease with which the initiative was channelled are simply not clear. The empiricism of the top political decision-makers, the irresponsibility of their economic back-room men, the blocked initiative of those below and, moreover, the arbitrariness of the models used and the omission from plans of important economic activities – all this is concealed in the authoritarian procedure of centralist planning. The main objection to this type of centralized planning is that it is not institutionalized, but is at the mercy of the political arbitrariness and bureaucratic whims of the central planning authorities, a state of affairs which creates the greatest tension between planners and planned, of all planning procedures.

Thirdly, there is the fact that planning in its centralized form is not a system in which rational methods can best be applied. Just because it is centralized the central authorities object to any kind of formalized models or prevent them from being used, preferring to remain within the framework of macro-economic empirical decisions made by political actors. In a system where there is a monopoly of power in one centre which is not checked or counterchecked, such a method of planning is not only possible but appears to be natural.

The fourth weakness of centralized planning is that such macro-economic planning is not the all-embracing system it is often supposed to be. Rather, it becomes restricted to some sort of internal closed system of balancing variables and objectives chosen in advance to suit the interests of the central planners, who leave out of the plan all activities which are not approved or recognized by them. It provides the perfect opportunity for concealing the actual biases of the central planner.

The decentralized model has its own rationality too, which is also limited. The inequality between the functions of a dominant *centre* and a (by definition) dependent *periphery* creates tensions which are an obstacle to rational planning, because the decision as to what should be the powers of the centre and what left to the periphery is usually arbitrarily taken. A system which does away with any such distinction and takes into account all centres of activity in an appropriate way will be more efficient and more successful than either a centralized system or a decentralized one.

The third method of planning is the polycentric method. It is less homogeneous than the centralized system seems to be, but its heterogeneity is recognized and institutionalized, so that it is recognized and from the start is automatically taken into account in an organized way. The polycentric system is less arbitrary just because of the possibility of using one dominant centre to check another.[1]

We shall now describe the three models of planning used in Yugoslavia by discussing certain basic elements of planning and the way in which they are organized in these three different models. This we hope will give a better understanding than describing the three types in chronological order. We shall

[1] For polycentric planning, see the author's book *Problems of Planning East and West*, Institute of Social Studies (The Hague, 1967), Part II.

consider the role of the actors, the means of planning the objectives, and the environment in which it takes place.

The actors
The rules of the constitution

As stated in the Yugoslav Constitution of 1946, in the period of centralistic planning the main planning agency was the state, which directed the development of the economy through the overall state plan.[1] The centralized state sector of the economy was intended to be the main field of planning action. In the second period, that of decentralized planning, instead of a *state* plan the Constitutional Law of 1953 speaks of a *social* plan. Instead of one overall plan providing the framework for all economic activities there were autonomous plans based on self-management in enterprises, and above these, self-government plans in the communes and districts, in the republics and finally for the federation as a whole. This social plan had as its aim the planned development of the economy as a whole, which in practice on the whole meant centrally planned investments.[2]

The Constitution of 1963 established new principles of planning, the purpose of which was to bring about self-management in enterprises, to serve the individual and common interests of the working people and to stimulate their initiative. Planning in working organizations was put on an equal footing with that of

[1] 'In order to protect the vital interests of the people, to further the people's prosperity and the right use of all economic potentialities and forces, the state directs the economic life and development of the country in accordance with a general economic plan, relying on the state and co-operative economic sectors, while achieving general control over the private economic sector' – *Constitution of the Federative People's Republic of Yugoslavia* (1946), Article 15.
[2] 'The self-management of producers in economic life consists of: "the right of business organizations to set their economic plans independently" (Article 6). Self government by the working people in communes, cities and districts especially consists of: "...the right of the people's committee autonomously to decide about the budget and social plan" (Article 7). "The social plan of the Republic sets aside only those financial resources determined by law for the people's republic; those which serve to implement activities, within the jurisdiction of the Republic, for assistance to cities, districts and to public agencies and business organizations which are of general interest to the Republic" (Article 8). "The Federation has the following rights and duties...to secure the unity of the economic system, and the planned development of the economy as a whole" (Article 9).' *Novi ustav Federativne Narodne Republike Jugoslavije* (New Constitution of the Federative People's Republic of Yugoslavia) (Belgrade, 1953), pp. 9, 10, 11.

the social-political communities (communes, districts, republics and the federation) – indeed priority was given to planning in the enterprises.[1]

The decision-makers

In the centralized system of administrative planning, all the agencies concerned were organized in a social pyramid in which decisions were made at the top and then relayed down to the bottom. The Five-Year Plan was made by the Federal Parliament, which was at that time entirely subservient to the Federal Government, which in turn was controlled by the Political Bureau of the Communist Party of Yugoslavia. A similar organizational relationship existed on the lower levels of planning in republics and districts. The basic characteristic of this system was that those concerned at the higher levels set the limits to the planning decisions of the lower levels in the social pyramid. Thus those on the lower levels could move only within the framework laid down by those higher in the administrative hierarchy.

In the decentralized system of planning, decisions no longer depended entirely on the line of communication from the top to the bottom of a pyramid. With regard to the agents concerned

[1] 'In order to attain self-management and to realize the individual and common interests of the working people, in order to stimulate their initiative and create the most favourable conditions for the development of the productive forces, to equalize working conditions, to achieve distribution according to work, and to develop socialist relations, the social community plans the development of the economy and the material foundations of other social activities. Planning is done in the working organizations by the working people as the bearers of production and of socially-organized work, and by the social-political communities in the performance of their social-economic functions.' *The Constitution of the Socialist Federal Republic of Yugoslavia 1963*, Basic Principles III. English translation published by the Secretariat for Information of the Federal Executive Council (Belgrade, 1963), p. 6.

'In order to secure conditions for the most favourable economic and social development, to equalize general conditions of work and the acquisition of income, to determine general standards of distribution, to realize the principle of distribution, according to work, and to develop socialist social relations, the Social-political Communities shall undertake, in accordance with their rights and duties, measures to develop a unified economic system, to plan economic development and the material bases of other activities, and to this end they shall adopt social plans. In order to achieve the relations determined by the social plans, the Social-political Communities shall pass regulations and other general decisions, set up social funds and social reserves, and undertake economic and other measures.' *Ibid.*, Article 26, p. 20.

the main differences were that there was a link built into the system making communication possible in a horizontal direction on the lowest level of the social pyramid, i.e. among socialist enterprises. This link was secured through the market mechanism.

The second characteristic of the decentralized model was that the federal plan did not set ceilings for the subordinate plans. Of course talks and discussions went on between the republic and federal planning authorities and the local authorities, but no normative ceiling existed. If a republic could find means to exceed an overall target set by the federal plan and to set its own target,[1] it was free to do so. The same was true of communal authorities. This change in planning decision-making and a certain liberalization of the position of the subordinate centres in relation to the higher ones was not only a matter of principle but also of political convenience. Since the central plan could not fulfil all the demands and expectations of those further down the hierarchy, it was necessary for planning units who wanted to make some additional efforts on their own to be allowed to do so and to set additional planning targets for themselves. Planning still suffered from the prejudice that over-fulfilling the plan was a good thing and not a sign of bad planning.

In the third model of planning, which has taken a polycentric pattern, not only can contact be made on a horizontal level, but the top centre has itself been split into many decision-making centres all on an equal footing.

It would be wrong to think that polycentric planning is a system where there is no central plan at all. Indeed there are several central plans, which differ in the agents involved, their targets, their size and policy instruments in different fields. The important point is that none of these central plans has power to over-rule the others or any indisputable priority in objectives set on the basis of a rational choice.

The first model of planning takes as its pattern a social pyramid, and the second a pyramid with horizontal rungs of communication at the lowest level. The centralist system operates only by communication up and down the pyramid. All planning links among economic units must take place through higher

[1] In this way e.g. the overall investments planned by the federal plan were over-reached by 40 per cent in all plans taken together in 1962.

levels in the hierarchy. In the decentralized system the market mechanism operates on horizontal enterprise-to-enterprise lines. The pattern of polycentric planning is a matrix, and this matrix provides interconnections between all decision-making planning agencies. It operates not only on the vertical commune-to-republic-to-federation line, but also on horizontal lines, and the republic-to-republic and commune-to-commune planning levels. In this system any planning unit can make its own plans; what matters is that all decisions are registered within the framework of a matrix and made consistent with such a matrix by check and countercheck. The effectiveness of planning depends on these interconnections and on the degree of social integration,[1] the extent of information on the economy and the speed and accuracy of the feedback of information between the planners and the planned.

Planning instruments

The nature of the tools of planning varies between the three different models. In the first model they were mostly of an administrative character: laws, rules, orders, government regulations, administrative acts and directives imposing planning targets and ordering what must not be done. There were also too many (14) kinds of regulations that had to be followed. The modest incentives which accompanied these imperative norms were moral gratification, awards of orders and medals and the presentation of flags or titles.

In the second model the instruments of planning were economic: wage bills linked to accumulation of funds in socialist enterprises; profit-sharing, income-sharing, interest rates, multiple exchange rates in foreign trade, etc. Workers' councils, pursuing the economic interests of the working collective of the enterprise, made their own autonomous plan and in doing so implemented the planning targets and so fulfilled the objectives of the social plan. Thus, instead of administrative instruments economic instruments were introduced, and at the same time the initiative of the workers was freed from the restrictions imposed by the state bureaucracy.

[1] By social integration we mean the degree of inter-connections between the pattern and allocation of outputs and of inputs.

It was expected that economic rewards would stimulate workers to fulfil social objectives. What happened in fact was just the opposite. In practice, indirect planning developed into a disguised form of direct planning, as a result of bureaucratic interference. Most of the enterprises had pressure put on them by local planning authorities, encouraged by those above, to accept planning targets which resulted in their paying into the government budget a certain global sum,[1] and to adjust their planning target to accord with this anticipated government income. In this way the government's share, instead of being a dependent variable, became a *constant*, round which all other elements of socialist income distribution turned. This was a *de facto* redistribution of anticipated, i.e. as yet unearned, income.

The half-hearted decentralization of the second period was upset by the development of workers' management. This had been introduced as a way of encouraging the fulfilment of social plans but by the middle sixties it had already developed into a system of business management and, further, into a system of overall social organization, so that the whole concept of socialism had come to be based on it.[2] This made the decentralization of the economic system essential, and new methods of planning had therefore to be introduced to fit this new system. One of the first principles which the new kind of planning had to take into account was that income could not be distributed until it had been actually realized on the market – i.e. no distribution of anticipated income to administrative bodies.

The spatial dimension

As far as the geographical organization of planning was concerned the centralized model meant that the overall state plan decided on by the federation was over-riding, and fixed the ceilings for the targets of the republic plans. Another kind of linkage was provided by departmental planning between the

---

[1] This pressure was applied by the local planning agencies immediately above enterprise level. This was because although jurisdiction had been delegated to them by the central authorities these central authorities had not at the same time delegated the funds, which they kept for their own purposes. Thus the local authorities tried to make good the loss by a global levy on the enterprises. They had in fact been given the authority but not the funds to implement their plan, and the whole fiscal system was based on flat-rate levy on enterprises.

[2] Statement of V. Bakarić, *Borba*, 24 July 1966.

three levels of administrative subordination: ministry–directorate–enterprise. There was a distinction between ministries of federal importance, which planned the activities of their subordinate enterprises only within the framework of the federal plan, and ministries whose jurisdiction was partly federal and partly at the republic level. The enterprises controlled by these ministries planned within the general framework of the federal plan, but were subject to the administrative control of the republics' ministries. Local authorities had only a small field of competence in handicrafts and some small local industries, in which no limits were set by the higher planning authorities. The local authorities were not expected to know anything about the plans of the federal or republic-level enterprises operating in their territories.

In the decentralized system the division of enterprises into federal, republic and local was abolished and all enterprises were brought into touch with the planning mechanism at the level of the communal authorities, through the intermediary of the communal plans. A spatial coordination in planning was achieved, as opposed to administrative heterogeneity of the planning in central planning, an achievement which prevented the situation arising in which several plans of different administrative levels operated in the same area without any institutional interconnection between them.

Since decentralized plans were limited territorially there soon developed a tendency towards a sort of autarchy based on administrative boundaries. Every republic and every commune had control over its own enterprises operating within its administrative frontiers. The federation followed an autarchic policy towards foreign countries, and the lower units tried to copy this within their own jurisdiction, basing their actions on the concept of a closed planning system. Moreover, as the enterprises were the source of fiscal income for local and republic authorities and also for the federation, a great struggle developed for possession of the income from taxation of the enterprises. One could say that administrative boundaries prevailed over economic linkages if it were not for the fact that even the economic considerations were politically biased, i.e. the course of action favoured by the central authorities was considered to be economically optimal simply because it was so favoured.

In order to counteract this, a polycentric system began to develop under the impact of the economic reform. In this poly-centric system autonomous planning by enterprises plays the main role and the authority of territorial administrative units over enterprises is reduced, so that it is possible for socialist enterprises to develop commercial and contractual (long-term) links with other enterprises across administrative borders and to take part in inter-enterprise activity to a much greater extent than before. They are led in this direction not by the command of administrative planning units but by economic interests.

This naturally brings about a difference in the role of the *initiative* of the planning agencies. The authoritarian system of centralized planning operated under the guidance of directives of the central, i.e. federal, authorities. Enterprises were severely punished if the plan was not fulfilled and the managers poorly rewarded if it was. This system sapped the energies of the work-ing people and the managers on the spot, and turned them into passive agents of the will of those above them in the administra-tive pyramid. Another consequence of this same system was that the lower actors were freed of all responsibilities except that of doing what they were told by the superior planners. The superior planning authorities had to provide them with the necessary resources, directives and means to implement the plans for current and investment activities, ranging from prices and wage rates to new patents.

When it was realized how much damage this sytem of bureau-cratic administration had done to the economy, workers' management was introduced in the factories, and spread to all socialist enterprises and public services. But in the system of decentralization the power of the workers' council was limited to planning *current* activities. It was considered to be the role of the federal social plans to direct centrally the policy of invest-ment for economic growth; in fact, of course, it was soon realized that it is not possible to separate current from growth activities. Successful management of current affairs tends to make an enterprise grow and this was hindered by obstacles set by the central planning of investment.

The enterprises now had control of planning in the current operational field, but had no freedom of decision-making in the organizational field or in the field of regulation, where they were bound by administrative decisions, many of which were aggregated or disaggregated by political orders. This began to be changed in 1965. Since the economic reform, planning of enterprises is seen as the auto-regulation of their activities. This again has led to a two-track policy, because although on one hand auto-regulation means that the enterprises are free to decide what to do, on the other hand they can no longer shelter behind the shield of the government budget, and make use of its funds and administrative subsidies. They therefore have to stand on their own feet and take the risks involved in their decisions themselves.

The time dimension

A significant change has taken place in the time dimension of planning. In the first period of administrative centralized planning there was one overall state Five-Year Plan with ramifications on both territorial and departmental lines. This perspective plan was split into five annual plans and these in turn were subdivided into quarterly plans, which were the smallest time units used in overall national planning. In the event this first Five-Year Plan (1947–51) had to be prolonged for one year. The plans of the enterprises were made not only on annual and quarterly bases, but also for monthly and ten-day periods. These short planning periods led to a *de facto* division of labour between those who continuously planned and had no experience in the implementation of plans, and those who carried out the plans in a merely routine way without taking part in their construction.

In the period of decentralized planning only annual plans were made during the first five years (1952–6), because the economy was in a transition period, searching for new patterns of organization. Quarterly plans were abandoned altogether, as it was felt that three months was too short a period for planning an economy on a national scale.

The next five-year period (1957–61) was included in the second Five-Year Perspective Plan, whose objectives were by and large achieved in four years (ending in 1960). The 1961–5 plan was abandoned because of a recession in 1961–2 and a seven-year plan (1964–70) only reached the project stage, because the centralist versus anti-centralist conflict made agreement impossible. The economic reform introduced a Five-Year Perspective Plan (1966–70) and abandoned operational annual plans altogether, as too short a period for planning. The idea of a two-year planning period was put forward, but not pursued.

In the struggle for stabilization of the economy, annual planning was abolished, since it involved frequent changes of economic instruments and rates, which were considered to be obstacles to stabilization, as was certainly true for the type of planning which had existed hitherto. On the other hand, it was held that planning in an economic system like the one introduced by the reform required further study.

Planning objectives

In the centralized system of planning the targets were stated in absolute figures. We would call this a system of *global planning*, whether the objectives are set in physical units or in value terms. It can also be called a system of direct planning. In the decentralized system direct planning was considered inadequate because it only set the targets and did not stimulate workers to produce more, to improve quality or to be more economical. Therefore the system was changed to a system of *parametric* planning. Parameters of action, called economic instruments, were set and it was left to those planning the enterprises to find their own optimum within the limits imposed by these instruments. If the planner was good at his job, the optimum arrived at by the enterprises should be close to the planner's target. A conflict developed between the enterprises and the social plans, about the way in which the optimum was to be found. A continuous game of hide-and-seek ensued and the gain was not always on the side of the planners, who tended to suffer from the disease of their profession: authoritarian over-optimism. In the decentralized system the parameters of action were each set separately and almost independently. There was no formalized model of planning to secure consistency in the setting of targets. It was therefore difficult to find a common yardstick by which to judge how effectively the plans were fulfilled. It was necessary to evolve a system which would take into consideration the activity of the enterprise as a whole. It is now felt that the solution is provided by a system where the parameters of planning are arranged in one consistent matrix, and which may therefore be called a *matrix-based* system of planning. Efforts to establish such a system are meeting with various kinds of resistance. Its consistency is attacked on many levels, from the politicians in the central government and its bureaucracy, to dictatorial managers of some enterprises. But there is no way out. It is my opinion that sooner or later such a system will have to be evolved in order to make the planning mechanism work efficiently. On one hand this system gives ample possibilities for developing the initiative of the workers managing the enterprises, and on the other it provides flexible links between their activities and connects them with other mechanisms (e.g. the market, firm, administration, etc.).

Prices

The centralized system was based on planned prices as instruments of distribution. All the constituent parts of these prices were planned and were fixed without reference to the real costs, for reasons we shall see later. As fixed targets were planned for all inter-enterprise relations, and each enterprise was told which other enterprises to supply at what prices, and what to obtain in return, any possibility of choice between products or criticism of the quality or selection of goods was ruled out. If it had not been for unofficial 'comrades' agreements' to circumvent the rules imposed from above, this thoroughly 'rationalized' system could not have operated at any price. There was a marked difference between the actual requirements of the enterprises for the implementation of imposed planned targets and the formal centrally planned resources, which the planned prices, based on averages of averages, could not bridge.

In order to avoid a breakdown of the economic system, it was necessary to abolish the centralized planning mechanism and to replace it with a more flexible and responsive framework for planning. The new system introduced market prices instead of rigid planned prices. Although the market was a very imperfect one, many of the elements of the price structure being defined by administrative methods, nevertheless it was a much more flexible and successful system than the centrally planned one. It came a little closer to real costs and expenditures than the earlier system. But the manipulation of prices on this imperfect market by administrative methods was a great temptation to 'create profitability by political means'. Therefore many enterprises were set up which were based on political decisions, and their prices were made to fit in with this imperfect market by subsidies and premiums, tax reductions and exemptions, deficit financing and crediting with no return and other methods of income redistribution by political means. Thus the whole system was eventually overburdened with so many exceptions that it required general overhaul. On the one hand, prices which were set administratively for socialist enterprises soon became monopolistic prices, although there were no capitalist owners behind the monopoly. On the other hand, such prices were much higher than real costs and very much higher than prices of comparable products in other countries (reflecting socially necessary labour). Some prices were deliberately kept low, e.g. agricultural prices (wheat, meat). Others were kept below the domestic profitability line by subsidies, but were still much higher than world market prices (e.g. pig iron, coal). On the other hand prices of manufactured consumer goods were kept high (e.g. textiles) and prices of capital goods rose rapidly. These were the results of planned maximization of growth and accelerated industrialization.

This system also enabled the federal authorities to give absolute priority to their own plans and to distribute the national income in their own way, taking the lion's share for their special interests – those of the central bureaucracy. The system soon created tension between the federal bureaucracy and business management of enterprises. The former favoured some general provisions in the social plan, which enabled them to act arbitrarily according to their own preferences; the latter had little use for such general rules; after paying their taxes and contributions and receiving their subsidies, the enterprises acted independently in their current transactions, hoping to be able to solve more of the problems created by past investment by asking for credits for new investment. This system finally became so inefficient that a crisis developed in 1961/2, which was temporarily overcome and the main issues postponed until 1965. By then it was no longer possible to delay any longer, and the economic reform was introduced, which had as its main target the stabilization of the economy and the creation of a more realistic economic system, by means of structural changes. After various attempts to introduce some sort of internal distributive system, along the lines of an income–price system, it was decided that the best objective measurement of the efficiency of the enterprises would be prices on the world market, which meant that enterprises should also plan production costs on the basis of world market prices, taking into account only normal tariff protection. Of course, this creates considerable difficulties in planning, but it does mean that a yardstick has been established, by which to measure the effectiveness of enterprises.

Gross national product distribution

The distribution of gross national product is extremely significant in these models of Yugoslav planning. In the first model the distribution was undertaken according to the decisions of the supreme political body deciding on the central plan. Distribution of every single product was achieved by first distributing the total quantity produced in the country (plus an anticipated 6 per cent 'planned profit') according to a system of weighted averages, from the top down to the lowest level of the economic unit, usually on a three-level scheme: the ministry, the directorate, the enterprise. This in effect meant that 16,000 groups of centrally planned commodities were distributed among 165 ministries, several hundred directorates and their 8,000 enterprises. The planning requirements of the six republics, with two autonomous units, 360 districts and 7,104 communal people's committees, ranked lower in priority. As there were so many levels, many of these averages gradually became more and more divorced from reality the further they were from the centre, and in the end they had nothing in common with the actual requirements of the population and the economy.

The system of centrally planned distribution thus had to be abandoned and in its place another system of distribution by planning was introduced. A 6 per cent general rate of interest was introduced on fixed assets and later on total working capital. The enterprises had to pay this annually into the general investment fund, in exchange for the use of the capital that society had put permanently at the disposal of the management of the enterprise. This rate was introduced by law and was not affected by the annual social plans.[1]

Another burdensome instrument of income distribution was the profit-sharing system by which the Federal Government took 50 per cent of all enterprises profits in the 1955–8 period. However, the turnover tax remained the main instrument of accumulation and the revenue it produced went directly to the federal budget. In fact the rates of turnover tax were changed so many times that eventually there were so many varied rates of taxation that no system remained. The turnover tax, which was originally meant to be the chief instrument for balancing effective demand with inadequate supply, lost its purpose almost entirely and retained only its fiscal character.[2]

Thus the workers' councils, after so many proclamations about self-management, were left with some 26 per cent of the income of the enterprise after the payment of all non-labour expenditure as the workers' personal income in lieu of wages. (The wage system was abolished in 1958 and replaced by a system whereby workers are paid out of the residual income after all other obligations are met.) The enterprise funds were allocated only 14 per cent of the income. The rest (60 per cent) was taken away and controlled by the social plans of the federation, republics, districts and communes.

In the third model the principle was accepted that the income of an enterprise belongs to the workers of that enterprise and that redistribution by the government is an imposition by an outside body. The principle adopted was that income should be disposed of where it is earned, i.e. in the enterprise, as required by the labour theory of value. It was considered reasonable that the government should take from the enterprise about 30 per cent of the gross income, but it was held that the division of the rest between the personal income of the workers and the investment funds of the enterprise should be decided by the

[1] Nevertheless, there were exceptions to this 6 per cent burden, which was too great for certain branches of industry, such as agriculture, or those with very intensive capital investment (hydro-electric power stations, etc.). Finally the capital tax reached an average of 2.7 per cent. It was reduced by the reform to a nominal level of 4 per cent.

[2] It was only in 1963 that the high tax on sales of textiles introduced in the times of clothing shortage was reduced, in order to lower the price of the already over-expanded production of textile goods.

workers' management. As a result, 70 per cent of enterprise income will ultimately be exempt from redistribution by the annual social plans and left to be allocated by the autonomous plan of the enterprise. The justification given for this is the need to modernize and replace obsolete capital equipment, which can best be done by the enterprises themselves. No central authority, despite its experts, can have such a detailed technical knowledge of modern innovations and as much information concerning the situation on the spot and the requirements for modernization in 8,500 factories as the business enterprises themselves.

The environment

Planned and non-planned activities

In the centralized authoritarian model the overall state plan operated in a universe of its own creation and the only problem was to fulfil the plan, ignoring what might happen outside this system. The number of planning targets was very great, but they still do not cover all the economic agents, objectives and forces in the country. The plan was based on a closed planning mechanism which did not take into account any activities except those which were planned; the only 'socially recognized' economic activities were those which were covered by the targets of the plan.

With the introduction of the second model came a great innovation. Activities apart from those which were planned were taken into account in framing economic policy, with the result that the monopoly of the plan was greatly weakened.

In the third model it was officially recognized that there are so many socially important activities apart from those included in the plan, and that it is the interest of socialism that such activities should be given due attention, whether inside or outside the planning mechanism.

This had already been stated in the 1958 programme of the League of Communists, which said:

The experience of Yugoslavia, and that of a number of other countries, indicates that a social economic plan, no matter how perfect it may be, cannot exhaust the limitless possibilities, forms, and initiative, afforded by the spontaneous development of economic forces. That is why the economic system and plan must not deprive the working man, enterprise and other social economic units, of that essential degree of independence without which no conscious initiative is possible and Man ceases to be a creative being.[1]

The 1964 programme of the League of Communists was still more explicit in emphasizing that the role of planning had changed and that it now gave guidelines for general conditions of development.

In a situation where direct producers themselves decide about investment and capital development, the function, system and method of planning are becoming an instrument in the hands of producers and of the community, for providing guidelines for economic development. The Federation, the republics and other socio-political communities should be primarily responsible for the creation of general conditions for harmonious economic development, but in doing so they should refrain from directly disposing of financial resources, this being the essential pre-condition for the implementation of the principles of income distribution according to labour input.[2]

Therefore a socialist economic policy must take into account not only the internal equilibrium set by the requirements of consistency with the formal plan, but also the external homeostatic equilibria between planned targets and non-planned activities. Such an approach involves changes in the methods of planning, in the direction of an open and polycentric planning mechanism. The plan has come to be considered only as a guide and an indicator of social objectives, rather than as an imperative or an obligation. Although the first model seemed to make possible the planning of many more economic activities, because the formal targets were much greater in number, in fact the number of activities planned is far greater under the third model, and only the planning methods have had to be changed.

Planning foreign trade

In the first model the volume of both exports and imports was

[1] *The Programme of the League of Communists of Yugoslavia* (Belgrade, 1958), pp. 158–9.
[2] 'The Programme of the LCY', *Yugoslav Survey*, no. 20 (March 1965), p. 2,907.

planned at planned prices. Between the internal planned economy and the external market there was no direct contact. Contact was channelled through the equalization fund, in which all gains and losses – mainly losses – between domestic planned prices and the prices achieved on foreign markets were centralized.

In the second model, planning of foreign trade was based on the commercial operations of various enterprises, which expected to be able to carry out their transactions by covering their costs from their proceeds. Thus the risk was decentralized. Central risk-taking by the equalization fund no longer existed after 1951 and enterprises could enter directly into commercial transactions and other relations with foreign enterprises, any income or profits accruing to themselves. Informal pressure was put on enterprises by government agencies in order to achieve planned export targets. This pressure varied from commodity to commodity and from country to country, depending on the various foreign trade targets. These targets were not set by the annual social plan, but were more or less operational targets arrived at by the government foreign trade agencies or the National Bank, with the aim of creating foreign currency funds and keeping the flow of payments abroad moving.

The first planning model was based on the assumption that national autarchy could be put into operation at once, and the closed centralistic plan was felt to be its political expression and main instrument. From the planning point of view this meant that the import targets (mainly of capital goods) needed for the fulfilment of plans were set up as essential planning requirements, which proceeds from exports had to cover at all cost. The second planning model extended the time period over which the objective of achieving national autarchy had to be achieved, and stated that it had to be achieved through balanced growth on the macroeconomic level. Commercial transactions with foreign countries were considered as temporary departures from national autarchy. Nevertheless their magnitude and duration demanded that the cost should be balanced by proceeds at the micro-level. Multiple rates of exchange took over the role previously played by the price equalization fund as the main planning instrument in foreign trade.

The third model was based on the attempt to structure foreign trade in accordance with the world division of labour with customs duties as the main instrument of trade policy and a uniform rate of exchange. The conception of autarchy has been abandoned, which implies further liberalization of foreign trade and gradual liberalization of foreign currency control until convertibility is reached. Planning has undergone a substantial change. In this field, as in others, enterprise planning plays the leading role and social plans are reduced to the role of an indicative instrument. There are two important exceptions: all purchases from centrally planned economies are made through one single enterprise which acts as distributor for each commodity from each separate country. The second exception is the bulk purchase of food and some raw materials by the state directories, for food and stocks.

Foreign trade planning is due to undergo yet further changes, in order to exploit the comparative advantages which Yugoslavia and its republics possess in various fields.

Main planning goals of various periods

It is interesting to make a brief comparison of the main planning goals of the various periods (see Table 3).

The *per capita* income in 1947 was about 200 dollars per annum. The second planning period, ten years later, started at the 325 dollars level, and the reform began at the level of 513 dollars per head, i.e. at a stage when countries generally move from underdeveloped models to developed ones.[1]

It is interesting to note the increase in complexity and the shifting of priorities between different planning objectives over the years. Backwardness was reduced from an overall problem affecting the country as a whole to a regional problem, and moved from first to last place in the list of objectives as the plans followed one another. It increased in importance again during the process of democratization in the reform period, so that it took third place out of seven in the fourth plan.

The building of the socialist sector was put in third place in

[1] According to the estimates of S. Stajić, who took into account the domestic purchasing power and the exchange rate of the dinar and put his estimates on a comparative basis with the western definition of the national income, the Yugoslav national income *per capita* reached 702 in 1964.

TABLE 3

Range of priorities of main planning objectives in the Yugoslav Five-Year Plans

Plan I, 1947–51	Plan II, 1957–61	Plan III, 1961–5	Plan IV, 1966–70
Rates of growth of national income planned and achieved			
planned 16.0% achieved 5.5%	planned 10.9% achieved 12.6%	planned 11.4% achieved 6.6%	planned 7.5–8.5% achieved 5.6%
1 Eliminating the backwardness of the country	1 Fast and stable growth of production	1 Fast and stable growth of production resources and capacity, especially key industries	1 Rise in the standard of living and personal consumption
2 Development of the economy and national defence	2 Stabilization of economic relations with foreign countries	2 Increase in personal consumption	2 Strengthening of socialism and development of self-management of direct producers
3 Development of the socialist sector	3 Improvement of the standard of living	3 Balance of economic relations with foreign countries	3 Accelerated growth of insufficiently developed republics and areas
4 Increase in general well-being	4 Aid to development of undeveloped areas	4 Development of undeveloped areas	4 Stabilization of the economy currency and prices
	5 Strengthening of socialism	5 Strengthening of socialism	5 Intensification of efficiency and total social and economic activity. Modernization and reconstruction of productive capacity by improved scientific and technical methods
			6 Convertibility of the dinar and wider integration into international division of labour
			7 Rapid development of education, technology and science

the first plan, as the basic measures of nationalization had already been taken before planning was introduced in Yugoslavia. It moved to fifth place in the second and third plans and re-emerged in second place in the fourth, as part of the problem of the development of workers' management.

Foreign trade was not mentioned as an objective at all in the first plan; in the second plan it took second place, and third place in the third. Its priority then sank to sixth in the fourth plan, but the objectives became more complex and complicated.

An especially significant ranking is that of the standard of living of the people. This was last priority in the first plan, moved to third place in the second, to second in the third, and in the fourth plan significantly rose to first rank of priority.

Stabilization of the economy took its proper place among planning objectives only in the fourth plan. Under the administrative methods in the earlier planning periods, it was not thought appropriate openly to admit the need for such a goal. It was felt that an economy claiming to be socialist and planned must by definition be a stabilized economy.

Finally, technological progress was stressed in the first three planning periods by implication only, as 'overcoming backwardness', the goal being to reach the level of the average 'non-backward' countries. In the fourth planning period it became particularly emphasized as a condition of economic progress. Education and scientific activity were similarly stressed. In the author's opinion these three objectives should be given overriding priority in the further development of the reform.

4
The evolution of the system of social control of the economic system

Administrative socialism

This was a centralized and authoritarian system in which all initiative was monopolized by – and all decisions taken by – the top Communist Party leadership, i.e. the Politbureau. This organization was set up during the war and during the subsequent revolutionary take-over of political, economic and social power. The party not only seized control of the top government machinery, but also took over the control of property, the operational management of business organizations and the running of the labour unions. All political parties other than the Communist Party were abolished in order to preserve a monopoly of power in the one-party system.[1] Control of all central, provincial and communal government agencies and of all autonomous public corporations and agencies, including their property and personnel, was completely centralized.

Thus there was a merger of government administration and business management under direct political Party leadership in each unit. Thus the principle of 'democratic centralism' was followed at all levels of the central state administration, in the six republics and in local government (the last having three levels: county, district and commune). In this authoritarian and strictly centralistic structure of authority all enterprises were classified as of federal, republic or local importance, and controlled by the corresponding state organs of authority. The business units themselves were organized on the principle of a chain with three links: ministry–directorate–enterprise. There were at one point (in 1949) 217 federal and republic ministries

---

[1] Nevertheless, besides the Communist Party of Yugoslavia there were six communist parties, one in each of the republics. These were linked together, although each had a strictly centralized organization.

with hundreds of directorates, running some 10,000 business organizations.

This system of control was modelled on the Soviet economic organization as it existed immediately after the Second World War. With some notable exceptions, exactly the same structure was set up in Yugoslavia in the second half of 1946, with the intention that it should start operating on 1 January 1947.

Business enterprises were run as if they were parts of the government administration and according to rules of administrative procedure. The favourite instrument of government was the directive, i.e. an order issued by a higher to a lower administrative level, which was binding for those below, but not for those above who had issued the directive. This made it possible for the superior levels to interfere continually with the running of current operations, issuing orders from above and indiscriminately interrupting the economic process from afar. Rules were not respected even by those who made them, and the personnel at the lower levels did not know whether to act in accordance with the formal laws or the informal directives. This situation resulted in great legal and administrative insecurity.

Soon this huge and complicated centralized monopoly of command and initiative began inevitably to show signs of organizational and operational difficulty. A huge central system was improvised to control the daily work of this triple monolith: party organization, state administration and business management. Its size bred inefficiency, its authoritarianism sheltered incompetence and its dogmatism led to arbitrary behaviour by thousands of inexperienced but self-righteous officials, each thinking himself to be the infallible organizer of the world revolution. The economic losses resulting from this system soon became evident, when revolutionary zeal evaporated and the mundane realities of supply, shortages of skilled labour and adequate machinery, began to emerge again. The first solution attempted was a new organization of the socio-economic system.

The new economic system

This moved in the direction of decentralization and legalization. Firstly, government administration was separated from business management of current operations. Rule by directives was to a large extent replaced by legal rulings, which fixed the rights and responsibilities for most current operations. The government administration no longer questioned the correctness of the decisions of the socialist enterprises, but only their legality. The administration stopped guiding the operational activities of business organizations and maintained only its regulative and organizing role. There was a considerable reduction in staff at the top levels of the government administration. Federal and republic ministries and their directorates were abolished and their place was taken by a small number of secretariats with reduced powers. Decentralization took place both functionally and spatially. In the functional sense new centres of decision-making were created in place of the many old ones. Political decisions were centred in the executive councils (federal and republic). These were policy-making bodies, the majority of whose members were elected by parliament from among its own ranks.

Federal councils were formed for different branches of the administration.[1] Parliament also elected committees which discussed the policies of the executive council or the government. The federal and republic secretaries were regarded as top civil servants, rather than political actors, as, with the two exceptions of the state secretaries for foreign affairs and defence, they were not members of parliament.

These three lines of social control – executive councils, parliamentary councils and secretariats and committees – together with a fourth and most important, the network of Communist Party organizations, created a complicated system of machinery, which was gradually reduced to some extent by merging the role of the federal secretariats and that of the members of the executive council. Its greatest deficiency was that it divorced decision-making from control over implementation.[2]

[1] Controversial decisions in which a joint agreement could not be reached were referred to the top political Party committee.
[2] This was a compromise achieved under pressure from the centralists, who favoured a central bureaucracy. In 1967 the law on reorganization of federal agencies did not support the idea of central government secretariats being policy-makers, and they were therefore excluded from membership of the executive committees and parliament.

In the spatial sense decentralization was effected by transferring a great deal of jurisdiction from the federal government to the six republics (and two autonomous provinces) and from them to districts and communes. This transfer was, however, carried out in such a way that legal responsibility was generally passed on, but without the funds which had hitherto been available to put decisions into effect, so that the subordinate units had to find new sources of finance.

The business organizations were now freed from administrative procedures and operated on the market, buying and selling as independent business entities. They were no longer classified as federal, republic or local enterprises and were put on an equal footing in the market. They were also granted the right to make their own autonomous plans. In place of the hierarchical links between enterprises and plans at different administrative levels, the territorial principle was applied and enterprise plans were linked with social plans at the level of the community. However, decisions were in fact very often imposed at all levels by the government administration at higher levels.

Purchases and sales on the market depended on decisions reached by the socialist business organizations run by managers and controlled by workers' councils. The workers' councils had the right to control their current business transactions, but investment decisions, both for the starting of new enterprises and for the expansion of existing ones, were taken by centralized government investment agencies. The position formerly occupied by federal ministries was taken by the General Investment Fund run by the Investment Bank. The business organizations now formed branch organizations within the framework of the local, republic and federal economic chambers. Originally there were several specialized chambers, but later they were merged into one economic chamber at each level.[1]

The organizational units of the League of Communists of Yugoslavia kept informal but effective control of all public administration and business management. This created some problems for business organizations, especially when self-

[1] At the federal level, there were chambers for transportation, construction and foreign trade. At the republic and local levels there were chambers for trade and catering enterprises and for agriculture.

management through workers' councils gained momentum. Party officials exerted significant influence on decisions, although financial responsibility lay with the enterprises.

The economic and social reform of 1965 further developed workers' management as the main instrument of social control. In this reform we can distinguish four lines of development in social control, which we shall symbolically call the four 'D's'. Decentralization, already started under the new economic system, began to develop *de facto* into a polycentric system of decision-making. De-etatization, developed along the lines of self-management both by the workers in their business organizations and by agencies for public services such as health and education, started to become the basis of the whole social system. Depoliticization aimed to reduce the role of the Communist League officials in economic decision-making, and created a need to redefine the role of communists in society and in the economy. Democratization began to develop into self-determination and independence for units within society.

The role of the League of Communists in social control

The role of the most important instrument of government, the Communist Party of Yugoslavia, also changed in the course of the three periods of economic policy and social development. In the period of administrative socialism the basic objective of the party was to create a state machinery for the establishment of the new social order and to control this order 'in the name of the proletariat, in the name of the working class and in the name of some of its allies'.[1] The authority of the state was the instrument by which the Communist Party expropriated the capitalist class, carried out the reconstruction of the Party after the war and organized the socialist economy. The socialist transformation of social relations was brought about from above by issuing laws and acts through parliament. Newly-created social property was subject to state control, which meant management by the bureaucratic apparatus of the state, directed by the Com-

[1] V. Bakarić, *Borba*, 24 July 1966. The interpretation of the role of the communists given here relies to a large extent on Bakarić's article.

munist Party. The Party officials controlled the state authority, which in turn was in complete control of the business enterprises.

This kind of all-powerful and all-embracing Party organization soon found itself in conflict not only with the basic Marxian principle of the withering away of the state, but also with the effective and efficient running of government. In order to justify its unlimited power it had to exercise continuous control over everything and everybody,[1] and to intervene in the daily running of business transactions in enterprises and government agencies. Such constant intervention by state and Party could only hinder the successful development of socialist social relations, rather than bringing such relations into being, which was the professed aim of the Party. The Party, acting from above, became increasingly isolated from the working class. Moreover, the centralized Party system of organization contradicted the principle of workers' management. The degree of continuous supervision and control increased as the economy grew in both size and complexity.

During this expansion the Party recruited new members mainly among the bureaucracy and the structure of its membership changed correspondingly. It consisted mainly of government officials and white-collar workers. Manual workers made up only one-third of the membership, and at the higher levels their number was considerably less. Since the main role of the Communist Party was to build socialism through command of the state authority, a two-way process took place as far as membership was concerned. On the one hand the communists who had the monopoly of command became government officials. Even though a large number of them were workers or peasants by origin, the fact remains that in order to play their role in building socialism they had to transform themselves into government officials. On the other hand the government officials, and those whose ambition was to become government officials felt that their chances of achieving a career or preserving their position would be strengthened if they joined the Communist Party.

---

[1] It was officially stated after the fall of Alexander Ranković that the political police had 1.3 million files on individuals in Croatia alone. Croatia had only 1 million male adult inhabitants at the time.

New social relationships were created by the introduction of workers' management in 1950, and this soon became the main agent of social change within the socialist society. Its aim was to change 'government on behalf of the working class into government by this class itself'.

In the period of the new economic system after 1953 workers' management became the main principle of the constitution. A large number of functions previously performed by the state were transferred to workers' management, which meant less power for communists in government agencies and more power for communists in working in socialist enterprises. In 1953 the Communist Party of Yugoslavia changed its name and became the League of Communists of Yugoslavia, in order outwardly to mark its changed role.

After the introduction of the new economic system a struggle began between the two concepts of continuing state control and developing workers' management. This struggle was apparent in every social organization and every measure of government policy. The role of the communist organizations was somewhat reduced and the privileges of their officials considerably diminished. They were divided into party organizations in government agencies and in business organizations. This division of function was stronger at the lower levels than at the higher. On the other hand the process of decentralizing party control from the top, but not transferring power to the lowest levels created a middle layer of state and party officials, who were very anxious to preserve their positions and therefore became pillars of dogmatism and the establishment.[1] As a rule, more liberal opinions and critical attitudes were found at higher levels. The struggle for legality was fought mainly by the top leadership of the League of Communists, and was chiefly directed against the state bureaucracy.

This struggle was intensified by the introduction of another form of self-government, that in the communes. Business organizations were not linked to government control at the lowest administrative level. This brought about a hardening of the administrative boundaries and the creation of economic barriers between different administrative units, each under the

[1] Marshal Tito addressed a letter to the communist organizations attacking the behaviour of these 'little Marshals', as he called them.

control of its Party committee, with taxes on business organizations as the main source of income for the administrative units.
Thus, in the name of democracy, antidemocratic administrative
limits were set on economic transactions.

The Constitution of 1963 formally proclaimed one-party rule
in Yugoslavia. Except for the League of Communists and the
Socialist Alliance, led by the communists, no political party is
legally allowed to exist, and indeed none had existed since
1945. Nevertheless, there was quite a wide difference of opinion
among the members of the League and of the various organizations representing the republics, on the issue of centralism and
the national question.

After the reform the further development of workers' management became crucial to the whole process of democratization,
decentralization, de-etatization and depoliticization. This
development was based on the principle that workers' control
automatically generates socialist relations. The basic issue soon
became, and still is, how the workers income is formed in the
process of distribution of the gross national product. The wage
system was abolished in 1958, since when the working collectives have distributed the income of the business organizations
according to the principle 'the greater the income, the more
developed the socialist relations'. Like the capitalist who must
invest part of his profits in his enterprise in order to survive and
to increase his income, so, under conditions of socialism, in
order to maintain the existence of the enterprise in which they
work and to increase their income, the workers must invest and
in this way extend socialist relations. Thus it was felt that the
weight of the membership of the League of Communists ought
in principle to shift from government offices to the workshops
and fields, and that the main effort of the Party should be to
alter the structure of its membership so as to include fewer
office workers and more producers. Thus the principle of
depoliticization, i.e. reduction of the decision-making power of
the Party with relation to the economic affairs of business
organizations at the macro-economic level, was generally
accepted.

At the micro-economic level the role of the League of Communists in business organizations was defined by Dr Bakarić
in the following way:

When it is a question of the current transactions of working organizations then it is evident that we must allow the decisions to be made by the organs of self-management which exist in all such organizations. . . When however the question is one that falls outside the framework of the normal conduct of business and is a source of difficulties in transition to the new system. . . then we can make use of other means, i.e. we can demand obedience to discipline from members of the League of Communists. . . they do not have to be made responsible as long as they act within the framework of what is not prohibited by law and as long as what they do does not interfere with the general course of affairs.[1]

Reorganization of the League of Communists along these lines began in 1967.

[1] *Borba*, 24 July 1966.

5
Industrialization

The policy of industrialization in Yugoslavia

By a policy of industrialization we mean measures of economic
policy for developing industry, i.e. manufacturing, production
of energy and mining according to the Yugoslav definition of
industry, at a certain tempo giving priority to the building up
of industry over other branches of economic activity (agriculture, commerce, housing, etc.) and taking account of the complexity of industrial activity, the complementarity in different
branches, and the horizontal and vertical connections among
industrial enterprises. Concentration on one branch of industry cannot be called a policy for the industrialization of a
country.

Objectives of industrialization

When a deliberate policy of industrialization was first formulated in Yugoslavia in 1947 five main objectives were listed, each
of which was given a specific meaning by the socialist character
of the policy.

The first objective was economic progress, which, as we have
already said, was taken to mean pulling the country out of its
state of backwardness, reducing the toil of human beings,
achieving greater efficiency with less labour on the production
side and increasing the standard of living and the quantity and
variety of goods on the consumption side. All this had to be
achieved by the industrial mode of production. There was to be
steam and electric power instead of animal traction, and
machines were to be substituted for human labour. In a country governed according to Marxist principles and the ideals of
socialism, economic progress was to all intents and purposes

identified with the development of industry – the more of it the better for socialism.

Second came the creation of an industrial working class. Here the objective was a political one. The system of government had been formed in the process of revolution and the social basis of the political superstructure was inadequate because of the small size of the working class. It was therefore intended through industrialization to create a working class which would provide the natural support of the political system, so that the dictatorship of the proletariat would follow on from dictatorship 'in the name of the proletariat'. This policy was helped by the existence of a high degree of agricultural over-population and an increasing demographic pressure felt in many parts of Yugoslavia.

Economic independence from foreign countries was the third objective. It was considered that a country that was not industrialized was at a disadvantage in relation to other countries. If a country which was dependent on imports for essential consumption goods and means of production wanted to be economically independent, it must learn to produce its own tools. It was thought that the terms of trade were against a country which was not industrialized. A policy of economic independence through industrialization was therefore conceived to reduce exchanges with foreign countries and substitute domestic products for imports. In a socialist country this trend was reinforced by the desire to become economically independent of the capitalist industrial countries.

National defence came fourth. Industrialization was intended to produce armaments for national defence. For a socialist country bordering on the capitalist world such industrialization was considered to be a condition of political independence.

The exploitation and processing of natural resources was the fifth main objective of industrial development. The socialist policy of accelerated industrialization was contrasted with the earlier slow process of industrial development in Yugoslavia, which was severely criticized for having allowed natural resources to be developed for the benefit of foreign financiers and their domestic agents.

To what extent were these objectives attained?

Three policies of industrialization[1]

There have been three different policies of industrialization in Yugoslavia over the last twenty years. We shall call them global, accumulative and selective industrialization.

Global industrialization. The first, global industrialization, lasted from 1945 to 1955. It was based on the Stalinist pattern as seen in the Soviet Union, and we would call it the first stage of industrialization based on nationalization, administrative planning and centralized management. It was a pattern thought to be universally applicable to all countries, whatever their level of development and endowment of natural resources. Its main characteristic was a rigid order of priorities in industrial development. First priority was given to industry over agriculture, transportation and other branches of the economy. In industry itself heavy industry had precedence over light industry; within heavy industry first place was given to factories producing machines and equipment.[2]

In this stage of industrialization, policy was considerably influenced by the needs of national defence which were chiefly supplied by engineering. Production of the means of production (the first of Marx's scheme of reproduction) took precedence over production of the means of consumption (or the second of the Marxian model). Between 1939 and 1955 the output of the machine-building industry increased eightfold, energy production 2.5 times and manufacturing production 1.7 times, while agriculture remained almost at the same level as before the war.[3]

---

[1] Where statistical sources are not otherwise specified, all data quoted in this chapter are taken from *Jugoslavija 1945–1964*, *Statistički pregled* (Statistical survey) (Belgrade, 1965), from the corresponding tables in the *Statistički godišnjak SFRJ 1966* (Statistical yearbook) and from *Indeks 1967*.

[2] Describing first how backward the old Yugoslavia had been in spite of its natural riches, and how it had been exploited and dependent on foreign countries, S. Vukmanović-Tempo, then the chief economic minister in the Federal Government, said that industrialization had to proceed by nationalization of existing industries and expropriation of capitalists. Attention was initially concentrated on essential tasks: the development of basic industries, such as metallurgy and machine tools, and the creation of sources of energy for the ever-growing consumption both of industry and of the population at large – *O zaključcima savetovanja o ekonomskim pitanjima* (About the conclusions of consultations on economic questions) (Belgrade, 1955), p. 26.

[3] *Ibid.*, p. 30.

Between 1938 and 1952 the number of industrial enterprises was reduced from 3,110 to 2,091, because the process of nationalization led to an increased concentration of industrial enterprises. By 1964 their number had increased only to 2,500, although production was almost five times greater. The tendency towards concentration can also be seen when pre-war data are compared with the later situation with regard to the number of workers. In 1936 industrial enterprises employing less than 60 workers numbered 1,654, and in 1963 only 335. The number of enterprises which employed more than 1,000 workers numbered 33 before the war and reached 297 in 1963.[1]

Building of new enterprises was centralized and the co-efficient of industrial concentration was high. The necessary prerequisite of this policy was to concentrate large sums in the central government budget and to spend them on a few large investment projects, without worrying about profitability or effective demand for the products in question. There was also emphasis on building the infrastructure of the country: railway lines, dams and power stations, metalled motor roads, new mines, etc. All these activities tended to be very capital-intensive and the labour force employed in building was mainly unskilled labour taken from the villages. Under this policy, the industries which were developed also required heavy investment in equipment industries. In order to build the machinery for the first power station, it was necessary to have all the equipment necessary to build many power stations. Therefore initial investment in the means to build the machines was out of all proportion with the product achieved for years to come.

Thus in the first period industries were built up regardless and costs were not competitive. No measurement of profitability was applied to them, with the result that resources were wasted and the period of construction was continually prolonged. Moreover, these industries were rather arbitrarily located for non-economic reasons (strategic or social considerations, personal influence, etc.), and almost the only criteria which were applied to them were political. Industrial enterprises were not connected with each other in an interdependent

[1] *Jugoslavija, 1945–1964, Statistički pregled*, p. 143.

system and did not encourage the setting up of further manufacturing plants for the final processing of products. Many were like rocks sticking up in the middle of desert plains.

The less developed the industry in an area the greater was the concentration of capital per person employed. This could be still seen for Yugoslavia in later years:

	National income per head 1962 000 din. (old)	Capital in industry per employed 1962 000 din. (old)
Yugoslavia	194	3,390
Slovenia	378	3,307
Croatia	232	3,307
Vojvodina	203	3,374
Serbia proper	187	3,420
Serbia (republic of)	175	3,570
Montenegro	142	8,848
Bosnia and Hercegovina	137	4,097
Macedonia	134	3,519
Kosmet	71	4,201

The first period was one of great sacrifice for consumers, because the development of consumer goods industries was neglected, and a high proportion of the national income was allocated to investment.

Accumulative industrialization. The industrialization of the second period might be called global or accumulative industrialization; this period started in 1955 and lasted until 1965. The policy was one of decentralized industrial development as envisaged by the new economic system.

At the Brioni meeting of top Yugoslav political leaders in 1955, which inaugurated a significant change in economic policy, it was decided that the foundations of advanced economic and social development had been laid. The needs of development hitherto – it was said – had demanded that a large proportion of national income should go to investment. However, this was no longer necessary and the structure of investment should also be readjusted, since previously most of it had gone to the basic industries and too little into consumer goods and agriculture. This had slowed down the overall increase in national income and the standard of living, and therefore the proportion of gross national product invested should in future be reduced.

A policy of decentralizing industry was now inaugurated, for the following reasons.

(1) The infrastructure of the country was to a large extent already laid down.

(2) The expense of setting up heavy industry out of the government budget was a very large financial burden which had to be shifted.

(3) The traditional defence industries had largely been built and after the death of Stalin in 1953, the threat of foreign aggression was much less.

(4) The demand for consumer goods had become so pressing that steps had to be taken to satisfy it. The consumer revolt which started in Western Europe in the late forties reached Eastern Europe in the mid-fifties (Poland, Hungary, 1956), and was prevented in Yugoslavia by a timely change in the policy of meeting consumer demand.

(5) The peasants who had been squeezed by the policy of forcible collectivization were no longer capable of providing sufficient savings to meet the increasing demand for investment funds needed in industrial development. Therefore the means of accumulation of such funds had to be transferred to industry, i.e. to the easily taxable consumer goods industry, which had to be given priority for that purpose.

The main change which took place in this period was the abandonment of the fixed order of priority for the means of production which had been set in the first period. The principle now followed was to build up first the industries which would accumulate income most quickly and which could then provide resources for the development of new industries, while simultaneously raising the standard of living and providing a source of fiscal income for the government at all levels (from central to local); these industries were called 'accumulative industries'.

Another aim in this second period of industrialization was to build industries which would rectify the imbalances created in

the first stage by non-economically-motivated growth industries – which would complement the heavy industries and
connect them into an interdependent and balanced industrial
whole. Thus the political emphasis shifted from developing
heavy industries to encouraging light industries, especially
those producing consumer goods which were heavily taxed.
Employment in the non-agricultural sector increased, and with
employment the demand for consumer goods and agricultural
products, which was not met satisfactorily because such goods
were not produced in adequate quantity or variety because of
the neglect of the consumer goods industry and because agriculture was still making great efforts to regain lost ground.
Housing and communal services were stagnant or regressing.
This created new disproportions, widening the gap between the
increasing purchasing power of the population due to employment and the lagging production of consumer goods and services, and was another reason for putting heavy industry
lower on the list of priorities and focusing primarily on light
manufacturing industries, agriculture, transportation and
other services.

The immediate post-war hunger for consumer goods had
already caused a considerable increase in their production in
the mid- and late-forties, mainly because of the activization of
unused capacities in existing pre-war factories, and the help
UNRRA provided in the form of raw materials. Thus the
emphasis on the need to develop capital goods industries
during the first Five-Year Plan was due not only to ideological
preferences, but also partly to the actual situation. Intensive
construction of heavy industries began in 1949, and required
heavy investment. Therefore the consumer goods industries
began to decline between 1948 and 1952 (where 1948 = 100
stood at 85). After 1952 the index number for capital goods
exceeded that of consumer goods by 5 to 18 points according to
various groups of industries. To redress this imbalance a change
of policy was decided on in 1955, but its effects did not materialize until 1962, when the consumer goods industries began to
move ahead faster than capital goods. The production of raw
materials and fuel was generally in line with the production of
consumer goods until 1956, when it began to differ. Up to 1962
the gap was moderate, but then it widened steadily until it

was substantially lagging behind the consumer goods index[1] (taking 1952 as 100). This had to be covered by increased imports of raw materials. Thus, unlike the classical pattern of development of other socialist countries, in Yugoslavia since 1962 the production of consumers goods has increased faster than the production of the means of production.[2]

At the same time the principle of decentralization of such light industries was accepted. Industry spread through all districts of the country and central investment funds were used to give all areas the means to develop such industries. This also meant spreading possibilities for the creation of a working class into all parts of the country, with a nucleus in each republic provided by the metal workers in the steel mills.

This policy had a number of consequences. In the first place, although industry expanded, in many cases the enterprises which were set up were of a size below the technological minimum required for efficient production. Secondly, these industries were linked to local administrative centres, where they were regarded as the main source of fiscal income for both the local centres and those above them. Industrial production, under such pressures, became expensive and non-competitive in wider markets. For this reason a policy of centrally subsidizing such industrial enterprises was accepted, so as to make them operational.

This policy of building industries in each locality was not aimed primarily at satisfying consumption. District officials wanted to increase the budgetary income[3] and generally the easiest way to do so was to tax industrial enterprises producing consumer goods, thus increasing fiscal income by the federal turnover tax. It was possible to raise prices because of unsatisfied demand in the artificially-created sellers' market. Thus inflated investment activity took place. This, in its turn,

---

[1]

	1946	1950	1955	1956	1960	1962	1964	1965	1967	1968
Capital goods	21	88	157	167	307	324	442	485	501	536
Raw materials	49	103	146	163	260	298	394	421	437	464
Consumer goods	59	117	146	162	289	346	469	511	536	570

(1952 = 100)

SOURCE: Statistički godišnjak 1969, p. 164.

[2] It was only in the 1968 plan that the USSR decided to allow the production of consumer goods to grow faster than the production of the means of production.

[3] See V. Bakarić's speech in O zaključcima savetovanja, pp. 42ff.

increased the price of investment goods and so investment required ever larger financial resources over and above those planned. Another pressure felt at this time was the growing inflationary gap between the steadily increasing labour force and the rate of the increase of the wage bill on the one hand, and the slower rate of increase in the production of consumer goods on the other (between 1952 and 1962). There was also a decline in the productivity of labour in the socialist sector and an increase in moonlighting among workers because of low wages.

In fact it was some time before the new industrial policy was able to produce results. Although it was established in 1955, it was 1962 before its effects began to materialize to a significant extent, by which time consumer goods industries had begun to expand faster than capital goods. There were several reasons for the delayed action of the new industrial policy.

(1) Factories producing capital goods, construction of which had started in the previous period (before 1955), came into production only after a long delay.

(2) Great efforts were made to supply these factories with raw materials and energy, and this was a competitive obstacle to the development of the consumer goods industries, to which less priority was traditionally attached.

(3) The established practice was followed of trying to make profitable capital goods factories which had been built on non-economic considerations, by increasing investment in accordance with the slogan that the main impediment to development was lack of capital and that further investment solved all problems of current production.

(4) On an average 30 per cent of capacity was unused, particularly in capital and consumer goods industries, because of lack of raw materials, energy, working capital and inadequate commercial services.[1]

(5) Centralized investment funds, political decision-making which showed an ideological preference for heavy industry (prestige steel mills, 'political' factories), the policy of low wages and salaries which provided inadequate purchasing power, all played their part as well.

Selective industrialization. The third stage of industrialization

[1] Savezna Narodna Skupština, *Industrijski razvitak Jugoslavije* (Industrial development of Yugoslavia) (Belgrade, 1957), pp. 11–13.

policy, which we have called the stage of selective industrialization, was inaugurated by the economic reform which started in 1965. The reasons why global industrial policy was changed were:

(1) Because many existing industries were inefficient and had to be subsidized. This was only possible as long as these industries were small and the subsidies did not represent a heavy burden on the national economy. But as the industries grew, so did the subsidies, until the financial burden became too great.

(2) Many enterprises were technically backward and there was no effective incentive in the country to change this. Thus well-protected domestic industries developed a tendency towards a small volume of production and a high rate of profit, or income, which was possible in a closed economy even at the existing technological level, which survived only because it was based on the monopoly of a domestic market of only 20 million people.

(3) It became imperative for the country to participate in the technological revolution taking place in the second half of the twentieth century. The fastest and most advanced way to do this was to break local and domestic monopolies, and to import technological progress into the country through world-market competition.

The guiding principle now became that of building up those industries which had the greatest comparative advantage from an international point of view (i.e. the industries with the relatively lowest labour (socially necessary) cost compared internationally). This meant, in the first place, promoting industries which could be incorporated in the international division of labour on a competitive basis. Therefore industrial policy had to be selective and had to abandon two previously-held ideas: that all industry is progressive, and that a country can afford to develop all branches of industry on an autarchic national basis. This meant changing from a closed into an open economy, exposed to both domestic and international competition. For this purpose the internal political boundaries created by the planning of administrative units had to be abandoned, and industrial enterprises had to be more exposed to forces. Parallel with this, a policy of integration of small enterprises began to be pursued, in order to make them stronger in the face of international competition and capable of rising from their low level of technology and aiming at continuous modernization.

This change in the policy of industrialization was necessary not only because of technological progress but for another and more specific reason, resulting directly from the industrialization policy itself. This had urged that all depreciation allowances should be concentrated into one central fund, out of which new industrial plants were financed. Adequate replacement of obsolete machinery in old industrial plants was not secured, a frequent failing of fast developing countries. Later the funds were decentralized and control was left to the enterprises themselves. But their spending was in effect often blocked, as these were the easiest funds on which the government could lay its hands. This problem was present at both the enterprise and the sector level (old versus new plant or sector), but it found its most evident expression on a regional basis. The depreciation of fixed, industrial assets was greatest in the most advanced republics (e.g. in 1962 for Slovenia 46 per cent, Croatia 36 per cent). By contrast, the percentage of the value of fixed assets depreciated was smallest where new individual plants had been built (in Montenegro only 25 per cent, in Macedonia 27, in Kosmet 26, while Serbia proper at 34 per cent was just below the Yugoslav average of 36). Thus the old industries complained that they had had to finance the construction of the new ones under the system of decentralized investment and now, with their obsolete machinery, had to compete with these new, up-to-date enterprises. Therefore modernization of existing plant had to take precedence over the building of new plants for quite some time. This policy met with moderate success, as we shall see later when we come to discuss investment policy.

The progress of industrialization

Surveying the development of these three policies of industrialization one can see a general tendency: from an undisputed dogma, industrialization has developed into a rational process and questions are asked with increasing insistence: 'Industrialization at what price?' 'Who benefits from which industries?' 'Which branches of the economy, which areas, which groups of the working population and to what extent?'

We shall now examine the extent to which the progress of industrialization over the whole period up to 1966 corresponded with the five objectives of industrialization mentioned at the beginning of this chapter.

Industry in Yugoslavia grew very quickly. Taking 1952 as the base year the index of the physical volume of industrial production increased almost five times by 1966 (index 474). In the same period the overall increase in the volume of production was three times (index 294). Trade services tripled, while agriculture (index 210) and handicrafts only doubled over these 15 years. The rate of growth of industry was one of the highest in the world.[1] But this overall successful expansion of industry needs to be examined in greater detail in order to see the advantages and disadvantages which it brought with it.

We need to ask which branches of industry in the Yugoslav economic system were leading the growth and which retarding it (i.e. which were above or below the general index for all industries). As already stated, the overall increase in the physical volume of industrial production in 1966 reached 474 (taking 1952 as 100), and we can see (Table 4) that the fastest growing industry was electrical equipment, with an index of 1,320. Next came the chemical industry (index 1,200), and then oil and oil products (1,167). Paper and pulp followed with 894 and then non-metallic minerals and products (including glass and cement, etc.) with 695. Electric power (633) was followed by rubber, food processing, iron and steel, and metal (including mechanical) industry. The most retarded sector of industry was tobacco, showing an index of 200, then came coal mining (219), building materials (288), non-ferrous metals (321), timber (373), textiles (385), and leather and footwear (414).

The overall picture then shows a general increase in the production of consumer goods over that of the means of production (indices 540:495). It is significant that an analysis by

[1] The rate of growth of industrial activity in Western Europe in the 1950–60 period was 5.6 per cent, and in the 1960–4 period it was 5.3 per cent. In Eastern Europe the average growth rates in the same periods were 11.9 and 8.4. The figures for Yugoslavia for these periods are 13.2 and 11.4. Latin America showed rates of 6.7 and 4.6 and North America 3.3 and 4.9. In the 1960s, among the 65 countries which are listed in the *U.N. Yearbook of National Accounts Statistics for 1965* (Table 4B), the only countries with higher rates of industrial growth than Yugoslavia were Panama (14.0), Ceylon (12.2), and Nigeria (11.6).

TABLE 4

Industrial production and labour productivity 1966 (index: 1952 = 100)

Leading branches	Production	Productivity	Lagging branches	Production	Productivity
Electrical appliances	1,320	227	Leather and footwear	414	155
Chemicals	1,200	235	Textiles	385	134
Oil and oil products	1,167	372	Timber industry	373	147
Paper and pulp	894	232	Non-ferrous metals	321	198
Non-metallic products	695	181	Building materials	288	141
Electric power	633	302	Coal, coke	219	178
Rubber	553	127	Tobacco	200	107
Food processing	550	181			
Iron and steel	535	225			
Metal-using industries	523	164			
Total industry	474	178			

industries shows the highest index for those industries producing the means of production, while many light industries and industries producing consumer goods were still lagging, with a few exceptions. Paper, food processing and the rubber industry were in the fast-growing group, and coal mining was among the slow-growing sectors.

A similar situation is found when the productivity of labour is examined. Between 1952 and 1966 it increased by 78 per cent, which is not very spectacular. Again petrol and derivatives, electric power, chemicals, paper and electrical equipment were leading the growth, while tobacco, textiles, timber, etc. were rather retarded.

The process of industrialization considerably increased the share of the Yugoslav economy occupied by industry. The industrial labour force increased from 33.4 to 37.3 per cent of the total. Fixed capital in 1952 represented 44.8 per cent of the total capital in the socialist sector.[1] By 1958 its share reached 52.7 per cent, although by 1964 it was somewhat reduced (to 49.4 per cent) because other, previously lagging, sectors of the economy were being given more attention. The proportion of investment allocated to industrial development also increased. This amounted to 38 per cent in the late 1940s, fell to 33.8 per cent in 1950, because of the eastern blockade but quickly increased to 65.6 per cent of total investment in 1952 (absolute reduction in other sectors) and then was gradually reduced to 31.9 per cent in 1959. After 1959 industry took between 35.5 and 38.5 per cent of total investment.

As we can see from these data the greatest drive for industrial investment took place between 1952 and 1956, when it represented the heaviest burden on the economy. The share of industrial production in the gross social product, which was 30 per cent in 1948, moved ahead more quickly than the shares of the other sectors of the economy, reaching 40 per cent in 1959, while in 1964 it moved up to 48.3 per cent (in 1960 prices).

Although the growth of industries in Yugoslavia was fast, it was not equally distributed over the whole country. The spatial distribution of the gross social product derived from industry

---

[1] Where total excludes agriculture, housing, non-business sector, etc. *Jugoslavija, 1945–1964, Statistički pregled*, p. 143.

shows considerable changes between 1952 and 1964. The position in Bosnia and Hercegovina and Croatia did not change much in relative terms; their gross product derived from industry remained the same, i.e. 27.0 per cent for Croatia and 13.6 per cent for Bosnia and Hercegovina. The largest relative increase was in Montenegro (from 0.7 to 1.8 per cent of the GSP) and the second largest in Serbia proper (20.3 to 24.0 per cent). There was a marked decline in the percentage of the industrial product accruing to Slovenia (from 24.9 to 18.7) and Kosmet, and a smaller reduction in Macedonia (Table 5). Thus the change in the relative share of the gross product showed various tendencies: a decline at both extremes and an increase in the middle.

Even more striking changes took place in the share of industry in the national income as measured within each of the republics and provinces. It is surprising over such a short period of industrialization, to find that the proportion of the national income originating in industry reached more than half not only in Slovenia (57 per cent) but also in Bosnia (52 per cent), and that the same percentage was almost reached in Croatia, with Montenegro actually overtaking Croatia and Kosmet approaching the same ratio. Serbia proper was also very near to the halfway mark (46 per cent). Vojvodina, a province whose wealth was predominantly agricultural, shows a much slower change in the relative importance of industry, and Macedonia still lags behind. The explanation of this is largely to be found in the pricing policy, which favoured industrial goods.

The share of industrial fixed capital at book value has, over the same period, diminished considerably in the most industrialized parts of the country (Slovenia and Croatia) and increased in the less industrialized (Bosnia, Montenegro, Macedonia and Kosmet). It remained at practically the same relative level in Serbia proper and Vojvodina.

Two complementary explanations may be given for these changes. One is the effect of relative prices set for various industrial goods produced in different areas. The other is the variations in the capital–output ratio, due to capital mix and technological progress. Nevertheless these two factors only partly explain the discrepancy between the relative shares in

TABLE 5
Industrialization of the republics of Yugoslavia

(units specified for each row)		Yugoslavia	Bosnia and Hercegovina	Montenegro	Croatia	Macedonia	Slovenia	Republic of Serbia	Serbia proper	Vojvodina	Kosmet
National income derived from industry (as % of republican NI)	1947	28.7	25.5	12.5	34.4	20.9	40.1	23.1	23.2	21.6	28.0
	1952	34.7	32.1	17.4	38.8	25.0	48.1	28.3	27.5	25.5	40.2
	1964	47.8	52.9	49.9	48.8	33.1	57.0	43.4	46.0	36.6	47.5
Index of industrial growth	1947	73	65	53	74	75	73	80		96	64
	1952 = 100	100	100	100	100	100	100	100		100	100
	1964	421	521	1,126	414	636	367	505	449	449	363
Gross social product of industry (in percentages)	1952	100	13.6	0.7	26.9	4.5	24.9	29.5	20.3	7.0	2.2
	1964	100	13.6	1.8	27.0	4.2	19.7	33.7	24.0	7.7	1.9
Employment (in thousands)	1952	562	85	5	155	20	116	181	120	49	12
	1964	1,319	189	24	341	70	224	471	318	126	27
Employment (percentage)	1952	100	15.1	0.9	27.6	3.6	20.6	32.2	21.2	8.7	2.1
	1964	100	14.3	1.8	25.8	5.3	17.1	35.6	24.0	9.5	2.0
Installed machinery (in megawatts)	1951	938	103	3	257	18	259	298	—	—	
	1964	3,187	578	93	725	112	633	1,047	675	273	99
Index (1951 = 100)		340	560	3,100	282	7,000	244	351			
Fixed assets in industries (1962 prices – mlrd dinars)	1952	1,129	145	15	306	33	249	373	262	89	22
	1964	4,378	754	180	1,032	193	755	1,464	1,011	334	115
Share of each republic	1952	100	12.9	1.4	27.2	2.9	22.2	33.3	23.4	7.9	1.9
	1964	100	17.2	4.1	23.6	4.4	17.2	33.5	23.2	7.7	2.6

(at constant 1960 prices)

the national income and the fixed capital invested in different areas. The chief difference results from the central distribution of capital investment and the influence of the replacement of depreciated fixed capital. Both call for a policy of autonomous financing of enterprises of decentralized investment, to allow modernization of industrial equipment.

If we now compare the progress of industrialization in relation to the power available, taking the latter as representative of technological progress, we find that here progress has not been very good. Motor power, measured in kilowatts per employed person, amounted to 1.7 in 1951. By 1957 it increased to 2.12 and in 1964 was still 2.13. This shows that the whole process of industrialization was more extensive than intensive. Replacement of men by machine-power has not been very satisfactory.

In this respect there are considerable differences between industrial sectors. For instance the paper industry has had the highest increase in motor power. Between 1951 and 1964 it rose from 3.1 to 9.8 kw/per man; second came iron and steel, increasing from 3.7 to 7.7 kw/man; third petrol and derivatives, from 5.0 to 7.5. On the stagnant side of the balance were the graphics industry with 0.3–0.4, tobacco with 0.2–0.3, textiles with 1.1, falling to 1.0 then increasing to 1.1. Generally speaking one can say that power per man had even been reduced in the electric equipment and food-processing industries, while increases took place in the paper industry, iron and steel, coal, chemical industries and ceramics. There was stagnation in timber, textiles, hides and skins, rubber and graphics. The drive towards global industrialization led to a situation where over-capitalization and excess capacity occurred in several branches of industry (textiles, metal, tobacco, food processing) which caused the factories to work at reduced capacity in 1966 (at 40 per cent and in some cases even less).

The reasons for this were:

(1) Capacity built below the technological minimum for economical production.

(2) Parallel building of factories competing with each other not only for markets but also for the same sources of raw materials, etc. Thus, bulk articles such as pulp, agricultural products,

livestock (pigs), etc. had to be imported from abroad in order to use the idle capacity.[1]

(3) In some cases out-of-date technological products and processes were introduced in newly-built enterprises – the products of which customers were not ready to buy.

(4) Sometimes factories were established on the basis of scanty information and through the influence of political functionaries who made the central investment funds available.

The second objective of industrialization was to build up a working class, and the number employed in industry did indeed increase between 1952 and 1966 from 562,000 workers to 1,360,000. Taking the 1952 level as 100 this meant an increase to index 235. The increase was largest in Macedonia (index 350) and second largest in Serbia (265); Bosnia was at the Yugoslav average, while the most developed republics, Croatia and Slovenia, showed smaller than average increases, i.e. to 220 and 193. Thus there was a considerable overall increase in the industrial labour force, but it was unevenly dispersed. Speaking in relative terms the percentage of the total number of workers employed in industry increased in the period 1952–66 from 32.4 to 37.3 per cent.

As we have already mentioned, the official policy was to spread industrial development over the whole country and wide decentralization of industries therefore took place. Indeed, if we look at the number of people in communes who were employed in industry, we find that in 1964 40.5 of all communes had more than 40 per cent actively employed in industry. The highest average for the republics was in Slovenia, where 66.6 per cent of communes had more than 40.0 per cent people employed in industry, followed by Bosnia with 45.2 per cent, Serbia with 44.5 per cent and Croatia with 41.5 per cent. Below the average were Kosmet, with 31.8 per cent and Macedonia, 37.3 per cent. In Vojvodina, which was a prosperous agricultural region, only 29.9 per cent of communes had 40 per cent or more of their members occupied in industry. Thus the working class employed in industry was pretty well dispersed,

---

[1] There were even cases where it was cheaper not to open a factory already built than to start production, e.g. textiles, wall-board, etc. Some such factories resold their equipment to other enterprises in Yugoslavia.

and the policy can be considered to have achieved considerable results.

Whether or not this dispersal was economically advantageous is another matter. This specific kind of decentralization of industry which followed the administrative division of the country had certain drawbacks. The rural exodus increased and resulted in intensified pressure on housing and communal services. Extensive use of unskilled labour in industry spread. Thus industrial over-population was substituted for agricultural over-population. On the other hand, along with the fast development of industrialization and urbanization and an absolute growth in the population came a decline in the birthrate, and demographic pressure was reduced. An explanation for this can be found in the fact that many younger people left the villages to obtain employment in industry; for a time they felt insecure while changing from a rural way of life to an urban industrial one, and there was therefore a decline in the birthrate, which was faster than the fall in the death-rate in this group of the population.

The number of industrial workers increased to a level which considerably exceeded the effective, economically justified demand for labour. The drive for industrialization as a means of creating a working class pushed the peasants from their villages and from agriculture faster than the manufacturing industry could absorb them. This was still tolerable in the first stage of industrialization, when the infrastructure was being built and giving employment to unskilled labour. But when the second stage came and skilled labour and technicians were needed, there was not enough work for all, particularly those who were unskilled. For a time the problem was suppressed and more labour than was necessary was employed. Soon, however, this disguised unemployment was forced into the open by the pressure of economic realities and visible industrial unemployment appeared, which could not be absorbed even by mass migration to other European countries. Jobs which should have been taken by skilled and technically trained people were occupied by half-trained and semi-skilled people, on the basis of 'first in – last out'. This further complicated the problem. The same difficulties were also encountered at the managerial level, where the tendency was to retain incompetent but politically well-entrenched management, which was supposed in this way to be rewarded for past loyalty.

The third objective of industrialization was the achievement of economic independence. It was expected that industrialization would reduce imports of raw materials and machinery, and increase exports of finished goods. It was in fact hardly realistic to expect foreign trade to decline with economic development when industrialization was such an important element of the development. In fact it increased considerably. In 1938 Yugoslavia imported only 11 dollars per head of the population. In 1956 this had increased to 26 dollars of imports per head, and by 1966 to 85 dollars (current dollars). On the import side foreign trade obviously had to increase because of industrialization. Raw materials become necessary to an ever greater extent, the demand for fuel increased, spare parts became necessary and new machines were ordered at an ever-increasing rate for the development of new and the replacement of old equipment. Thus imports had to increase in absolute terms.

Exports also had to increase, not only because of pressure to export in order to pay for imports, but also in order to sell the surplus industrial products over and above effective domestic demand. In the third stage the process was begun of integrating domestic industry into the world market, which brought about an increase in exports. At this stage, exports were losing the character of 'surpluses' and taking on the nature of regular production for foreign markets.

For these reasons there was a change in the concept of national independence as it related to the industrialization process. It was no longer seen to lie in the decline of foreign trade but rather had to be redefined in accordance with the way in which goods were to be exchanged with foreign countries – i.e. whether the equivalent value was being received in exchange, and the way in which the terms of trade developed during the process of industrialization.

Under the impact of industrialization the structure of foreign trade showed a considerable change. A significant indication of the nature of this change can be seen in the second part of Table 6, where goods are compared according to the degree of processing incorporated. This makes clear the extent to which

TABLE 6

How industrialization has changed the structure of foreign trade
(in percentages)

	Exports					Imports				
	1939	1947	1951	1964	1966	1939	1947	1951	1964	1966
Industrial materials	78	67	77	42	43	49	73	53	62	58
Capital goods	—	—	—	12	18	28	18	16	22	22
Consumer goods	22	33	23	46	39	23	9	31	16	20
Raw materials	55	45	34	17	14	20	24	45	24	25
Semi-finished goods	39	38	58	39	33	26	33	19	24	23
Highly-finished goods	6	17	8	44	53	54	43	36	52	53

SOURCES: *Jugoslavija 1945–1964, Statistički pregled*, p. 207; *Statistički kalendar SFRJ* (1967), p. 71.

the policy of industrialization was instrumental in changing the structure of foreign trade; the degree of processing of exports increased considerably, and that of imports also rose. Both imports and exports of non-processed goods declined markedly. It had been expected that exports of raw materials would decline relatively as domestic industries began to process them and this did indeed happen. It was also expected that imports of some raw materials would disappear altogether, because they would be produced from domestic natural resources, but this happened only to a certain extent. Another expectation was that imports of consumer goods would decline as domestic industries began fully to satisfy domestic demand. This expectation did not materialize. However, as expected, exports of finished consumer goods did increase relatively.

Both exports and imports of capital goods rose, although a rise had been predicted only for exports. All these tendencies were largely determined by the administered relative prices. As relative prices changed during the first stage of the reform, some changes were to be expected.

Another important indication of the progress of industrialization is provided by a comparison of developments in the production of machines and equipment, raw materials and consumer goods. From 1948 to 1951, over the period of administrative socialism,[1] there was a very marked relative increase in the production of machinery and equipment, which rose to 153. This increase continued at the same rate from 1952 to 1954, when the index was 157. The greatest jump ahead was from 1956 to 1960, when the index reached 184. Between 1961 and 1965 it fell back again.

Production of raw materials and semi-finished goods was rather slow. In the first period, between 1952 and 1955, it decreased considerably (index 146); it then reached its peak in the period 1956 to 1960, when it was 160, and fell slightly again in the period 1961 to 1966, echoing the change in the production of machines and equipment. Production of consumer goods was somewhat below average in the 1948–51 period. In 1955 it increased by almost 46 per cent and in the period 1956 to 1960 by 78 per cent. The increase slowed down between 1961 and 1966 to 64 per cent.

Thus we may say that the greatest advance in the process of industrialization in Yugoslavia took place in the period 1956–60. After that there was a slowing-down, but more orderly and gradual than in the previous periods. The limit to the unsophisticated conception of the economic independence of a

[1] From Table 6 we can see that from 1947 to 1966 the percentage of total exports accounted for by industrial materials declined from 67 to 43 per cent while the share of capital goods (non-existent in 1947) amounted to as much as 18 per cent by 1966. Exports of consumer goods increased from 33 to 46 per cent of total exports in 1964 and then fell to 39 per cent in 1966.

On the import side there was first a decline in the percentage of industrial raw materials and fuel, from 73 per cent in 1947 to 51 in 1956. This was during the period of explicitly autarchic policy. From 1956 to 1964 the percentage increased again to 62 per cent. This was clearly due to the policy of global industrialization. The movement in investment goods is also characteristic. Imports of such goods amounted to 18 per cent of the total in 1947 and declined to 14 per cent in 1956, when they received a new impetus and moved up to 28 per cent in 1960/1, falling again to 22 in 1966. A reverse tendency took place in imports of consumer goods. These were very low because of the autarchic policy in the forties, and did not amount to more than 7 to 10 per cent of the total. In 1956 they increased to 35 per cent and then, with the development of the domestic consumer goods industries, fell gradually to 16 per cent.

closed economy was found, as has already been said, in the high cost of production, the struggle against monopoly prices and an obsolescent technology, all of which acted against an autarchic policy.

The fourth objective of the policy of industrialization was to strengthen national defence. In this respect changes in aims were quite considerable after 1955. The main reason for this was that the army and navy very quickly built up a capacity for national defence purposes which met their requirements. In addition the danger of foreign aggression was considerably less after Stalin's death, and there was no other threat to Yugoslavia's frontiers. A certain number of machine and shipbuilding enterprises, which were originally under the control of the Ministry of National Defence, were transferred to civilian administration for the production of civilian goods and organized on the lines of workers' management in socialist enterprises. As far as national defence is concerned it can be said that industrialization has served its purpose and that the goals have to a considerable extent been achieved.

Industrialization may be said to have achieved considerable success in the exploitation of natural wealth (Table 7). The utilization and processing of the natural wealth of the country have extended to many new fields, with both vertical and horizontal developments. Production of many new goods was started (Table 8).

In the exploitation of new natural resources the greatest success has been in drilling for oil in Croatia. Although these oil wells are not particularly rich, production is already two million tons a year (a total of 2.2 million in Yugoslavia in 1966) and there are definite prospects for oil drilling and natural gas in Vojvodina and in the Adriatic Sea. Already over half the oil processed in the country for domestic consumption is obtained from domestic sources. Next on the list comes coal, with particularly rapid development in the first period of industrialization, from 7 to 29 million tons, though now competition from oil is being felt and there is a slowing down. A variety of non-ferrous metals are already processed and production has expanded greatly. Yugoslavia holds second place in Europe in copper production, third in mercury, and fourth in lead and bauxite. Production of both iron and steel passed the million-ton mark

TABLE 7
Exploitation of natural wealth, 1939–66

Production of		1939	1966
Electric energy	mlrd kWh	1.2	17.2
Coal and lignite	M tons	7.0	29.3
Crude oil	M tons	0.0	2.2
Natural gas	M m³	2.6	402
Iron ore	ooo tons	667	2,493
Pig iron	ooo tons	101	1,143
Steel	ooo tons	260	1,867
Copper ore	ooo tons	984	5,624
Copper	ooo tons	54	134
Lead and zinc ore	ooo tons	775	2,439
Lead	ooo tons	11	98
Bauxite	ooo tons	719	1,887
Zinc	ooo tons	5	51
Aluminium	ooo tons	1.8	42.0
Magnesite	ooo tons	33	527
Manganese ore	ooo tons	5.7	8.6
Forest cutting	M m³	22.7	17
Timber (III phase)	M m³	7.1	10.3
Agricultural land	M ha	14.7*	14.8
Cultivable land	M ha	10.1*	10.2
Arable land	M ha	7.6*	7.6

SOURCES: *Statistički godišnjak Jugoslavije, 1969*, pp. 135,
158–9, 166–7; *Jugoslavija 1945–1964, Statistički pregled*, pp.
99, 132.   * Average 1930–9.

in 1957 and steel is approaching its second million, with the
prospect of reaching 3.2 million in 1970.

The traditional wealth of the country lay in its forests and
timber and these are still among its greatest riches. But there
has to be careful husbandry and processing if the rate of replacement is to be maintained, even though the forests are no longer
being over-felled, as they were during the first years of industrialization.

TABLE 8

Some of Yugoslavia's new industrial products since 1947
(statistical groups)*

First year of production	Product	Production in 1966	
1947	Electric transformers	000 tons	11.9
	Bicycles	000	345.5
1948	Railway wagons	000	4.8
	Lorries	000	8.9
	Telephones	000	102.3
	Radios	000	369.0
	Electric meters	000	717.0
1949	Ball bearings	000 tons	2.3
	Tractors	000 pieces	8.9
	Petrol	000 tons	9.7
	White spirit	000 tons	16.3
	Railway lines	000 tons	10.5
	Asbestos sheeting	000 tons	7.6
1951	Milk powder	000 tons	4.2
	Buses	000 pieces	2.9*
	PVC powder	000 tons	15.0
	PVC raw product	000 tons	18.5
1952	Coke	000 tons	1,227.0
	Sinter magnesite	000 tons	189.0
	Electronic tubes	000 tons	7.3
1953	Sheet iron	000 tons	213.0
	Seamless tubes	000 tons	77.3
	Benzene	000 tons	11.3
	Roto paper	000 tons	52.8
	Ammonium sulphate	000 tons	17.1
1954	Nitrogen acid	000 tons	267.0
	Ammonium nitrate	000 tons	7.1
1955	Cars	000	37.3
	Fluorescent tubes	000	1,495
	Refrigerators	000	207
	Washing machines	000	58.1
	Sewing machines	000	108

TABLE 8—*contd*

First year of production	Product	Production in 1966	
1956	Motorcycles	000	48.8
	Margarine	000 tons	22.8
1957	Detergents	000 tons	53.5
	Powdered soups	000 tons	5.2
	Plastic footwear	000 pairs	2.8*
	Plastic clothing	000 m²	2.1*
	Refrigerating equipment	000 tons	1.6
1958	Cellophane	000 tons	1.0
	Artificial fibres	000 tons	28.5
	Television sets	000 pieces	286
	Plastic footwear	000 pairs	2,844.0
	Plastic clothing	000 m²	2,124.0
1959	Wall board	000 m²	155.6
1962	Hollow bricks	million	373.0
	Building blocks	million	176.0
	Concrete elements for building	million	218.0

SOURCE: *Statistički godišnjak Jugoslavija, 1969*, pp. 166–70.
* Products shown as special groups in the statistical monthly review, *Indeks*. There is usually some delay in recording the production of new goods, i.e. they appear only after they have begun to reach the market in some quantity.

The expansion of agricultural land has also reached a limit, as far as the area under cultivation is concerned. The future lies in careful intensification of crop cultivation and livestock breeding. Nevertheless there are great possibilities for improving the 4.5 million hectares of extensive pasturage. There are also another half million acres of cultivable land and fallows, being mainly submarginal.

There are some open questions with regard to natural wealth which are similar to problems in other parts of the world. Some mines are threatened with exhaustion, and the substitution of oil for coal has raised the difficult question of the redundant coal miners. There are recurring shortages of electric power, because the supply cannot keep up with the constantly increasing demand. Use of water power has still a great deal of potential for development, especially the great rivers of the south, which represent a vast source of energy for domestic consumption and export, which is beginning to be tapped in such schemes as the great Danubian Iron Gates power station. Agriculture's greatest problem is to create storage facilities adequate to cope with the excess capacity of the flour mills and industrial slaughterhouses. The scale of slaughterhouses is a particular problem, as their capacity is far greater than of the domestic livestock industry to provide raw materials.

There are still some beliefs left over from the old concept of national autarchy which are considered to be questions of national patriotism rather than economic calculation. One of these is that it is always more profitable to export products in their final processed state. A second is that industries based on imported raw materials are 'not a good thing' (i.e. refineries on the Danube based on imported oils, steel mills on the Adriatic Coast using imported ores).

The figures below show to what extent the aim of developing natural wealth has been achieved. They show the growth of the extractive industries compared with that of manufacturing.

	1939	1952	1955	1966
Extractive industries	100	182	250	506
Manufacturing industries	100	164	251	820

Up to 1955 the extractive and manufacturing industries developed at more or less the same rate, which is an indication of a closed economy. From 1955 onwards (in fact the break-even point was in 1957), the manufacturing industries went ahead considerably faster than the extractive ones. After 1957 manufacturing achieved a much faster rate of development and by 1966 had reached a level considerably higher than the extractive industries (indices 820 to 506). The fact that the production of the means of consumption developed faster than that of the means of production is a sign of the extent to which Yugoslavia developed into an open economy.

Comparative advantages

The direction of industrial development in the Five-Year

Plan 1966–70 depends on finding the industries in which Yugoslavia has a comparative advantage on both world and domestic markets. This of course is a difficult and long-term process.

It is considered that comparative advantages exist in the following branches of industry: production and processing of copper, lead, zinc and bauxite; shipbuilding and equipment; production of consumer durables made of metal; advanced stages of production in the timber industry; some food-processing branches, especially meat and livestock products; some commercial crops; tourism and the hotel and catering industry, etc. Faster than average rates of growth are planned for power-generating plants, basic metals, the chemical industry, ceramics, building materials and tourism.

The comparative advantages of different branches of industry are even more explicitly stated in the plans of the republics. For instance the social plan of the Socialist Republic of Croatia for 1966–70 explicitly enumerates the following branches of industry as having comparative advantages: maritime transport, shipbuilding, production of some basic processed foods, equipment and installations for processing industries and electrical engineering, highly finished timber products and tourism.

It is expected that the domestic market will particularly encourage increases in the production of steel, some modern building materials, oil and gas, fertilizers and plastic products. The garment industry and knitwear, leather and food-processing industries are all expected to have a high level of demand, comparable to consumption in the rest of Europe.

As a general rule it has been left to individual business enterprises to establish their places in both the foreign and domestic markets; and for this reason they have been given a degree of initiative.

The Federal Five-Year Plan 1960–70 (p. 115) stated the policy of selection in the following way:

there will be more scope for choice between producers. Some products will have to be abandoned as non-profitable while others will develop more quickly. During this process a certain number of business organizations will develop into up-to-date, well-equipped enterprises with highly qualified personnel. These will achieve a high level of labour productivity, which will allow them to compete on the world market. Business organizations which cannot adjust themselves to the new conditions will run into difficulties. Some will have to switch to other products or associate themselves with the more advanced groups of industries.

6

Some aspects of the policy of workers'[1] income in Yugoslavia

The general framework within which the policy of the formation of workers' incomes is put into effect in Yugoslavia is that of a socialist economy with specific characteristics, i.e. all industrial enterprises, banking, commerce, transport, etc. are socialized and so is the 20 per cent of agricultural land which is not in the hands of small, private family holdings. Within this institutional set-up these characteristic features are found:

(1) An accelerated process of industrialization.

(2) A large proportion of the national income devoted to investment (20–27 per cent) and a high level of expenditure for general government and public consumption (13–23 per cent), with personal consumption accounting for 52–57 per cent of the national income.

(3) Intensive pressure on employment because of the exodus from agriculture by the economically active population, the transition from agricultural to non-agricultural occupations proceeding faster than urban concentration of population.

(4) A high proportion of workers' income (indirect income) redistributed through the wide range of social-welfare benefits including free education.

(5) Practically all workers are members of trade unions; neither collective bargaining nor strikes are practised, but the workers find other ways to express their dissatisfaction, e.g. widespread slow-down of work, reduction of productivity, decrease of working discipline, etc.

The consequences of this general situation are that the incomes of workers and employees are low not only in absolute,

[1] In Yugoslavia the term 'workers' is used in two different ways: as a term differentiating those who do physical jobs from white-collar workers; and in a wider sense to cover all employees including the top personnel. In a still wider sense all civil servants are also included in the term.

but also in relative terms. Therefore most workers' families cannot manage on the wage or salary of one wage-earner alone, but have to supplement it by having two or more income earners in one family. Forty per cent of all workers and employees in non-agricultural occupations live on peasant family holdings. Many workers take complementary second jobs, working on 'fauche' jobs, increasing fringe benefits, working overtime, taking temporary assignments, etc. in the socialist sector, or private jobs doing repairs, etc.

In the beginning this tendency was encouraged by a government policy in which everyone was urged to work as much as possible. But later it was realized that such efforts by the workers do not simply add to their product but compete with their regular employment. Thus the worker's attention is often divided between two jobs, which are usually located in two different sectors, the socialist and the private. The competition is for working time, for money income, but above all for the energy and physical strength of the workers.

In Yugoslavia the workers' wage – or rather income – policy is dominated by the fact that the workers are employed by socialist enterprises. The policy is, therefore, part of the policy for the distribution of the revenue of socialist enterprises. There are two main periods in which different policies must be distinguished.

One is the period of administrative socialism on the Soviet pattern, which lasted from 1947–51. The second is that of the specific Yugoslav socialist system, which can be sub-divided into three phases: the wage-bill saving and social funds rate system (1952–3); the profit-sharing phase (1954–7); and the income-sharing phase (1958 to the present).

The administrative management of the national economy

In the first period (1947–51) the policy regulating workers' incomes was a comparatively simple one: all wages and salaries were decided and strictly regulated by the state for all branches of industries and all groups of workers and employees. Neither the workers and employees nor the management of the enterprises where they worked had any say. In this period of the post-war reconstruction of a war-torn country, the wage policy was dominated by inexperienced enthusiasm and revolutionary drive in their prime, and material incentives to work were considered counter-revolutionary. Consequently (and because of low *per capita* production levels) wages were low, hardly enough to meet essential needs. No personal saving was supposed to take place even from earnings from work, and the financing of all investment was meant to be by compulsory saving through the medium of the overall state budget.

The whole system of rigid, planned proportions, where the wage level played one of the most important roles, first broke down in the field of wages. Managers of enterprises, anxious to fulfil the plans, and in fear of the consequences if they did not do so, began to compete for skilled labour in short supply, and to pay 'black' wages over and above the stipulated level. The productivity of labour which had no material incentive and was regimented and regulated by a hastily-formed bureaucracy, decreased further as the difficulties of living became prolonged. In the course of a few years planned, average wages became far removed from the realities of economics. This, and the economic blockade of the country ordered by Stalin in 1948, caused the whole system of administrative management to be abandoned and replaced by a new socialist system.

The saving-wage-bill-rate system (1952–3)

The new economic system was not established overnight from a ready-made blue-print. It was built during the struggle with day-to-day problems, and with it a renewed ideological outlook was adopted. Gradually prices were freed from government regulations; enterprises came to be managed in a more and more business-like way, acting autonomously on the market on a profit-and-loss basis; deciding on their micro-economic plans within the framework of the macro-economic social plan; released from operational, administrative management by government departments, and run by workers' councils. Socialist enterprises could increase their sales and increase their returns, but the division of these returns was strictly regulated by law. They could employ labour according to their own decisions, and pay it from income gained by the enterprise itself.

The last elements to be freed from administrative control were wages and salaries. The reasons were, firstly, that the government did not want to take the risk of letting wages be decided by what were at that time inexperienced workers' councils, and, secondly, that no workable system had been found which could be trusted with such an important role in the new type of socialist economy.

The system of wages and salaries was based on Marx's formula:

$$y = c + v + m.$$

Returns equals constant capital, plus variable capital, plus socialized surplus value. This principle, transformed into policy measures, prescribed that the income of the enterprise gained on the market should be distributed according to the saving rate imposed by the plan; the residual represented the workers' aggregate wage-fund. It meant that aggregate saving and contributions to social funds were deducted from the income of the enterprise at a rate determined in advance by the yearly federal plan. This amounted to an overall average of from 122 to 597 per cent in manufacturing industries, and for certain enterprises was as high as 2,000 per cent of total wage-bill.[1] Nominally the workers' wages were determined by the wage rates or tariffs of the enterprises, but in fact they were decided by the controlling administrative department. What was left after deductions represented the wage-bill. If this sum was not sufficient to cover a certain level of minimal wages set by the plan the difference was made up by the government. The plan prescribed the minimum capacity of production for every enterprise. A contribution, at progressive rates, had to be paid into the state budget to drain off most of the income above the level corresponding to this prescribed minimal capacity of production.

This system, called the saving-wage-bill-rate (*stopa akumulacije i fondova*) was in existence for only two years. Its main defect was that it concentrated the whole income distribution of the enterprises into one single policy instrument, and if this was wrongly fixed there was no way to compensate for the error

---

[1] In other words, to increase the workers' wages by one dinar, the enterprise had to increase its income by six dinars or more.

by other instruments. In point of fact these saving rates were chosen with little preparation, and often very arbitrarily, which greatly distorted the whole economic process. Many changes in the rates, sometimes depending on the 'pull' of the managers and their VIP friends, created uncertainty and dissatisfaction. The difference between branches was too big, and the whole system had no upper ceiling, thus leading to inflation. Progressive rates taxed away all gains from increased productivity. On the other hand every increase in the workers' wages automatically led to a multiple increase in prices in an economy starved of goods. As the prices of consumer goods were not controllable in the private sector (food), and scarcities of industrial consumer goods prevailed in the socialist sector, workers' wages had to be increased, and this led to inflationary pressure.

This system was abolished by the end of 1953, and a new system, that of profit-sharing, introduced in 1954.

The profit-sharing system (1954–7)

The profits of socialist enterprises were considered to be a result of the institutional set-up of the socialist society, and therefore to belong to society as a whole. The wage policy in the profit-sharing system was based on the division of workers' wages into two parts, one fixed, the other variable. The fixed, or regular wage, had the function of covering the essential needs of the worker and his family. Its sum total formed the basic wage fund of the enterprise. The variable part of the wage was designed to play the role of a stimulant to the productive efforts of the workers. It was derived from a share in the profits of the enterprise. The share was a percentage of the basic wage-fund decided on by the district social plan. Later the federal plan fixed its maximum and minimum rates (8 and 16 per cent). There was constant competition between the district authority, the enterprise funds and the wage-bill for bigger shares in the net profits after deduction of the federal income tax. The Federal Government secured top priority for its own share, and played the arbiter for the rest between the competitors, protecting the workers' share from the district authority, and strengthening the funds of the enterprise against the claims of the workers for bigger shares.

In 1954 the wages were still 'accounting wages', fixed by government orders according to 'classification by skill', and made dependent on the aggregate wage-fund, and on the structure of this fund according to the skill and level of the wages of the workers. If, for instance, a manager wanted his salary increased, the workers' council had to raise the whole wage-fund proportionally so that the proportion of the shares of the highly qualified, the skilled and the unskilled workers remained constant. This block system of wage structure made it more difficult to increase the incomes of higher paid workers and employees. In practice it resulted in the tendency to increase unnecessarily the number of unskilled workers in the lower pay brackets.

After 1955 wages and salaries were no longer determined by the government. The decision was left to the enterprises themselves. Every enterprise had to evaluate a norm for each of the jobs it provided and include it in a tariff which was part of the statutes of the enterprise. This tariff, on whose composition many workers and experts cooperated, had to be agreed on by the local trade union council, and confirmed by the district people's committee (= district authority). In principle, each enterprise could decide independently about fixed wages, and therefore about the size of the aggregate wage-bill as part of the costs of the enterprise. The net revenue, after deduction of taxes and other contributions to social funds, etc., was shared by the Federal Government (which took 50 per cent), the republics and the district authority. The workers' share amounted, in 1954, to 4.8 per cent of the net profits of the enterprise, and this percentage gradually rose to 9.2 per cent in 1957. In proportion to the workers' fixed wages in the enterprise it usually amounted to the value of one monthly wage-payment (called the 'thirteenth pay-cheque'), and sometimes to two, three or even more.

This policy gave the workers' councils a much greater say in the fixing of wages.[1] It was a very considerable improvement over the system of administratively-regulated wages. Nevertheless, guidance was given by the trade unions, which at that time

[1] In 1957 there were 6,134 workers' councils in enterprises of 30 or more workers. They held 74,391 meetings and the following items appeared on agendas the number of times shown: workers' tariffs, 16,457, investments, 18,377, use of the fund of the enterprise on which workers' council decides, 15,476, distribution of profits, 11,684.

mainly transmitted the wishes of the government to the workers' councils and worked as equalizing moderators, bringing some system into the decisions of particular workers' councils and trying to keep wages down. To this system of job evaluation premiums were added for special performance by workers, and also overtime bonuses, etc.

But the main interest of the workers remained in their variable share of the profit, which especially in large enterprises, they could not directly influence. It tended to be regarded more or less as a windfall profit, sometimes depending more on the skill of the chief accountant than on their efforts or those of the technical manager or the commercial director. Sometimes temporary results for the year were distributed as interim or anticipated profits which, once distributed, it was difficult to recover if the balances for the whole accounting year showed a smaller profit than expected. In some enterprises enjoying a monopoly and especially in commercial enterprises, profits rose very high, and in some cases amounts equal to as many as eight extra monthly wage-payments were distributed. This contributed to the inflationary pressure which also arose from other causes (investment demand, etc.).

Another preoccupation of the wage policy was to stimulate the productivity of labour and to prevent further increases in employment, which were encouraged by the way the profit-sharing system operated in practice. The profit-sharing system was altered to a greater or lesser extent every year in a game of hide-and-seek between the Federal Government, the local authorities, the managements of the enterprises, the workers' councils and the workers themselves, all competing for better gains from the profit-sharing legislation.[1] The system was finally abandoned in 1958 and the income-sharing system introduced.

Income-sharing (1958)

The basic principle of income-sharing in Yugoslav socialist enterprises is that the workers who run socialized property

[1] For an analysis of this competition, see the author's 'Interaction of macro-economic decisions in Yugoslavia, 1954–1957, in G. Grossman (ed.), *Value and Plan* (Berkeley, Calif., 1960), pp. 346–59.

through workers' councils do not receive wages and salaries, but get their earnings in the form of personal incomes. In other words the workers are not considered to be hired personnel who have the right to be paid, but receive from the enterprises the amount which they have earned by their work. The wage system has been completely abolished. In this situation the workers' earnings do not represent costs of the enterprise. The workers are operators of socialist funds who choose the workers' council and therefore have to carry the risks of management. Thus the workers' wage policy has become a more general workers' income policy (concerned with that part of the workers' income derived from work in the enterprise). In other words the workers' personal income is no longer an independent variable, but a function of the proceeds, business gains and losses of the enterprise. Their share of the gross revenue of the enterprise is calculated after deduction of all costs of running the enterprise, i.e., costs for raw materials and energy, depreciation allowance, taxes, contribution to the general investment fund (6 per cent of the working capital per year) etc. This may be called the first, or external, distribution of the gross revenue, by which the income of the enterprise is established.

This income is divided between the funds of the enterprise, and the aggregate workers' gross personal income. From this sum (after deduction of the tax for communal budgets, and contributions to social insurance) the aggregate net personal income of the workers is obtained. This is the second, or the internal redistribution of the revenue of the enterprise, and is decided by the workers' council. It amounts to roughly 40 per cent of the gross revenue, of which some 25 per cent was allocated for the workers' net personal income and 15 per cent to the funds of the enterprise. The tendency is to bring the ratio to 28 to 12 per cent (70:30) of the internal income of the enterprise.

In this second redistribution the gross income of the workers is determined in the following way.

(1) All jobs are internally evaluated by points which show how much a worker's work is worth for the enterprise, including assessment of payment by effects of work.[1] These points are

---

[1] As an illustration we give here the points evaluation of a number of workers in a Zagreb textile factory. The factory has 2,800 workers altogether and points evaluation is given for 440 different jobs. [Contd. on p. 109

converted into money when the final accounts of the business year are closed. In the course of the year the worker gets a monthly advance on his income, depending on the preliminary estimates of the final outcome. In my opinion these points will necessarily develop into some sort of internal money of the enterprise (the 'certificates' of old socialists), having a rate of exchange with the national money, and it will be interesting to follow the effect of changes in these rates.

(2) The second principle is that of economic units. In order to secure a more direct interest by the workers in the effects of their work, most enterprises are divided into economic units either on the technical principle (workshops, plants), or on the functional, operational principle (transport department, book-keeping service, etc.), and the effect of work is calculated not only per individual worker, but also per economic unit as a whole. Each economic unit has, in most cases, its own workers' council with somewhat limited autonomy. There is a quasi selling and buying of products among economic units within the enterprise, calculating internal costs and benefits. This has greatly increased the interest of the workers in the problems of management. Collective productivity is further developed into the work of the whole enterprise. Thus there are three levels at which the worker's income is decided: his personal efforts; the

	Education	Ability and experience	Management	Responsibility	Physical effort	Mental effort	Working conditions	Total points
General manager	100	170	150	190	10	100	10	730
Technical manager	100	140	140	160	10	90	10	650
Works manager	100	130	100	120	10	90	30	580
Foreman	80	60	40	50	10	40	40	320
Skilled weaver	50	40	—	40	35	30	40	235
Semi-skilled spinner	30	20	—	20	30	10	40	150
Sales manager	100	130	100	140	10	90	10	580
Book-keeper	100	100	50	90	10	80	10	440
Lorry driver	80	60	—	70	30	40	40	320
Cleaner	20	10	—	10	40	10	40	130

There are also premiums for lowering of costs, quality of products, increase in the productivity of labour in economic units, measured by actual performance above that planned. The top personnel get premiums of up to 10 per cent of income by points for successful management.

collective effort of the unit; and the efforts of the enterprise as a whole.

(3) The third principle is concerned with safeguarding a minimal income for the worker. Although it is an accepted principle that the workers must bear the risks of their own work and management, there is nevertheless an underlying basic principle that the existence of the worker and his family depends on his income from work, whatever the performance of the enterprise in which he works. Therefore two safeguards have been introduced: a guaranteed personal income level, and a minimum personal income. The first is established by the government on the basis of the last yearly average personal income per person employed in the corresponding branch of industry (varying in 1963 from 17,600 to 23,800 dinars per month). If any enterprise cannot pay the guaranteed minimum there is a communal reserve fund, to which all enterprises contribute, and out of which the sum is forwarded to the enterprise to provide the difference. This sum must be returned to the communal fund after the enterprise has improved its position. If the results of the enterprise show no improvement, workers' management can be suspended, and ultimately the enterprise can go bankrupt and be liquidated. This guaranteed income is distributed within the enterprise according to its own points system. The other safeguard, the minimum personal income, is fixed by law and is the same for all industries and all enterprises. It is paid out of the funds of the commune.

There is a special fund in each enterprise called the joint consumption fund, into which a part of the income allocated by the workers' management is paid. This fund is used to increase the general welfare of the working collective, e.g. to provide health dispensaries, workers' houses, children's crèches, reading rooms, sports clubs, etc.

Practical problems

There are a number of problems in the actual operation of the system described, and in its long-term development. These are partly related to the specific workers' income policy, but to a large extent reflect the effects of general economic policy on workers' income.

(1) In implementing the general socialist principle 'to each

according to his work' a difference of opinion arose which became manifest when the new constitution was debated in 1962–3, and in discussions concerning the causes of the 1961–2 economic recession. One trend of thought felt that in practical terms 'to each according to his work' should be translated 'to each according to the intensity, effort and sacrifice in his work'. Those holding the opposite opinion, mainly from the more industrially-developed areas, claimed that the principle meant 'to each according to the results, i.e. productivity, of his work'. The constitution provided a compromise formula by using both interpretations, but present government policy rightly puts weight on productivity, although there are voices representing the other view.[1]

(2) Workers' incentives are based on increases of income dependent on increases in productivity, and on the rise in the level of living dependent on increases of income.

The question arose whether the enterprises' returns, and consequently the workers' aggregate income, should be taxed at a flat or a progressive rate. One opinion, held mainly in less-developed areas, was for the progressive rate, maintaining that socialist taxation policy had already upheld progressive rates. The other opinion was based on the fact that the incentive effect on workers is greatly reduced by progressive rates, and that the state would be penalizing the most advanced enterprises and productive workers for the benefit of the least successful. Moreover, it was stressed that different principles must be applied under conditions of workers' management of socialist enterprises and income-sharing than under private, or even state-owned enterprises, where the workers get wages and salaries, which are part of the costs of the enterprise. The principle of flat rates has been applied, and the extraordinary contribution to the state budget, which had been based on a kind of progressive tax, was abolished in 1963.

(3) The different productivity of individual enterprises, and particularly the different average productivity of labour in different branches of industry and different regions has necessarily

---

[1] The new constitution introduced a 42-hour week instead of a 48-hour week. Efforts being made to achieve this reduction of working time under the same system of income-sharing seem to be having success, as there are reserves of working efficiency in many enterprises.

led to a problem about the basis on which the comparative productivity of labour should be assessed. This problem of the starting basis is still being discussed, and an acceptable solution has not yet been found.

(4) The range between the lowest- and highest-paid workers in the enterprise has also given rise to various difficulties, particularly when all income and direct and indirect benefits are taken into account. As always in a period of inflation, there is a tendency to level out the workers' incomes by increasing first those of the lowest-paid groups. Indeed the percentage of workers in the lowest-paid groups has been halved since 1961, and that in other low-income groups greatly reduced. On the other hand some of the managers and highly trained experts secured excessive incomes (producing a variation of 7:1 between the highest and the lowest group within a single enterprise).[1] Political pressure was exerted to end some excesses, and this was interpreted as a sign of a general movement towards *uravnilovka* (levelling) of all personal incomes in enterprises, hitting the technical experts hardest. This primitive concept of socialism soon showed its negative effects, as many of the experts, always in short supply, moved to better-paid jobs, and the tendency was reversed again, but with less excessive claims being made.

(5) There is a constantly felt competition between the share of the revenue which the enterprise can distribute between the workers as their personal income, and the funds of the enterprise (the working capital fund, including depreciation allowances, the reserve fund and the joint consumption fund).

In 1962 the workers' councils were given the right to use the net revenue more liberally, which they did by allocating more to workers' incomes with no adequate increase in productivity. As prices also began to rise quickly, workers' councils increased the share distributed to the workers at the expense of the funds of the enterprise.[2] Administrative intervention was considered

[1] The differences of the net monthly average income of workers varied in 1963 from 58,000 dinars in maritime transport and 54,000 in construction drafting bureaux to 19,000 dinars in the timber industry and 19,800 in the textile industry, the overall average being 25,000 dinars. The average per worker per month in Slovenia is 37,000, in Croatia 30,600, in Serbia 27,300 and in Macedonia only 23,000 dinars.
[2] From 1960 to 1961 the share of net personal income rose from 25.2 to 26.4 per cent, and that of the funds of the enterprise fell from 18.7 to 16.7. In 1962 the corresponding figures were 23.9 and 15.4.

necessary, and indeed government commissions were set up at all administrative levels to advise the enterprises how to distribute their revenue between the two main uses. Besides subjective guidance a formula was prescribed giving the right proportions. This was considered an encroachment on the rights of workers' management, and in 1963 the government set up machinery by which an agreement was reached between the Federal Secretariat of Labour, the Federation of Trade Unions and the Chamber of Commerce (representing a federation of managements of all socialist enterprises) on the indicators to be applied in that part of the internal distribution of the revenue of the enterprise which was left to the workers' councils.[1] These indicators were not combined into one consistent model, and thus workers' councils were left to make final decisions using the indicators only as a guide.

This tripartite agreement is the first instance where the Trade Unions Federation openly stood as an independent and separate representative of the workers' interests, side by side with the state authority and the representatives of the management of socialist enterprises.

(6) Another problem of workers' income policy is the macroeconomic distribution of the national income. The question is asked whether the present generation should carry the main burden of economic development, or whether some of it should be passed on to future generations. In terms of economic policy it is a question of whether the investment quota of the national income should be increased or made smaller, to the benefit of personal consumption. The question used to be discussed in rather academic terms, and a step forward was taken in 1956 when the burden of investment was made somewhat lighter. But there was no pressure from organized labour, partly because at that time the workers still represented a minority of the population. But since the early 1960s the workers have made up more than 50 per cent of the active population and the macroeconomic distribution affects them more clearly than ever before. Therefore their influence is being felt, and in the discussion

[1] These indicators are combined in three groups, each consisting of four to six indicators, such as: comparative net product per worker; the rate of saving and of workers' income per head; the used capacity and productivity of capital; gross volume of production per worker; total sales compared to total costs, etc.

concerning the more recent social plans the Trade Unions Federation is putting more and more stress on the desirability of increasing the percentage of the national income allocated for personal consumption. Personal consumption is low not only in absolute terms, but also in relative ones, amounting to 52 per cent of the national income, while in 1952 it was 56 per cent. There is a feeling that a general re-examination of the national income distribution policy is due.

(7) Competition between work in the socialist sector and private, extra work is still a major problem. In order to make workers concentrate their energies on their regular employment greater stimulation and the possibility of increased earnings are required. This has partly been met by the introduction of a system of stimulative payment by effect. One great problem is the fact that 40 per cent of all workers live in peasant families on holdings which are additional sources of income, and also require additional efforts. Any speeding up of the process of vertical and horizontal mobility is hampered by the fact that the largest part of the workers' budget is spent on food, expenditure which is greatly reduced in the case of the worker-peasants who are supplied by the peasant family holding. This is even more true for rent, as housing is in such short supply that many workers are unable to move to towns and factories even if they want to. Increased building activity since 1958 has not yet been able greatly to improve the situation.

(8) The rural exodus was fostered by the government as a movement favouring their policy of creating a working class in a predominantly peasant society. The indirect consequence of this movement was that it made possible the policy of low wages. What was once surplus agricultural population is now to a certain extent being transformed into surplus industrial, commercial and administrative population.

Since the combined effect of the economic recession, the policy of deflation and increased workers' influence on income-sharing in the enterprises (revealing surplus labour) is being felt, a reversal of policy is beginning to take place. The effect of this policy must necessarily be towards increasing the workers' personal incomes.

(9) Practically the same is true for the increased, open un-employment into which some agricultural and industrial con-

cealed unemployment has been transformed. When the manu-facturing industries were only a little developed and on a low level of productivity, unskilled labour was good enough and with a little training could become semi-skilled. But as indus-tries have progressed quite a number of unskilled workers have become superfluous, although it has become difficult to meet the need for highly trained personnel. Therefore registered unem-ployment had risen by 1963 to 7.5 per cent of all employed. Emigration of labour to some Central European states has partly eased this pressure. The tendency is to increase the development of services that have so far been poorly equipped in order to employ surplus labour after retraining.

(10) The consequence of inflationary pressure is a lowering of real income. The gap between the nominal and real personal income of workers has been widening again since the beginning of 1961. It looks as if inflation–deflation tendencies affect dif-ferent sectors of the economy in different ways, and the workers' income is caught between the hammer of increased living costs and the anvil of the policy of deflation. Some more energetic measures than hitherto will have to be applied to escape from this situation.

Conclusions

The workers' income policy in Yugoslavia now depends on the workers' management of the socialist enterprises, as it operates within the general framework of the economic system and cur-rent economic policy.

The effect of workers' management depends on the maturity of the working class and the experience of workers' councils, in which up to now more than one-third of all workers have taken part over the last twelve years. Maturity grows with responsi-bility and as experience is gained. In the beginning the main interest was centred on personal problems and labour relations. It shifted to commercial problems of prices and the quality of products in order to improve sales. This led to investment problems, and at one time it was thought that investment would solve all difficulties. But as, on the one hand, public funds were insufficient to cover all claims, and on the other hand, the autonomous funds of the enterprise were increased, so workers' councils had to rely more on their own resources. In 1953 investment out of autonomous enterprise funds amounted to 21 per cent of all investment. In 1962 this figure was 30 per cent. But this increased freedom of action was paid for by increased demand for responsibility and more farsightedness on the part of workers, especially when decisions posed the dilemma between increases in personal income or in enterprise investment funds.

So far it could be said that the result has proved successful. Moreover, there are many cases where workers have decided temporarily not to take the variable share of their income, but to put it partly or wholly towards increasing investment. Whatever the ambitions of the managers or the guidance of the local authorities may be, there is no doubt that the final decision is borne by the workers' councils. But their behaviour is influenced by two major considerations: the relationship between their nominal and real income which depends on monetary policy and the price of agricultural produce in the first instance; and the equality of treatment in economic policy.

Two tendencies are felt. The first is to try to solve all difficulties by demanding exceptions and privileges, thus shifting the burden on to others. The other is to demand equality of treatment for all according to certain objective criteria such as productivity of labour and rationality of investment. One could say that the workers' councils follow the principle 'we do as all do'. So if there is a feeling that others are being given investment credits out of public funds in an easy or privileged way, then they will put forward their claims for getting credits too ('not to be left out'), without much rational examination. The competitive spirit is a corollary of the willingness to bear sacrifices and to cut down their share of income. Thus decisions made in an authoritarian or arbitrary manner would cause dissatisfaction and a trend towards increase of personal income. If, on the other hand, decisions are made in a democratic way and participants are persuaded of the rationality of decisions, then the interdependence is felt more directly, and the growth process is more favourably influenced.

Thus the workers' income policy in a system like the socialist system of Yugoslavia is closely connected with the whole problem of economic growth. Moreover, it becomes the major political issue for which the new constitution has endeavoured to provide the basic principles and the political machinery.

7

Economic growth and investment policy

The motivation of growth policy

The over-riding principle of the policy of economic growth in Yugoslavia after 1945 was to build socialism and, following that, communism. Economic growth meant an accelerated development of the production forces in the country in order to achieve these aims, so that ultimately a level of affluence would be reached in which everybody would have goods and services supplied to them according to their needs. The impulse for the policy of maximizing economic growth was supplied by four main motives:[1]

(1) Ideological: the greater the economic growth the faster the country would progress towards socialism and communism.

(2) Economic development: to maximize growth meant to increase socialist production and consumption in the country, and to increase the income and living standards of the working population. This idea was originally linked with the policy of pulling the country out of its state of backwardness and submission to capitalist exploitation.

(3) National independence: to make the country strong (i.e. resistant to foreign influence) by making it economically developed. This was also linked to the strategic goals of the economic policy of world socialism.

(4) Class or social; in order to end exploitation of the labouring classes and to create a situation in which the working population would need to work less and could enjoy the benefits of technological progress, to reduce demographic pressure and to create a working class on an expanding and self-augmenting scale.

---

[1] These motives almost correspond to the four objectives of the first Five-Year Plan. See p. 61 above.

In the course of time experience was gained of the speed, complexity and interaction of changing factors in the growth process. With regard to the above-mentioned motives this process may be seen to have developed in the following way:

(1) Those guided by the ideological approach realized with time that the road to socialism is not a direct, linear one, with a single leading sector (industry) determining everything. One pattern would not meet the optimal growth requirements and each country had to find its own road to socialism. Yugoslavia was the first socialist country to stand for this principle. It became an increasingly general experience that the more the economy grew, the more growth developed from a straight line into a complex matrix of interdependent human relationships. As time went on several turning points in the developmental process appeared, which had to be taken into account.

(2) Consequently the emergence from backwardness, which was achieved with considerable success but at great sacrifice, did not lead to overall harmonious growth. It proved that unbalanced economic development is not a law only of capitalist economics, but that a socialist economy is also subject to it, and that uneven growth comes to be of greater importance the higher the level of development and the more differentiated the choice of technologies. The assumption that there would be steady, uninterrupted, linear growth was proved wrong by research into the process of socialist economic development, which showed varied fluctuations and cycles of different kinds (developmental, seasonal, administrative, inventory, etc).

(3) It became evident that national independence, as conceived in the national bourgeois autarchies of the nineteenth century, was no longer practicable under the impact of modern technology, which is first exploited by the strongest powers, who cannot, however, preserve a monopoly of knowledge. Thus resistance to great power leadership in economics became important. The aim of national independence developed into international interdependence. Sometimes this was institutionalized in the activities of the United Nations agencies, and a policy of non-alignment was pursued; sometimes it took a more operative form, as seen in the different processes of integration taking place to the west and east of Yugoslavia. The essence of national independence in economics was no longer isolation of one's own

political territory but development of technology towards the international level. This painful education process, through which the whole world is now going, is of particular significance in a multinational state such as Yugoslavia, with areas at various levels of development. Thus the urge for Yugoslavia to follow her own road to socialism was partly derived from experience gained from internal problems of social transformation within the country itself, experience which has made Yugoslav leaders very sensitive to the complexity of growth problems.

(4) Finally the fourth objective, that of freeing working people from social exploitation through economic progress, developed after the revolution into a struggle against the machinery of the socialist state and its bureaucracy. This resistance changed the role of the state and substantially contributed to the development of workers' management, economic democracy and social self-government. These developments took place in accordance with the experience that economic progress is not necessarily obtained by squeezing the population through compulsory saving, and that modern technology can give ample opportunities for progress towards abundance without continuous shedding of blood, sweat and tears.

Investment policy

Investment policy was the instrument used to attain the aims of economic growth. In various periods there were different ideas about the best way to achieve these objectives and practical political measures differed. We shall divide our analysis, according to our method, into three different periods, which correspond to the years of administrative socialism, the new economic system and the period of the economic reform.

Within the three periods we will follow changes in the immediate objectives of economic growth, in the actors and the institutions, in the means of their allocation.

Objectives

In the first period of administrative socialism we can say that economic growth was achieved by arbitrary methods. This meant a policy of growth without regard to cost. It was a policy of command and not of demand. Growth was an end in itself, which expressed the revolutionary aim of speeding up the building of socialism as much as possible. But this was a policy of economic growth in only one direction. It meant the growth at all costs of the socialist sector, while growth in the non-socialist sector was opposed. It was a policy of destroying or preventing any potential growth in the capitalist sector, and of carefully controlling the growth of the private sector based on personal labour, where production forces were gradually declining. Thus there was no maximal overall development of all production forces, but a building up of the socialist sector (defined in a normative sense) and a prevention of growth in the non-socialist sector. This was carried out by institutional expropriation of old classes and a transfer of saving into the centralized socialist sector, leaving the rest with very meagre investment funds.[1] The federal budget financed investment in the business enterprises which were under central jurisdiction, and the republic and local budgets did the same for their respective business enterprises.

The sums allocated by the Federal Government amounted in 1947–51 to 216 milliard dinars or 60 per cent of total investment. The six republics spent 111 milliards or 31 per cent in investment, while local authorities disposed of only 34 milliards or 9 per cent of the total sum invested. Thus there was a policy by which administrative methods were used to achieve ideologically and politically motivated results and little importance was attached to economic factors.

The new economic system followed a policy of maximizing economic growth. At that time (1952) the capitalist sector had been completely destroyed and its property transferred to the socialist sector. The private sector was so small in comparison with the socialist sector that it represented no threat and was

---

[1] Gross investment in the private sector derived from the social sector amounted to 8.6 milliard dinars in 1947 and to 6.8 milliard in 1948, mainly for repair of damages suffered by the victims of war, but from that year to 1953 it rose only from 0.8 to 1.6 milliard dinars a year. The private sector invested from its own resources 8 to 20 milliard dinars annually, while total investment in the socialist sector amounted to 87 to 147 milliard dinars (all at 1956 prices). I. Vinski, *Procjena rasta fiksnih fondova Jugoslavije od 1946 do 1962*. (The estimate of the growths of fixed assets of Yugoslavia) (Zagreb, 1964), p. 320.

allowed to exist and vegetate,[1] in spite of the regeneration of peasant family holdings after 1953.[2]

We could say that this was a period when maximizing overall economic growth in a particular way was the objective of a policy which was interpreted as the growth of the socialist sector, leading the others. The expected effect of the investment policy was to increase demand by command. The purpose of the policy was by centralized investment decisions to stimulate an increase of demand in the controlled, imperfect, sellers' market. Indeed in this period maximization of the rate of growth became the main objective and the yardstick of the success of the economic policy. It was assumed that economic growth was proportionate to the sum spent on investment. In this sense the investment policy met with considerable success, as the rate of growth became one of the highest in the world. The effect of the growth policy was measured by the increase in net material product per head.

In the reform period the policy of maximization is turning into a policy of optimization of growth, which means that a constraint was introduced, requiring growth to be subject to the principle of rationality set by the international division of labour. The policy changed from one of overall global growth into one of selective growth, which means that growth should be stimulated in those sectors where there are the greatest comparative advantages for Yugoslavia, from a world point of view. These comparative advantages have to be measured by prices on world markets. Thus autonomous growth which determines the demand gave way to induced growth which is determined by demand, and the market became a buyer's market.[3]

[1] From 1953 to 1964 the size of the socialist sector more than tripled (index 319), while the private sector grew by only 29 per cent (1953 taken as 100). The private sector grew moderately in agriculture (index 132) and construction (394) which chiefly represented the building of family houses, but fell sharply in handicrafts (72).

[2] The upturn of the investment swing in favour of the private sector took place in the early fifties, so that by 1960 private investment had risen to 44 milliards, which was still only 13 per cent of the total gross investment (from 8 to 11 in the previous period), although the private sector contributed 25 per cent of the gross social product. Vinski, *Procjena rasta fiksnih fondova*, p. 320.

[3] The growth rate was planned to be smaller in the next Five-Year Plan, 1966–70, i.e. 7.5 to 8.5 per cent, and an even slower growth was proposed for the first two years of the plan, until the new policy took hold. Indeed the rate of growth which was 3.5 in 1965 and planned for 1966 as 4.3, was predicted by some for 1967 to be

Consequently the main stress in economic growth began to be laid on technological effects, and on increasing labour productivity by improving the productivity of capital.

The actors

In the period of administrative socialism the main agent in growth and investment policy was the state, represented by the Federal Government as the supreme centralized administrative authority. In this period macro-economic and micro-economic growth were merged into one huge micro–macro system, where the growth policy was implemented by acts of the government, as if the Yugoslav economy were one single enterprise.[1]

In the new system period there was a split in the growth policy. Macro-economic growth was maximized by the central authorities, which kept control of decisions about global direction and sectors of growth; the micro-economic growth of enterprises was governed by the principle of profitability in competition for fund allocation. Micro growth in the enterprises depended on the redistribution of the gross social product by macro decisions arrived at through the central federal plan. Thus there was a system of centralized growth decision-making and decentralized running of current economic transactions in the business enterprises.

With the economic reform the bodies concerned in growth policy changed again. The Federal Government is no longer the main actor in economic growth, nor is there a centralized system of gross product redistribution by administrative decision, or by central plan. There is a federal economic policy in which economic growth plays an important part, as it also does in each of the republics and other socio-political units. But the operational decisions have now become centred on the business enterprises. Next in importance in investment decisions come the socialist banks, which accumulate the financial resources of

4 per cent, which was only to be expected in an initial period of structural change, when some sectors were declining while others were increasing. *Društveni plan razvoja Jugoslavije* (The social development plan of Yugoslavia) (Belgrade, 1965), p. 19.

[1] The aggregate rate of growth of the Yugoslav economy reached 8.5 per cent in 1950–60, and rose in the early sixties to 8.9 per cent, which represented, with Romania, the second highest rate in the world, surpassed only by Japan and Israel (both 10.8). *U.N. Yearbook of National Accounts Statistics, 1965*, Table 4A.

the enterprises on business lines and invest them in other enterprises according to business management principles. The influence of the public authorities in these banks is in principle limited, as we shall see later. However, the complaint is still (1967) heard that these banks do not operate on strictly business lines, but are subject to pressure from local political functionaries. With regard to macro-economic decisions the role of the republics was strengthened *vis-à-vis* the role of the Federal Government. The Federal Constitution was changed in 1967 and the federation can now make no investment decisions except by a special federal law, which has also to be agreed on[1] by a special House of the Federal Parliament, the Chamber of Nationalities, in which each republic votes through its delegation so as to ensure that the interests of each nation and constituent republic are adequately treated.

Therefore we can say that in this system the main decisions about investment are taken by the enterprises, whose decisions are based on self-management and that a policy is now followed of induced rather than autonomous growth.

The institutions

The policy of economic growth under administrative socialism was decided by the overall state plan and the overall state budget, which embraced all budgets from the federation and republics down to all districts and communes, and also included all social insurance. All the accumulated investment funds were paid into this budget which then paid out the sums to be used for investment by lower units. Thus investment policy operated on the basis of income redistribution by the state budget. This budget was defined as a 'unified fund of state financial resources' and roughly half of it was allocated to investment. The State Investment Bank was no more than a technical institution through which these financial operations were carried out. The reasons why this overall state budget could not operate satisfactorily were several:

(1) The budget was so big and so complex, ranging from

---

[1] Amendment III of the Federal Constitution adopted in April 1967 said: 'In pursuit of its objectives and obligations as enacted by the Constitution, the Federation can, with their own means, take part only in financing of investments for specific purposes decided upon by a federal law.'

taxation to social insurance, and from foreign affairs to village schools, that adequate care could not be given by any state agency to any particular objective; this led to a situation where special attention was given to objectives chosen by influential politicians or favoured by bureaucratic personnel. In other words it led in fact to favouritism and subjectivism in the disguise of the overall, rational, globality of an all-embracing centralism.

(2) The rules by which the budget was run were rigid administrative regulations which, because of their ridigity, were not practicable for everybody, but nevertheless could be strictly applied when the high economic and political bureaucracy, wished it. This intermingling of ridigity and laxity led to arbitrary administration. Less rigidity, less regulation by the centre and more adaptability of day-to-day administration was required to keep up with the rapid changes in economic growth.

(3) The central decisions were made at a level so far removed from the business organizations on the spot, both in the locational sense and as regards administrative stepping stones, that it was clearly necessary to simplify procedures and to bring the decision-makers closer to the production units. Instead of improvised short-cuts circumventing the central system, a new decentralized system was envisaged.

In the new economic system investment policy was organized on two different lines: according to the system of investment funds (1952–63/5) and later through administratively-established banks until the beginning of 1965.

The first policy, which we shall call the investment fund system, after a short transition period consisted of one General Investment Fund (1954–63), which had to provide for the main lines of economic growth centrally decided upon by an annual Federal Social Plan.

Other special funds were created in great numbers, the most important of which were the Social Investment Funds at federal, republic and commune level. The centralized General Investment Fund run by the Yugoslav Investment Bank carried out investment policy at the micro-economic level, i.e. which investing enterprise should get the money. Decisions at the macrolevel – how much money was to be allocated to different sectors of the economy – were made annually by the Federal Social

Plan and the Republic, District and Communal Social Plans. There was a special procedure by which micro-decisions were made by the General Investment Fund. The Fund would announce how much money had been allocated for a certain type of investment called 'investment circle' (e.g. sugar refineries) at a certain date. There was then public bidding in which enterprises interested in getting investment funds in this 'circle' competed by offering rates of interest. Then the Investment Bank awarded the funds to the highest bidders, after evaluation of the project by a committee of experts, which included government officials. The whole procedure was in fact liable to more or less informal but effective pressure by politicians and final *de facto* control by the political bodies.

Parallel to the General Investment Fund there were investment funds in each republic, district and commune. Each enterprise also had to have its own separate investment fund,[1] and some specialized funds were created to finance investment in other sectors, e.g. investment fund for agriculture, roads, forests, housing, etc.

This system had certain advantages over the allocation of investment funds by ministries through the budget. On the one hand the funds were exempt from administrative decision-making and rigid budgetary procedure. They were not wound up at the end of each budget period but continued in operation. But the government bureaucracy was replaced by the central banking bureaucracy, and there was no democratic control of their operation and funds.

On the other hand the decentralized funds were strictly confined within the boundaries of administrative units in the territorial (republic, district, etc.) or functional sense (housing, agriculture, schools, etc.). This made them highly dependent on corresponding political officials, territorial or departmental. The splitting of investment and other funds on administrative

---

[1] As early as 1952 a fund for the allocation of autonomous resources of enterprises was set up and later other investment funds were created for government institutions and business enterprises (in each administrative unit, etc.). Specialized banks (for investment (1956), for agriculture and land reclamation (1959), for foreign trade (1955), etc.) were created on a functional basis to allocate decentralized investment funds for various projects. Some very large projects, such as land reclamation in the Danube area and in Macedonia, were approved and organized by special federal laws.

lines into so many hundreds of funds, and on functional lines into so many thousand separate funds, approached more closely the individual enterprises, but did not secure a proper functioning of effective investment policies.

The constant fear that their investment funds would be blocked or expropriated by the central government for its own purposes encouraged the agencies and enterprises administering them to allocate funds to the first project they could think of.[1]

This was called the system of decentralized investment. But when all the sums spent on investment were taken together the result was that the General Investment Fund, which centrally collected and allocated the investment resources, handled (in 1958) 764 milliard dinars or 81 per cent of the total, the republic funds 163 and local investment funds 12 milliard dinars.[2]

This situation was expected to cease when the General Investment Fund was abolished in 1964. Some changes were introduced when communal and republic banks were reorganized on along more territorial lines after 1961, but this change affected the technique of financial operations rather than concrete decision-making. Instead of the politicians at the top, those able to influence communal banks became most important. The banks were small and numerous (more than 200 in number) and political officials in all administrative units persisted in maintaining 'their own' banks as financial adjuncts to their policies

These territorial banks represented a small step towards the much advocated or criticized (depending on the point of view) financial decentralization in 1963; they had total funds of only 1,135 milliard dinars, while the three centralized functional banks kept control of 2,115 milliard dinars or 65 per cent of the total.[3]

The reform introduced a new investment policy. In the first place self-financing by socialist business enterprises was introduced. The enterprises accumulate investment funds from income and allocate them according to the decisions of the workers' councils. Secondly, the decisions as to how the funds

---

[1] In 1963 50 per cent of enterprise funds were transferred to the General Investment Fund as a 'compulsory loan'.
[2] Jugoslavenska investiciona banka, *Godišnji izvještaj* (Annual Report) (1958), p. 90.
[3] *Yugoslav Survey* (July 1965), p. 3,221.

paid into or deposited with the newly-created investment banks should be allocated for investment financing are now made by the banks on business principles and are no longer influenced by political considerations, as under the previous systems.

The reform brought about a reorganization of investment financing, by creating special investment banks, which are organized by business enterprises and socio-economic communities as capital subscribers and also financed by long-term deposits such as insurance and social security funds, etc. These banks extend over political administrative boundaries and operate throughout the whole territory of the state. Nevertheless, there are still official complaints that the banks operate under political influence, especially since the credit squeeze of the deflationary policy has put many enterprises in a difficult position and they have mobilized their political friends to put pressure on the banks in order to lessen the anti-inflationary measures. The size of investment funds handled by federal institutions reached a ceiling in 1961, declined slowly until 1963 and then fell very rapidly until 1965. The investment activity of other social investment funds was small on the whole. After 1960 it began to increase slowly until 1964, but after that year fell back again.

In contrast with the declining investment expenditure of socio-political communities, there has been since 1963 a sharp movement upwards of investment by banks, which have taken the place of other investors. Above all there is now investment by business organizations. This was almost stagnant until 1959, but from that year started to expand steadily. This expansion was pushed steeply upwards by the legislation of the reforms of 1965 and 1966.

Bank funds are in fact divided into those allocated by central banks and those under the control of non-centralized business banks, which are not instituted by a central government act. There is, however, a marked difference between the amounts distributed by these two kinds of banks, and most investment credits are still allocated by the central institutions.

Allocation of investment funds

In the administrative period the effectiveness of economic growth was considered to be proportionate to the size of investment funds spent, irrespective of costs incurred or gains achieved. In the second period the criterion of profitability was introduced and later the principles of cost minimization and income maximization began to gain importance (therefore we call it 'accumulative industrialization'). But the principle of profitability was limited to the micro-level, and no such criterion was adequately applied at the macro-economic level of the General Investment Fund. Macro-investment decisions were still made on empirical and arbitrary grounds and they also influenced the decisions at micro-levels. The decision to invest depended on the calculations of the enterprises, and on whether they considered investment to be profitable. But again there were certain limitations to the application of the criterion of income maximization. In one sense the enterprises considered that all investment was productive, provided they could get the funds and that there would always be a way of alleviating the burden of repayment, by increasing the price of the product, by subsidies or by tax reductions. The result was an unlimited demand for investment.

As investment was identified with economic growth and growth was in turn identified with the road to socialism, it was considered that all investment was a good thing and that a socialist enterprise could not go bankrupt, in spite of all the legislation in this field. Thus the principle of income maximization was blurred by other considerations of an extra-economic, or at least 'extra-business', character. After 1954 the principle of profit maximization was applied until 1958, when it was replaced by a principle of income maximization. Priorities in the investment policy were no longer determined by rigid order as in the first period. The priority was given to those projects most likely to have the greatest accumulative effect, i.e. income maximization on the micro-level. Among other subsidiary criteria used were: the employment effect, the export effect, the import substitution effect: the greater the effect the more favoured the project.

Under the third system the economic reform is developing an investment policy based on selective investment and comparative advantages, which have to reconcile the micro and macro maximization of income, using non-administered market prices as a common yardstick. Thus instead of a micro-policy of income maximization at domestic administered prices there is cost-benefit maximization, developed at both macro and micro levels. It remains to be seen how the matter of social costs and benefits will be handled. So far the tendency is to reduce all social costs and benefits as far as possible, to avoid income redistribution by the state and to use the market mechanism as the only means of income distribution and investment allocation.

Accumulation of investment funds

In the first period primitive socialist accumulation prevailed. It was an accumulation of funds taken from the private sector (including the peasants) and the consumer, with no regard to the effect on production and the standard of living and with very high priority for investment. The main instrument for enforcing saving was taxation, in three forms: a progressive income tax for the non-socialist, private sector, together with a turnover tax and planned profits in the socialist sector. Consumption goods were taxed at a very high rate, in order to accumulate funds for investment, leaving producer goods free or almost free.

In the second period, that of the new system, accumulation for the central investment fund was derived mainly from a 6 per cent tax on the fixed assets of the enterprises, which was later extended to the whole of working capital. But as the burden of 6 per cent on the whole of capital was very heavy, an exception had to be made for certain sectors of the economy where capital investment was very intensive, such as hydro-electric power stations and agriculture, or where the gains from accumulation were very low for extra-economic reasons (the graphics industry). The turnover tax remained the largest source of funds for the federal budget. The third form of accumulation was the income tax on socialist enterprises, which amounted to 15 per cent of the income of the enterprises. Previously, when the profit-sharing system still existed, there had been a fifty-fifty distribution of the profits of the enterprises between the Federal Government funds and the enterprise, as well as the turnover tax. Even when the income-sharing system was introduced in 1958, based on workers' management of socialist enterprises, about 60 per cent of the total income of the enterprises still went to the state and only 40 per cent was left to the enterprises. This was

then divided by the workers' councils between the personal income of the workers and investment funds (about 13 per cent)
of the enterprise.

Under the third system, that of the reform, saving for investment was based on the revenue of the enterprises and the distribution of the net income of the enterprise by the workers'
council. The capital tax remained, but was reduced to 3.5 per
cent. As there was a revaluation of the capital of all enterprises,
this in fact contributed more to the federal funds than the previous 6 per cent. But in other respects a great change has taken
place, and redistribution by the state of the income of the enterprises is greatly reduced. In fact, the 1966–70 social plan provided
for an almost reversed position, that is, up to 70 per cent was to be
left to be allocated by the enterprise and 30 per cent was to be
taken by the government on all levels. This would not and did
not mean that the enterprises could do as they like with the 70
per cent left to them, but only that they would have the right to
decide how much to allocate for different purposes, including
investment, laid down by law. In this distribution they have to
preserve the value of the social property (fixed and circulating
capital) under their management.

The extent to which the policy of maximizing economic
growth became a fetish is shown by the way the depreciation
funds were handled. In the first period they were entirely centralized in the state budget, including the central depreciation
fund; this was not allocated to the enterprises from which it had
been collected or given to those which needed to replace worn-
out machinery and equipment. Out of these funds new enterprises were built while the old ones were left without replacements. Under the second system there was a depreciation fund,
but it was kept with the National Bank like all other assets of
the enterprises and was therefore easily appropriated by the
government. Part of this replacement fund was often blocked by
the government in order to obtain finance needed for government policy or at least to prevent the enterprises from spending
it. In the third period the enterprises are free to set their rates of
depreciation according to their own policy and moreover they
are encouraged to put the depreciation high, in order to provide
resources for the modernization and re-equipment of their
factories.

Criteria of the quality of growth

There are three standards by which the quality of economic growth can be tested. The first is the choice between intensive and extensive growth; the second is that of the capital coefficient, or the productivity of capital in economic growth; and the third is the problem of the productivity of labour.

Extensive and intensive growth

The dilemma of intensive versus extensive growth was resolved differently in each of the three periods. In the first period the use of labour in combination with capital was extensive. An ever-increasing number of workers were employed in the socialist sector, and their numbers rose faster than the stock of capital goods increased. Thus, there was an increase in the ratio of labour to capital employed, and increases in production were achieved by human labour rather than capital. The rate of substitution of capital for labour was therefore comparatively low. This policy was facilitated by the fact that growth in the first period consisted of building up the infrastructure, which required masses of unskilled labour for the construction of railways, roads, dams, power stations, etc. There also were cases of a backward movement, where manpower was used instead of machines (e.g. in agricultural cooperatives, building trades, etc.). These processes were brought about by the government's policy of cheap labour. It was felt to be more important to employ more labour than to use capital efficiently. This was reflected in over-employment, particularly of clerical and administrative staff (white-collar jobs), and of course in public administration.[1]

In this first period capital had no price, in the sense that no burden was put on the user for its use. Therefore neither those who decided how capital should be allocated nor those who handled capital acted responsibly. Although there was a shortage of capital in the country, its allocation did not reflect this shortage. Instead, it was redistributed by the government, and

[1] The urge to employ more people was very strong for extra-economic reasons as well (employment for demobilized soldiers; employment for victims of war, whose houses had been burnt down and families dispersed or victimized; employment for political patronage, etc.).

this redistribution was determined by political criteria, i.e. extra-economic reasons. Capital was therefore wasted.

The new system brought a change in policy and an effort was made to move from an extensive to an intensive economy. As a result, at one and the same time could be seen tendencies towards intensification, i.e. using less labour and increasing capital faster than the number of employed, and also sectors where labour increased faster than capital. This mixture of a capital-intensive and a capital-extensive economy created difficulties in carrying out economic policy. The more capital-intensive enterprises were overtaxed, because they had to pay a threefold contribution to the state. Firstly, they had to pay the rate of interest on capital stock, secondly the depreciation allowance fixed by law and removed from the control of the enterprise, and thirdly the rate of interest on long-term capital loans.

Productivity of capital

Capital was scarce in the economy and demand for investment funds was therefore very high. Capital was not cheap, but it was provided by society; the burden of indebtedness was shifted on to the consumers and alleviated by inflation. In other words, the rate of interest was not a distributive criterion for allocation of capital. Instead capital was distributed according to the centralized decisions of redistribution at the state level. Once the factories were built demand shifted from unskilled to skilled labour, but workers were not needed in such large numbers as in the first period.

It was not easy, however, to push people back into the villages from which many of them had come, and concealed unemployment therefore developed in many sectors of the economy. Also the procedure for dismissing workers became more controlled, and workers' solidarity helped to keep in employment many more workers than were really technically necessary. The proportion of surplus labour in the factories amounted in many cases to 20 per cent of the people employed.

Although considerable efforts were made to improve the proficiency of workers and technicians, a large number of improperly-trained workers still remained. Many jobs which should have been done by fully-trained workers, qualified technicians and university graduates were in fact taken by people with fewer skills and inadequate training. Originally, this was because such personnel were in short supply, but later the principle 'first in, last out' prevailed and people holding jobs were reluctant to give them up. Thus a paradoxical situation developed, in which trained workers and experts were unemployed, while people with inadequate training remained in jobs which they could not perform properly. This situation remained to some extent unnoticed during the period of inflation and autarchic policy, but world competition quickly brought such shortcomings out into the open. Even so, the process of replacement proceeds very slowly. There are several reasons for this: one is the misunderstood solidarity of the workers (sometimes the majority of workers in a factory are unskilled). Another reason is legal: the procedure for dismissing a worker involves an enormous number of formalities. The third reason is of a political nature: sometimes the political functionaries themselves are untrained, or take the side of the untrained so as to preserve their influence. The process of replacing unskilled by skilled labour is clearly more difficult than the technocrats realize, and therefore a process of growth results in which the ratio of labour to capital used is very high.

The intention of the new measures introduced in the reform is to allocate capital according to economic criteria, which are measured by the rate of interest and the extent of participation by the banks in investment: capital is becoming dearer, and therefore it is expected that the economy will grow by using relatively less capital more intensively. This requires that the price of capital must increase, so that the law of demand and supply of capital comes into effect.

It seems extraordinary that capital allocation, after twenty years of socialist experience, should come back to supply and demand. But this is because capital allocation by the budget and capital redistribution by government decision have proved ineffective in practice. This third system has come into operation in order to meet the demand for an intensive economy, i.e. an economy where the amount of capital will increase faster than the employment of labour, so that the economy becomes more capital-intensive. In connection with these problems we propose to undertake a somewhat more detailed analysis of the limitations of investment. Firstly we shall discuss the reasons why a country which had such a high rate of growth had to change its policy and pursue a policy of reduced investment.

Limitations of investment

Investment policy in Yugoslavia, although it was considered to be the main-spring of economic growth, in fact encountered objective limits. These were sometimes neglected in economic plans, but had to be taken account of later in political considerations. This policy of growth by investment was in fact confronted with objective upper and lower limits.

The upper limits of investment

One upper limit was provided by the actual physical volume of production and imports of investment goods, and the extent of building activity. When this limit was exceeded an inflationary gap appeared, as we have already seen, and sooner or later inevitably put a brake on the volume of investment.

Another upper limit was the receptiveness of the economy – the volume of investment goods which it could absorb at any one time. This depended on the capacity of the building trades and the speed of assembly operations. Indeed, the fact that the gestation period was so protracted – normally lasting 2 to 3 years – demonstrates that this limit was frequently exceeded.[1] This overstrained gestation period was one cause of the extension of the investment programmes. It also meant that large amounts of assets were frozen in the form of unfinished production, providing another example of the growth fever.

The third upper limit to investment was the size of the investment quota in relation to personal consumption. There is a level of income and of consumer demand which if it eventually reaches an almost zero level cannot be further reduced, and if pressure is put on the consumer to reduce consumption further the whole social fabric begins to be strained. This can happen either in an indirect form; by slackening of work discipline,

---

[1] In the mid-fifties the gestation period in industrial construction was usually four years. Of 834 projects financed by the General Investment Fund and terminated between 1959 and 1962, only 256 (30 per cent) were finished in time, 402 were delayed by up to one year and 176 for more than a year. B. Depolo, *Neki problemi u fazi realizacije investicija u SFRJ* (Some problems in the phases of realizing investments in SFRY) (Belgrade, 1965), p. 125.

carelessness, demoralization in work, economic crimes and corruption, or by a slowing-down of work and a decline in the productivity of labour.

In some cases it can lead to open rebellion if the safety valves are not opened in time (Poland, Hungary in 1956). Indeed the share of the Yugoslav gross social product allocated for capital formation (the investment quota), was raised to such an extent that there were signs that the limit was approaching. The sensible growth policy in this situation was to reduce the tension, which happened in Yugoslavia in 1955. The years 1950 to 1954 were the most difficult, for it was then that the consumer had to bear the burden of rearmament under the pressure of Stalin's blockade, agricultural collectivization and accelerated industrialization. Personal consumption fell to 46 per cent of the gross social product in 1950. When in 1952 investment was reduced, personal consumption rose to 55 per cent. In 1953 it fell again to 51 per cent of the gross social product, and remained at 52 per cent in 1954. Gross investment rose to 33 per cent of the gross product. This was the critical year for investment policy, and in 1955 it was decided to reduce investment and to switch to a policy of favouring consumer industries.

Investment pressure increased again in the 1960s. The investment quota increased to 35 per cent of the gross social product in 1963 and then fell slightly in 1964 (to 31 per cent), when the reform became necessary. This time there was not a diffused consumer rebellion, but action took the form of political pressure from the regional authorities against a centralized and undiscriminating growth-maximizing policy. There was in fact collective resistance from within the socio-economic system, by management, workers' councils of enterprises, republics, governments and commercial administration. The response was the triple policy of the reform: limiting the overall volume of investment; spreading investment over the country by self-financing at enterprise level; a formal prohibition of the allocation of federal assets for investment.

Public consumption (i.e. the part of gross national product spent by budgetary-government organizations on consumption including subsidies and grants to enterprises) was reduced from 23 per cent of gross social product in the early 1950s, to 13 per cent in 1961 and 11 per cent in 1964. There was also a change in the net inflow of goods and services from abroad (excess of imports over exports), which moved from 1 per cent in 1948 to 6 per cent in 1953 and 3 per cent in 1964, of the gross social product. The national accounts showed a residual sum consisting of differentials between domestic and foreign prices, covered by state budget subsidies to domestic prices, customs duties, change in inventories, etc. This residual gradually increased in the mid-1950s and in 1957 amounted to 10 per cent of the gross social product. It was only 1 per cent in 1961 and 1962, the years of recession, but in 1963 and 1964 the recovery period rose again to 5 and 10 per cent respectively. The absolute value in 1964 was 638 milliard dinars, which was more than all the budgets of public authorities, social and health services and educational expenditure, put together.[1] From the above it is evident that most of the gross social product was in the hands of the central authorities and their bureaucracy, which redistributed it as they saw fit. Eventually it became imperative to clear away the 'residuals' and start a clean sheet; this was the time of the reform.

The lower limits to investment

The lower limit to investment also had a considerable effect on growth policy.

There are three indicators determining the level below which investment cannot fall. One is the replacement quota, which has to be covered by the depreciation allowance. Below this limit disinvestment takes place. In a socialist society, where all depreciation allowances were put into one centralized fund allocated by the federal planning authorities, this had different effects from those produced in other countries. We have already described this process.

The second indicator is population growth. If impoverishment of the country and a simultaneous decline in national wealth per head are to be avoided, the investment quota must be raised to match the rate of population growth (demographic investment rate).

If we add these two rates together and deduct them from the rate of actual gross expenditure on investment, we obtain some sort of net growth rate per head.

[1] *Jugoslavija 1945–1964, Statistički pregled*, p. 83.

The tensions created by the investment policy in Yugoslavia in the 1960s and the controversial problem of growth policy can be better understood if changes in the upper and lower limits of growth are taken into account. The conflict between centralists and anticentralists and the problem of changes in the investment quota contributed something to the national tensions, as did the problem of underdeveloped areas. These all had their basis in changes in the rates of investment.

At this point, the reader's attention is drawn to some relevant facts. Net expenditure on investment was 9.7 per cent of the gross social product in Croatia and 9.3 per cent in Slovenia in the fifties, while the average for Yugoslavia was 17. In the underdeveloped republics the rates were 38.5 for Bosnia, 64 for Montenegro and 18.1 for Serbia.

In 1964 the situation changed and the depreciation funds became much larger in the areas with newly established industries and a large capital infrastructure. (Note that the depreciation rates were fixed by government regulation.) In the country as a whole they were reduced, but they represented a heavier burden for the less-developed republics, which were nevertheless developing quickly. As a result, there was increased pressure for central funds (i.e. overall income redistribution by the Federal Government).

The demographic investment rate was also reduced. The natural rate of population growth in Croatia fell by more than half (from 1.32 to 0.61), a fall which was only to some extent anticipated. The fall in Serbia, from 1.67 to 0.9, came as a shock to many people. The sacrifice to urbanization and industrialization is heaviest in the transition stage. Bosnia and Macedonia, and above all Albanian-settled Kosmet, still showed a very high rate of population growth, well above their capacity to cope with it.

When we come to the net rate of investment the most striking decline occurred in Bosnia and Hercegovina from 1952 to 1964. The reason was that they were no longer considered to have first priority in the allocation of centralized investment. This was the reason for the first appeal to the Chamber of Nationalities in the history of Yugoslavia. Net investment in Montenegro was still very high, but the highest rate was in Macedonia (63 per cent of the gross social product). Slovenia and Croatia improved on their very poor showing over the previous 12 years, but were still well below the overall average.

The following table indicates the magnitude of the change in the investment policy of Yugoslavia:

Gross investment as percentage of gross social product

	1952	1958	1961	1964	1966
Yugoslavia (average)	28.8	27.2	32.0	30.9	21.4
Bosnia and Hercegovina	52.4	24.1	31.3	31.2	22.7
Montenegro	72.6	68.9	78.4	60.6	29.5
Croatia	22.5	22.4	26.5	28.0	18.3
Macedonia	31.9	30.5	45.5	73.1	39.1
Slovenia	20.9	21.6	24.2	27.5	18.2
Serbia					
of which					
Serbia-proper	—	—	—		21.6
Kosmet	—	—	—		44.2

SOURCE: *Statistički godišnjak, FNRJ*, 1955; *Statistički godišnjak Jugoslavije*, 1968.

The most substantial changes from 1952 to 1966 are for Bosnia and Hercegovina and Montenegro. Croatia and Slovenia succeeded in increasing their investment rates very substantially as compared with 1952. These increases were due more to the gradual decentralization of investment and the reduction in the reallocation of funds collected in these two republics, than to the increase in saving which also took place. The fall in the demographic rate and in the depreciation rate could not make up for this decline in actual investment in Serbia. As a result there was an increased pressure on central investment funds.

Maximizing or optimizing the rate of growth

Why did the maximizing growth policy have to be discontinued? The immediate reason was the inflationary gap created by investment.[1] The policy gave priority to growth, regardless

[1] The index of gross capital formation at current prices rose in 1964 to 710, and the overall index of the gross volume of production reached 431, while the general index of prices remained at index 116. Investment goods showed a marked inflationary influence; the production of building materials rose to an index of 276 and their prices rocketed to 173. The prices of capital goods reached 120 (all figures for 1964; 1952 = 100). These figures do not reflect the real depth of the issues because the markets concerned were very sheltered.

of cost. But further factors soon came to light indicating that a reform of the whole growth policy was necessary.

An anti-inflationary stabilization policy required that investment expenditure be reduced, because it was covered neither by physical production and the import of investment goods nor by financial resources (investment credits or budget allocations). In too many cases such funds were neither allocated nor earmarked, and yet their granting was optimistically anticipated by investors or arbitrarily ordered by local political officials. Thus discontinuation of indiscriminate and inflationary expenditure on investment was part of the stabilization policy.

In order to reduce the rate of investment, very drastic measures were used, such as restricting credit, freezing prices, introducing budgetary restrictions, etc. The effect was comparatively small. Investment stopped increasing in all republics except two, but the volume of investment was only slightly reduced. However, the rate of growth of gross social product fell quite substantially in 1966, though less in 1967.

It must be said that this policy met with widespread and diffuse but determined resistance, which was difficult to overcome. The main reason was that investment was still considered to be the easiest escape from all difficulties of current production and that political influence was used to impose investment spending on the public authorities and, more significantly, on the banks.

At the same time the reform policy envisaged some changes in long-term growth policy. The attempt to combat inflation brought out the following facts:

(1) That by 1965, although industrial capacity was growing quickly, as much as 40 or 50 per cent of it stood idle; why therefore accelerate growth?

(2) A large number of industries had to be subsidized to an ever-increasing extent in order to reduce exorbitant costs or to cover losses. (These subsidies reached 400 milliard dinars in 1965.)

(3) There was open unemployment of as much as 8 per cent of the labour force and disguised unemployment in some sectors of up to 20 per cent of employed labour; on top of this 300,000 workers worked abroad (1965).

It was not possible to squeeze consumption any further for the benefit of growth, and a policy of rebalancing the labour force became imperative.

Industrial production continued, but many enterprises were operating only to fill their own stock-rooms. In 1966 total stocks of raw materials and finished products reached the equivalent of half of the national income. In such circumstances there was no point in continuing growth along the same lines as before. A policy of selective growth was needed. But such a policy cannot simply be put into effect in this changing world of technology, integration and politics, unless it is known which combination of industries is optimal. Many years of experience are required for the thorough testing of a long-term policy. A policy of selective, rather than of maximum, growth was needed.

Production costs of industrial goods were high because of lack of competition; goods were highly taxed because of high tax burden; social services were exorbitantly expensive, though of poor quality.

International competition seemed the surest way of reducing domestic prices to a realistic level. The cost of production *of all* products could not be sufficiently reduced to make them internationally competitive. Therefore the principle of comparative advantage was introduced into growth policy.

The policy of maximizing economic growth was based on several theoretical assumptions: unlimited demand for consumer goods and services; unlimited demand for capital goods; unlimited demand for labour; unlimited supply of managerial skills; unlimited protection of growth by society. These assumptions were wrongly assumed to be principles of socialist economics. They proved to be ideological aspirations which built an element of inflation into economic policy.

Unlimited demand for consumer goods and services. Unlimited aggregate demand for any kind of goods and services was supposed to be inherent in a socialist society. Therefore there should be no concern about the choice of goods produced; any quantity of any quality at any price would be welcomed. Such a theory could only have originated in a very poor society and it became increasingly unrealistic as production developed. It brought about agglomerations of unsold stocks, of which large amounts were also unsaleable.

Unlimited demand for capital goods. It was thought that there was no physical limit to the use value of capital goods and that the only limiting factor was financial resources, which should be overcome, preferably by inflation or the redistribution of the national income by the state. As a result, capital goods were acquired at any cost. (The costs were supposed to be shifted onto the insatiable consumer.) There was also an unlimited demand preference for imported capital goods. No concern was paid to technological research, and domestic demand was shut off from foreign and domestic competition. The end result was over-capitalization and idle capacity in the economy.

Unlimited demand for labour. The assumption of unlimited demand for labour was based on a vulgar interpretation of the Marxian labour theory of value, that only labour creates value and that therefore increases in industrial employment bring about proportional increases in income.

Therefore labour's income pushed its aggregate cost up and brought about a preference for unskilled labour; a policy of cheap labour, with over-employment and unemployment co-existing; an excessive rural exodus and temporary emigration in search of employment abroad. The consequences were unemployment, under-employment and low productivity of labour.

Unlimited supply of managerial skills. The assumption of unlimited supply of managerial talents led to protection, conservatism and bureaucracy in business management. The production process continued to be organized on the basis of the traditional factory crafts, in contrast to modern management methods. It was held that any experienced worker or man with some organizing ability, specially if he had proved himself in the administrative or political field, could also be a good socialist business manager. Political reliability therefore took precedence over technological skill and managerial training. This resulted in an unnecessarily low level of managerial capability, in spite of the fact that qualified managerial talent was available.

Unlimited protection of growth by society. When the principle was applied that all growth is good for socialism, a logical consequence was a belief that everything which existed should be protected as a product of socialist society. In addition to the right to work proclaimed by the constitution and the automatic right to social services, there were also: the right of the enterprises to exist indefinitely and to obtain support from society at all costs; the right to a level of subsidy sufficient to ensure survival; and the right to protection from foreign and domestic competition. This principle lay behind the resistance by political pressure groups to the deflationary policy of the authorities and banks.

Some of these difficulties were attributed, mainly by the supporters of growth maximization, to workers' management. But it would be more accurate to say that any economy managed on such maximization principles will either collapse or run into serious difficulties if attempts are made to reduce personal incomes and increase the burden of growth on the population. Forcible redistribution of the national income by the repressive political machinery of the state will be less effective the more developed the country.

Thus constraints had to be introduced to the policy of maximizing growth, account had to be taken of the limitations of effective demand and consumer preferences, as manifested on the market, and demand had to be gradually expanded by means of an income redistribution policy. In addition, the demand for capital had to be limited by making the cost of capital goods realistic and sensitive to technological progress; labour had to be employed productively, by creating new openings for employment, mainly in services, and by freeing the initiative of enterprising men to earn their living without endangering the efficiency of the socialist economy; the right managers had to be selected and tested for organizational ability, skill and experience. These are exactly the measures the reform has taken in pursuit of its objectives.

Productivity of labour and economic growth

Although actively propagated as one of the main levers of economic growth, the fact is that productivity of labour has not been of such importance in the growth process of Yugoslavia as one might expect.

In the administrative period it was considered that economic growth would automatically improve productivity, by shifting population from the private to the socialist sector. Economies of scale were expected to have the effect of concentrating production forces. Although the Marshallian fourth factor of production is not in accordance with Marxian economic theory, nevertheless the transfer from the non-socialist to the socialist sector was considered to be a means of increasing productivity. Therefore an administrative push to achieve this policy for industry after nationalization was achieved by the concentration of labour and equipment in larger units, resulting in an increase in the productivity of labour. Economies of scale were expected to be even more important in agriculture, where collectivization was meant to achieve wonders by assembling working peasants in large collective farms. Wages were low and there was not much stimulus to increase productivity by other than psychological means, e.g. prizes, competition for labour championships, medals and flags, etc. These should not be underestimated, but the economic system lacked any material means of stimulating increased productivity. Moreover, as nobody could live adequately on his salary there was a constant pressure on workers to find other sources of income in order to survive (living with the family in the village, moonlighting, several members of the family working, etc.). This prevented the workers from concentrating on their main work. Labour was cheap and therefore substitution of capital for labour was ineffective. There were even cases where machines bought at great expense were not used, because the cost of labour was less than the cost of maintenance of the machines. This happened most frequently in agriculture, in the collective farms during the period of collectivization, and in the building trade.

Under the new system wages and salaries increased so that income from employment was considerably higher than income earned from other sources (on the family farm) and therefore there was a constant flow of labour from the villages.

Under the new economic system the productivity of labour was expected to increase as a result of having better-qualified workers with improved skills. Great emphasis was therefore laid on schooling, passing of exams and acquisition of formal qualifications. Indeed, much was done in this respect. Special schools were created and the system of payment according to results was improved. But this improvement of the workers' skills at the individual level did not have the desired effect on global productivity. Workers' management created some excellent opportunities for improving the situation, including payment by economic units. In fact workers' management was extended down to a lower scale of enterprise organization, and was introduced in the smallest organizational units which could operate as production or working entities. These were called the 'economic units', and each kept its own accounts, so that workers' earnings could be computed for the unit as a whole. It was hoped that this incentive would increase the productivity of labour to a considerable extent, and it did in fact become one of the main institutional means of improving the productivity of labour in the reform period. But it spread very slowly, meeting many obstacles, of which resistance from enterprise managers was not the least. The official opinion is often expressed that economic growth has been due more to an increase in the number of workers and employees than to an increase in the productivity of labour.

In the third period increasing the productivity of labour became one of the leading principles of growth policy.[1] The policy of more intensive use of labour has led to an increase in the cost of labour, and labour productivity has therefore become much more important as capital and labour have become more expensive. Thus the reform has used as its main instrument for improving the productivity of labour the modernization of the equipment of existing factories and enterprises.

In our view much is still to be done in the sphere of organization and managerial planning. There is room here for much improvement, in spite of the many obstacles, which include the resistance of the managers and the present hierarchy of the business organizations, who fear new methods of management which fall outside their own experience.

[1] Of the economic growth in the decade 1953 to 1962, 58.7 per cent was due to the increase in the number of employed and 41.3 per cent to the improvement in the productivity of labour. V. Farkaš, *Ekonomika Jugoslavije* vol. II (Zagreb, 1964), p. 65.

8
Foreign trade policy

Like the overall economic policy of Yugoslavia, foreign trade policy can be divided into three periods. At first there was a state monopoly of foreign trade, coinciding with the period of administrative socialism (1945–51). Then followed what we have called the commercialization of foreign trade, which covers the period of the new economic system of 1952–65. Thirdly came the policy of integration into the international division of labour, which meant the restructuring of foreign trade, a process which was sanctioned by the economic reform of 1965, although in fact some elements were already to be seen in the partial reform of 1961.

We shall now consider: the basic principle of foreign trade policy; the organs by which this policy is put into effect; the role of the foreign trade enterprises; planning and foreign trade; and prices in foreign trade. We shall then go on to consider the relationship between the Yugoslav economy and the world economy.

The basic principles of foreign trade policy

In the first period a *de facto* monopoly of foreign trade existed and was exercised by the state. The Constitution of 1946 (Article 14) laconically decreed that foreign trade was under the control of the state. In fact, since 95 per cent of total foreign trade was at that time under operative state control, one can say that state monopoly of foreign trade, according to the Soviet pattern, already existed in 1946.

This state monopoly had three objectives:

(1) To put an end to all previously (i.e. before 1945) existing direct foreign trade business relations between domestic (although nationalized) enterprises and foreign firms.

(2) To interpose a barrier between the domestic, planned economy and foreign market economies (and other planned economies as well), so as to protect the planned economy from cyclical fluctuations of the market in the capitalist world. In order to achieve this, foreign transactions were strictly separated and isolated from domestic economic flows.

(3) To put into effect a policy of economic autarchy, identified with economic independence for the Yugoslav socialist economy. The basic long-term plan for foreign trade was to create economic autarchy in Yugoslavia in the form of a closed, socialist, planned economy. By autarchy was understood a situation in which all the needs of the country could be satisfied by domestic products, and all domestic materials could be processed into finished products in Yugoslavia, with exports and imports reduced to a bare minimum. On the basis of such an economic objective, foreign trade could only be regarded as a necessary evil.

These ideas prevailed in a situation where imports were the leading sector. One could almost say that the dominating aim of this policy was to import, within as short a period as possible, the whole industrial revolution. When we say 'imports' then, we are thinking mainly of imports of machines and other capital goods needed for the industrialization of the country. Imports of other goods were to a large extent supplied by the generous allied aid of UNRRA (500 million dollars). Exports were relegated to the subordinate role of merely paying for the import.[1] Yugoslav exports in this first period consisted predominantly of agricultural products and raw materials, especially ores and timber. These were called export surpluses, but the idea of a surplus, in relation to exports of such a high priority, is relative. For instance, exports of food surpluses, from a country in which the standard of living was very low and the shortage of food acute, in fact represented a small part of production which could easily have been consumed domestically. To this we must add that the export of timber in this period was increased to such an extent that not only was the growth

[1] 'It is necessary to secure, by an increase of exports, a sufficient amount of means of payment, sufficient foreign currency, in order to pay in time and in full for the raw materials, machines and equipment bought.' N. Petrović, Minister of Foreign Trade, as quoted in *Spoljna trgovina Jugoslavije* (Yugoslav foreign trade) (Belgrade, 1947), p. 13.

of the forests reduced for years, but the basic stock of timber was felled and exported.

Another characteristic of Yugoslav foreign trade in this period was that commercial trade relations with other countries developed on a strictly bilateral basis. This was the type of foreign trade which the Soviet Union practised, balancing imports and exports with each state separately, which hindered the expansion of trade.

At this time there was also an expectation of socialist solidarity, and a belief that ideology would direct flows of foreign trade among socialist countries. Disappointment soon came and after it the economic blockade by the Soviet bloc countries (1948–55). Disagreement with the foreign trade policy of the Soviet Union, which was based on strict utilization of every opportunity to make gains, even to the point of exploiting new fellow socialist countries, was expressed in the following way:

> The Yugoslav side stood for a different ideology of foreign trade among socialist countries, which had hitherto been based on capitalist principles and which in the future should be based on the following principles: real, and not formal, economic equality among the countries which have abolished exploitation. This is a condition for the creation of a world socialist economy. Marxists must recognize the fact that undeveloped (agricultural and raw-material producing) countries are exploited in foreign trade by industrial countries and by a capitalist way of trading, whatever the social system of the country; backward countries have the right to non-profit-making aid, and developed socialist countries have an obligation to give such aid.[1]

In 1952 the new economic system introduced the principle of opening up Yugoslavia to foreign markets, but this could not be carried out to any great extent until 1965, because many forces opposed it, mainly on the grounds of a preference for socialist and nationalist autarchy. In 1965 Yugoslav foreign trade with other countries still amounted to only 10 per cent of the gross social product, and it was only 0.4 per cent of total world trade.

In support of the liberalizing policy in external economic relations the following arguments were put forward: Yugo-

[1] M. Popović, *On Economic Relations among Socialist States* (London, 1950), p. 60.

slavia was increasingly lagging behind the world in technical development; the closed economy lowered the standard of living with regard to the quantity of goods and services available, and their quality and variety in comparison with neighbouring countries in the West; the existing capacity of industry could not be fully employed nor developed rationally because of the smallness of the domestic market; the natural riches of the country could not be fully exploited with domestic capital resources; employment could not be secured for the growing domestic population; efforts to achieve increases in the productivity of labour could be effectively put to the test only through international competition.

The arguments *against* a liberal foreign trade policy were: that economic growth could be achieved most quickly in a closed economy, under conditions of restrained personal consumption; that under conditions of liberalized international exchange the standard of living would rise to the extent of allowing the consumption of unnecessary goods and even luxuries; that increased trade with the world market would further alienate Yugoslavia from the socialist bloc; that in the long run the productivity of labour would decline under the impact of foreign imported goods.

During the second period, foreign trade was based on a system of commercialization. An autarchic foreign trade policy existed at the macro-economic level, but at the micro-economic level this trade was commercialized, although this commercialization could only be considered marginal in its operation. This meant that the market was used only as a stimulus to foreign trade. The direction and size of trade was determined by the aim that it should serve the planned balance of economic development of the closed economy. In other words it was considered that the macro-economic, fixed objectives would be best achieved if the foreign trade enterprises operated on a commercial and not an administrative, directed basis. Goods were bought and sold according to the law of supply and demand on markets where profitable transactions could be achieved. This was therefore a policy which made use of absolute cost advantages in foreign trade; these advantages were measured on one (the external) side by international prices, and on the other (the internal) by domestic, administered prices. Administered prices were those charged on the home market and many of the elements of the price structure were determined by administrative instruments.

In this period too, imports were the dominating sector, but to the import of machines were now added increasing imports of fuel and raw materials. Also, two more factors affecting trade became apparent which had not been present before, and which had not been taken into account in the formation of foreign trade policy. These were imports of food, which increased over time, sporadically at first because of natural disasters (drought in 1950, 1952), and later because of shortages in domestic production and changes in population structure and consumption habits; and the policy of keeping agricultural prices low and thus failing to stimulate domestic agricultural production. The losses resulting from the Soviet-organized economic blockade were compensated for by tripartite aid from the US, the UK and France, and later by American agricultural surpluses and other aid.

Foreign trade policy in this period was based on the principles of international trading, i.e. goods were bought and sold according to a programme of accelerated economic growth, with the intention of achieving the best possible prices abroad. In order to do this, a policy of multiple rates of exchange and of subsidies and premiums was introduced. Imports were still controlled through the central distribution of the foreign currency, but exports were duty-free, except for certain articles which were scarce on the domestic market, and whose export was regulated by administrative export permits. At this time industrial products and capital goods also began to be exported.

The relationship between Yugoslavia and other states was no longer on a bilateral basis, but to a large extent on a multilateral one, i.e. the objective was no longer to balance current annual imports and exports with each country separately, but to balance the multilateral foreign trade of Yugoslavia as a whole. Nevertheless, two kinds of countries were distinguished. One group had convertible currency (i.e. currency which could be converted into the currency of another country) and trade with such countries was regulated according to the principles of a free market. This group was made up largely of the countries of Western Europe and America. The second group consisted of countries with a clearing system of payments, and contained the countries of Eastern Europe and a certain number of under-developed countries. There was an ever-growing necessity to balance imports with exports for each group of countries separately; but an increased active balance with the countries with convertible currencies was stressed as an objective of policy, because imports from those countries were especially in demand in Yugoslavia and exports to them lagged considerably behind.

Towards the end of the period (in the mid-sixties) exports to the countries of Eastern Europe became favourable because of price differences, but imports from these countries lagged because of the less competitive quality of their goods, so that Yugoslavia had a positive balance of payments with the Eastern European countries, while the balance was negative with the convertible-currency countries.

In the third period, foreign trade policy was guided by the basic principle of integration into the international division of labour and the restructuring of the Yugoslav economy. This required certain changes. Relations now exist with an ever-increasing number of other states and efforts are being made to achieve special commercial agreements with integrated groups of states. In this period it is no longer a question of short-term benefits from current commercial transactions following the profit line wherever it appears, but of the long-term structural integration of Yugoslav production into the international division of labour, the dominant principle being the liberalization of foreign trade, i.e. the removal of obstacles set by state policy to the international exchange of goods and services. The policy of autarchy is being completely abandoned on both macro- and micro-levels and is being replaced by an open market policy. This is based on comparative advantages according to world market prices, i.e. advantages by which Yugoslavia's interest lies in exporting to foreign countries those goods which she produces most cheaply, in exchange for goods which are produced more cheaply abroad than in Yugoslavia.[1]

[1] But there is, for instance, still a controversy as to whether Yugoslavia should expand the output of wheat, which she produces at higher than world market prices, and accordingly restrict the production of maize, or concentrate on maize in which she has a comparative advantage. Here political argument conflicts with economic gain.

The liberalization of foreign trade follows the principles of multilateral relationships introduced by GATT.

If it exploits comparative advantages, business integration between domestic and foreign enterprises is encouraged, even though it cuts across the national frontiers of Yugoslavia. This encourages the development of more permanent international cooperation and the opening up of markets.

In the first stage foreign trade was reluctantly tolerated, in the second it followed the principle of commercial gain, but in the third it has developed a new dimension beyond the above-mentioned objective of the reform – integration into an international division of labour. Two more specific problems must now be faced in the internal policy of Yugoslavia. These are the following:

(1) As a result of foreign competition domestic enterprises which produce at high costs and use more than the socially necessary amount of labour, judged from the world point of view, must lose their monopoly of the domestic market. Acceptance of this is completely contrary to the attitude held during the period of state socialism, when monopolistic exploitation existed on the Yugoslav market by Yugoslav enterprises which produced their goods more expensively or did not care to produce them more cheaply than foreign firms.

(2) The second new problem results from the import of technical progress into the country. Foreign trade brings goods which are more efficiently produced and these, by competition, force local producers to accept technological progress – or perish. On the export side the same policy has the effect that goods can be sold abroad only if they can withstand the competition of goods produced in foreign countries, in both quality and price. Thus on both sides – export and import – technical progress is introduced and spread through the domestic market by the removal of barriers between foreign and internal markets. Such competition is most effective when trade is with the countries which are most progressive technologically and have the most open economies.

Foreign trade organization

During the first period foreign trade was as far as possible sub-ordinated to the state organs through the state monopoly of foreign trade. The most important administrative body was the Federal Ministry of Foreign Trade.[1] This ministry was organized on a strictly centralized basis, not only for purposes of administrative control and detailed planning of operations by subordinate business enterprises, but also to carry out actual business transactions. All payments were made by the National Bank of Yugoslavia. Although there were republic committees of foreign trade, their only function was to be responsible for the implementation of federal export and import plans, as set by the ministry, with regard to quantity, quality and kind of goods, terms of delivery, etc.

In the second period the Ministry of Foreign Trade and its numerous branches were abolished and in their place, after a certain period of transition, a Federal Secretariat[2] of Foreign Trade, with limited jurisdiction, was set up in 1956. Its task was to make the foreign trade plan and control its implementation. Transactions with foreign countries were carried out by special foreign trade enterprises on a business basis. Instead of an administrative hierarchy the business enterprises had joint organizations for special sectors of foreign trade under the auspices of chambers of commerce, through which informal but effective government control was exercised.[3] The issuing of import and export licenses was discontinued and business with foreign firms was now carried out on a commercial basis. Nevertheless, operations with centrally planned Eastern European countries were made dependent on permits issued by the Secretary of Foreign Trade. In this period a special Yugoslav Foreign Trade Bank was founded to provide foreign trade enterprises with credits for imports and exports, and to carry out various banking operations in connection with foreign

[1] At first (1945) direction of foreign trade was under the Ministry of Commerce, and then in 1947 a special Ministry of Foreign Trade was organized.

[2] In 1956 the Secretariat of Foreign Trade was abolished and a Foreign Trade Committee was introduced. This was a coordinating body, since there were some 15 central government agencies which took part in the administration of foreign trade. Finally the Federal Secretariat of Foreign Trade was re-established to take care of the greater part of the administrative activities connected with foreign trade.

[3] We have translated *privredna komora* as 'chamber of commerce' and not 'economic chamber', as is more usual, because we consider that in this context *privredna* means 'business' and not 'the economy'.

trade. Thus bank and chambers of commerce replaced directorates and ministries.

In the third period the function of crediting and financing
foreign trade has been extended to a number of newly-created
socialist commercial banks. Payments abroad are still concentrated in the National Bank, and the financial handling of all
imports of equipment is undertaken by the Yugoslav Investment Bank. Exporters are obliged to deposit with the National
Bank within 90 days all their foreign currency receipts with the
exception of a small proportion of earned foreign currency
which is retained by exporters, out of which importers are
allocated currency to pay for imports.

In the third period, although jurisdiction in matters of
foreign trade is retained by the Federal Government, according
to the 1963 Constitution the role of the republics in foreign
trade has increased and social planning of foreign trade by a
federal secretariat has been abolished. Besides the National
Bank, which remains the central bank for foreign trade, some
other banks are now empowered to undertake banking operations in connection with foreign trade.

Foreign trade enterprises

In the first period all enterprises dealing with imports or
exports were under Federal Government control, i.e. all
foreign trade enterprises carried out transactions as if they were
part of the state administration which planned and licensed
them, although in their relationship towards third parties they
were considered legally to be autonomous persons. In 1950 there
were 110 foreign trade business enterprises altogether – of
which 74 were only commercial, 14 were also producers and 22
were general directorates of various economic ministries. In fact
the bulk of foreign trade was concentrated in the hands of a
dozen large centralized business organizations, acting under
the direct control of the Federal Ministry of Foreign Trade,
and according to a fixed state plan.

In this period no foreign trade transaction could be carried
out except by these special enterprises, and for each there had
to be a payment permit from the National Bank and a preliminary export or import licence from the Ministry of Foreign

Trade. On top of this, every commercial contract or agreement affecting foreign trade transactions had to be submitted for approval to the Ministry of Foreign Trade, its Directorates for Exports and Imports or its representatives abroad. This centralization of trade put the enterprises in a very difficult position. On the one hand they were bound to implement their parts of the state import and export plan and to follow administrative regulations, while on the other hand they had to trade abroad, where market forces prevailed. They were under pressure to fulfil their plans by a certain date and more experienced partners abroad knew how to exploit the fact that they were always anxious to meet these deadlines. Enterprises were not therefore in a position to take quick and effective advantage of any market situation, so that the state monopoly of control turned from a theoretical benefit into an actual drawback.

In the second period the enterprises became autonomous in their trading operations and had to do business according to the principle of profitability, i.e. they had to cover their costs with their proceeds, and also achieve a profit. The foreign trade enterprises were freed from dependence on a ministry or secretariat, in the sense that they no longer had to seek permits or approval for planned orders from the ministry, but were free to act for the good of their own business and to decide for themselves about the choice of goods to be imported, the markets in which to buy and sell, the time to act and the partners with whom to transact business. All this was now their own responsibility. Foreign trade enterprises, like all other enterprises, had the right to decide on their own autonomous plans within the framework of the social plan. This was particularly so after 1950, when workers' management developed in business organizations, including foreign trade enterprises.

To ensure the business reliability of foreign trade enterprises, a system of registration of firms was introduced.[1] This registration obliged commercial enterprises to limit their trade to the framework of commodities for which they were registered (i.e. timber, textiles, machinery, etc.). Production enterprises trad-

[1] From 1953 to 1962 this registration was carried out by the federal foreign trade organizations, but there were many objections to the way in which it was handled administratively and since 1962 the function has been transferred to the commercial courts.

ing on the foreign market were permitted to export only their own products, and to import only products necessary for their own production.

In this period of commercialization the number of foreign trade enterprises increased greatly. Thus by 1954 there were 485 registered business enterprises in foreign trade – of which 283 were commercial, 144 productive and 58 representatives of foreign firms. Ten years later this number had fallen to 391 – of which 204 were commercial, 143 were productive and 44 were Yugoslav representatives of foreign firms. Thus there was a tendency to reduce the number of enterprises dealing with foreign countries, so as to strengthen their position and reduce competition among Yugoslav organizations doing business on foreign markets. Such competition had in fact been brought about more by an unsophisticated and short-term outlook in business than by the number of enterprises. Registration was several times revised in order to reduce the number of business organizations trading abroad, but this reduction was done in an unsatisfactory way because of political intervention, so that it was carried out not according to economic criteria of concentration and integration, but by administrative alterations of the conditions of registration.

It could be said that decentralization in foreign trade was implemented in this period, but not to a very good extent. One has to take into account the fact that only 400–500 of the 10,000 business enterprises in Yugoslavia were allowed to trade abroad, so that the overall number was very small. But even within this small number of enterprises, concentration of transactions remained very pronounced. This was an after-effect of the period of administrative regulation, on both the import and the export sides. The formerly centralized monopolists retained the lion's share of foreign trade for themselves. Thus there was an increasing divergence between foreign trade operations and commercial and business transactions on the domestic market. The division, which was administrative, was illustrated in the institutional dimension by the number of enterprises which were privileged to deal on foreign markets, and in the payment dimension by the fact that transactions earned exaggerated profits at the expense of the domestic market, by exploiting a monopolistic situation.

In the third period the predominant principle has become that of workers' self-management in foreign trade enterprises, so as to remove both market and administrative monopolies. The policy now is to abolish the boundaries between enterprises trading only on the domestic market and those dealing on foreign markets. In this way the distinction between internal and external commerce is being reduced for domestic enterprises, not only in the transaction of goods and services, but also in the monetary field (convertibility). In particular, production organizations can deal freely on foreign markets. Domestic enterprises are now acting according to the business principles of an open market. A new arrangement in this system is the development of more long-term cooperation in production between Yugoslav and foreign enterprises.

Planning and foreign trade

In the period of state monopoly the foreign trade plan was part of the overall state plan. On the basis of the overall plan an operational plan was worked out by the Ministry of Foreign Trade, which decided when imports or exports of different kinds of commodities had to be carried out, by which enterprises, and what the quantity and the country of origin or destination should be. This state plan had three typical characteristics of a foreign trade monopoly:

(1) It was an administrative plan, which had to be carried out according to central directives – detailed decisions about the nature, origin, destination and timing of all imports and exports were made – decided by the federal administration.

(2) It was rigidly fixed by planning indicators which were decided by law and by the government and which could not be adapted to changes on foreign markets or to changes in domestic demand during the planning period.

(3) Targets were set in terms of physical volume, i.e. the plan had to specify in detail for each import and export firm the physical properties of the great multitude of goods it was to import or export. This made the plan very inflexible, although it could not be made sufficiently detailed to satisfy the varied needs of the population and of the large number of business organizations in Yugoslavia. One has to bear in mind that there

were some 16,000 centrally planned groups of articles, in a country where the number of different items produced ran into millions.

In the period of commercialized trade the implementation of the plan lost its state character. There were now social rather than state plans for foreign trade as for everything else. Planning was now called 'preparing the programme of foreign trade', and was carried out by the Federal Secretariat in collaboration with the chamber of commerce and with the cooperation of the branch organizations of business firms. Nevertheless, there was still a central plan for the whole state, of which some parts were more rigid than others. For instance, some kinds of goods could be freely exported or imported to and from particular countries, while others were still administratively planned. Some commodities were still purchased and distributed centrally by state agencies, but most were bought on the market.

There was a special type of organization for trading with the centrally planned Eastern European countries. State monopoly of a kind still existed in trade with these countries. In most cases the branch organizations of the exporting or importing Yugoslav firms would, by common agreement, empower one of their members to act on behalf of the others and represent them when trading with the centrally planned countries. In this way purchases were made and goods sold by this one firm on behalf of all other Yugoslav enterprises in the same industry, in order to implement the state-level commercial agreements.

The social plans and the enterprise plans were drawn up in this period as if there were no longer a strong planning discipline, but there is no doubt that the organs of state administration used economic incentives and informal pressure in order to ensure that their programmes would be carried out as far as possible.

Under the third system the enterprises have their own plans and are free to trade on the world market. The federal social plan is now only a suggestion for action for the enterprises. Nevertheless, certain restrictions of a planning nature do exist, because there is a constant lag of exports behind imports, so that special obligations have been introduced for certain kinds of commodities. Enterprises which want to import these commodities from abroad have to pay for their imports with their exports. There is a sort of compensation for transactions with foreign countries. In this business a special role is assigned to the State Directorates for Food and for Industrial Reserves, which have to buy bulk imports of certain foods and raw materials (such as cotton, wheat, etc.). These are distributed to domestic enterprises within the country mainly through the branch organizations of the chamber of commerce.

Prices in foreign trade

In the first period two kinds of prices affected foreign trade. Domestic prices were planned prices determined by the state planning system. They were rigid and did not change during a planning period. All elements in these prices were fixed by administrative procedure. On the other hand the prices on the international market were free prices and subject to change. Therefore there was an asymmetric tension between the rigid, planned prices and the flexible, free market prices. The difference between one system and the other was covered by a special instrument of foreign trade called the Prices Equalization Fund, which will be described later.

In the second period the market prices of imported and exported goods were used not only abroad but also within Yugoslavia in business relations between foreign trade enterprises. These domestic prices were basically market prices, but because of the large number of elements in them which were determined by the state (different kinds of contributions, taxes, interests, etc.) we have called them administered prices.

In the third period there is a tendency for both the foreign trade and the internal trade of the country to be guided by world market prices.

The opening of the Yugoslav market to the influence of the international division of labour and competition in foreign trade on the world market is expected to have two further results. First, it is expected that the effect of competitive world market prices will be to raise production capacity in Yugoslavia above the technological minimum.[1] It is expected that the import of mass-produced commodities at low prices will bring

---

[1] Legislation dealing with dumping, monopoly practices and similar problems is being considered.

down the prices of domestic goods, which were previously protected by a domestic monopoly, and that the quality of domesti-
cally-produced goods will also improve. Prices are expected to
be reduced to the level of external prices plus the normal
customs protection. In other words, economies of scale are
expected to be imported into the country.

It is also expected that the prices and the cost of production
of export goods will be reduced to the level prevailing on the
foreign market under conditions of world competition. This is to
be achieved by expanding the domestic capacity of production
for external markets. In reality the full effect of imports will
only be achieved if they are substituted for home-produced
goods wherever domestic production is technically backward
and costs of production are higher than abroad. Home-produced goods must become better and cheaper than imported
goods or they will have to cease being produced. The market
system is expected to encourage the import of technological
progress into the country.

Instruments of foreign trade policy

We have already mentioned that in the period of state direction
of foreign trade the differences between planned domestic
prices and free market prices abroad were equalized by a
special instrument called the Prices Equalization Fund, which
existed from 1946 to 1951 as the main instrument of foreign
trade. The difference between higher domestic and lower
foreign prices was paid into the fund, which also made up the
difference the other way round. As all price differences were
left to the care of the fund, Yugoslav enterprises did not have
to worry much about them. They neither had to make additional efforts to achieve better prices and become competitive
on the world market, nor had to try to buy import goods abroad
at low prices. To do so was a question for their moral and
socialist consciences, but not of immediate economic interest.

There was a marked preference and a high demand for
foreign products. The result was that the Equalization Fund
very soon turned into a fund which paid out on both the export
side and the import side. Both exporters and importers asked for
payments from the fund so that, as foreign trade increased, it

took more and more funds from the government budget, until finally the expenditure became too great, so that at the end of 1951 the fund was abolished.

The main foreign trade instruments in the period of commercialization were what were called currency import and export coefficients. These coefficients consisted of certain multipliers by which the prices of imported or exported goods were multiplied when foreign currency was exchanged for domestic. For this purpose an accounting rate of 632 dinars for one American dollar was introduced in 1954.[1] The coefficients applied to this accounting rate favoured exports if they were higher than one and discouraged them if they were less than one. On the import side the opposite took place. Imports were discouraged if the coefficient of imports was high and favoured if it was low. In this way the coefficient acted as a kind of simplified customs protection, in addition to being an instrument of currency policy. These coefficients, by which the rate of exchange was multiplied, numbered twelve on the exporting side, ranging from 0.6 to 2.0, and ten on the import side, ranging from 2.0 to 3.0. In the earlier plans of 1952–4 they had ranged from 0.4 to 4.0 on the export side, but in 1954 they were reduced in order to make the multiple rate fit the smaller firms. The goods therefore cost the importer 1,264 dinars for each dollar. By contrast, on the export side, if the coefficient was, say, 0.6, when the exporter exported his commodities he received for each dollar earned abroad and handed over to the National Bank the sum of 632 dinars multiplied by 0.6, i.e. 379 dinars. In other words, he received less than the accounting rate equivalent from the National Bank. If his coefficient of export was 2 then for one dollar's worth of commodity sold abroad he got 1,264 dinars. Accordingly, for an export with the same foreign price, the exporter might receive only 60 per cent, or as much as 200 per cent, of the value, depending on the coefficient which the state granted for the export of the commodity. Effective import prices ranged from one to three times higher than the accounting rate of exchange.

From the point of view of currency there was a large number

---

[1] For instance, if a commodity had a coefficient of 2 on the import side, then the importing firm had to pay twice the accounting rate of dinars when he bought foreign currency from the National Bank in order to pay for it.

of different rates. These coefficients eventually came to play the role of an undeveloped system of customs duties, which was not really comparable with other customs systems, which have thousands of different rates.[1] These multiple rates of foreign exchange were not a very developed or efficient instrument of foreign trade policy. As they represented multiple rates of exchange for domestic money they led to a situation where nobody could figure out what the effect of the exchange of goods on international markets was, i.e. whether and when the Yugoslav economy gained or lost through its transactions.

A second consequence of this system was that it separated macro-economic gains from micro-economic profit, i.e. many commercial transactions which were favourable for the enterprises from the point of view of prescribed coefficients were in fact unfavourable for the national economy, while other operations which would be macro-economically favourable were not undertaken because the foreign trade enterprise received no profit from them. The cause of all this was that these co-efficients, which had been introduced in a difficult temporary situation, were then retained after the situation had changed. They were decided on by the Federal Government, whose decisions were often subject to the influence of large enterprises and influential political persons or the intervention of socio-political bodies. As foreign trade increased in volume these coefficients did more harm than good, because they were in-flexibly and arbitrarily set and arbitrarily changed by the administration. These multiple rates of exchange were finally abolished in 1961, partly because of pressure in Yugoslavia to join GATT.

In the system of commercialization of foreign trade it was possible to stimulate exports by giving special premiums for the export of certain commodities. These premiums had to cover the difference between the higher domestic prices and the prices on the world market. On the import side, for commodities where the prices were higher than the Yugoslav market could support, prices were reduced by state subsidy. This system was introduced in 1962, when commodity trade with foreign countries was reorganized by a partial reform. Exports became

[1] Even the pre-war Yugoslav customs tariff had some 2,300 customs rates and that of 1961 had some 4,500.

completely free, but imports were subjected to a regime of import duties according to a classification of goods by the intensity of domestic requirements. Nevertheless, the Federal Secretariat for Foreign Trade was granted the right to introduce physical control of foreign goods in the form of quotas and licences if necessary. The premiums and subsidies continued the balancing of the difference between domestic and world market prices in a new way. So foreign trade went on in spite of the existing differences between domestic and foreign prices. As this price differential increased so the subsidies and premiums had to be increased; finally in 1964 they reached a sum of 400 milliard dinars, an amount which represented a very heavy burden for the federal budget. On the other hand the system gave the federal administration power to redistribute the national income by means of foreign trade instruments, because what one group was given as a subsidy had somehow to be obtained from others. This is basically contrary to the socialist principle of workers' self-government – to each according to his work – which was embodied in the new 1963 Constitution. Moreover these subsidies were used to stimulate an increase in turnover in foreign trade. So the deficit grew bigger than the financial means allocated for the purpose. This policy also involved favouring or discouraging particular branches of industry by administrative rules of the central government. It led to an ever-increasing deficit in the balance of trade.

The import of commodities was too small to meet total demand because of the shortage of foreign currency, which also became a limiting factor on economic growth. The costs of production of domestic goods were high, but the unsatisfied domestic demand was of low elasticity, which made it possible to transfer the burden of high prices of imported goods on to the domestic consumer, since there were too few imported goods to provide effective competition for domestic production and create a substitution effect. Thus the import effect was not sufficient because of the low elasticity of substitution. Indeed one could say that imported prices tended to adjust to high monopolistic domestic prices, rather than to reduce them. But the real gain from this economic monopoly in connection with imports and exports did not accrue to the enterprises. This was because on one hand they were overburdened with contributions and taxes paid to the state, and on the other they could not carry out investment from their own funds and expand in order to satisfy demand, because the accumulation and investment funds were still centrally allocated. Therefore there were no capital gains from this monopoly in the sense of a further increase in production brought about by investment. The monopolistic enterprises gained only in the sense that they were able to keep the costs of production high in the absence of competition, because there was not enough incentive to reduce them. In this way they had some sort of guaranteed income from society, in return for expensive domestic production.

The central redistribution of the national income through the foreign trade policy, and particularly through the instruments of premiums and subsidies, was based on the creation of a constant disparity which was lower on the import and higher on the export side, and which favoured final products, even though they were produced at high cost.

The subsidized exporting firms did not create income by exports. They exported because of administratively granted subsidies or premiums for export; they did not therefore increase the national income by gains from foreign trade, but rather transferred domestic income abroad. Foreign countries bought Yugoslav goods more cheaply than local consumers because the exporters got a subsidy from the state. In this way the exporting firms also increased the domestic prices of imported goods, for which demand was inelastic, and this again increased the level of domestic prices and had a multiple effect on increases in export premiums. Thus inflation was imported into the country.

In 1961 a system of customs duties was provisionally introduced. An accounting rate of exchange was also introduced for foreign currency, on the basis of one dollar to 750 dinars. But the system of subsidies and premiums distorted this exchange rate so that the reform of foreign trade was not fully effective and was soon invalidated and discontinued. One of the main reasons why this happened was that reform was attempted only in foreign trade, while the domestic system of production and prices remained substantially untouched. Therefore new difficulties were created for the national economy.

The situation improved for a short time but inflationary pressure, an indication of many accumulated problems in material production, increased more and more and, in 1965, began to get out of hand. It was therefore necessary to extend the 1961 reform, and to discontinue an economic system which was out of step with reality and pulled the whole economy back to administrative income redistribution, out of which other socialist countries had already started to find their way.

In the third period subsidies and premiums were abolished, which meant a further step towards liberalization of foreign trade. One need say only that the upper limit on premiums for foreign trade is 10 per cent of the value of the goods.

Customs duties have now become the main instrument of foreign trade policy. This protection is carried out according to a new customs law and a new tariff of duties for various kinds of imported goods. There are no longer a few coefficients with 20 different rates, but a full system of some 4,500 rates of customs duties.

This, then, is a much more differentiated system of foreign trade protection and more nearly corresponds to similar systems in other countries. Customs duties used only to play a very small role. There were duties even under the state monopoly system, but they were only symbolical, and were too small to have any effect. The socialist sector did not have to pay them at all, i.e. they were not paid by the importing and exporting enterprises, but only by private persons, who imported insignificant quantities of goods into the country.[1] The customs duties before the reform (i.e. from 1961 to 1965) represented an average rate of taxation of 23 per cent of the value of imports, when the accounting rate of the dinar, 750 dinars a dollar, was applied. But when Yugoslavia joined GATT in 1965 customs duties were reduced to an average of 10.5 per cent and this was applied to the rate of 1,250 dinars to the dollar (see, in particular, different rates of customs duties).

The new uniform rate of exchange for all import and export

[1] The state income from customs duties in the federal budget amounted in the last year of the state monopoly of foreign trade (1951) to the insignificant sum of 25 million dinars, while the federal budget was 160 milliard dinars. In 1961 import duties were reorganized. Socialist enterprises had to pay them too and therefore the income increased to 130 milliard dinars or 14 per cent of the federal budget in 1961. In 1964, customs amounted to 227 milliard dinars, or 13.4 per cent of the federal budget. In 1965 they were reduced, and in 1966 amounted to 203 milliard dinars, i.e., 10.6 per cent of the total federal budget.

transactions and the new permanent system of customs duties introduced by law constitute a stable instrument of foreign trade policy. As a result, the enterprises have a much more secure basis for their calculations, not only with regard to commercial transactions, but also for long-term production policy for both foreign and domestic markets.

Trade relations with other countries

Table 9 shows the difference between pre-war and post-war imports and exports, and also the accelerating growth of foreign trade from 1963 onwards. Table 10 gives the relationship between groups of goods imported and exported.

In 1964 Yugoslav foreign trade was still less than 0.5 per cent of world trade; it was at the same level as that of Mexico, Venezuela and Finland, a little lower than Austria and a little higher than Bulgaria. Exports per head of the population in 1937 were 8 dollars; by 1956 they had reached 18 dollars, and by 1966 66 dollars. Corresponding figures for imports were 7 dollars in 1937, 27 in 1957, and 81 in 1966.

The framework of an autarchic policy became too narrow for the further economic development of the country. In addition, the speed of Yugoslav development, with one of the highest rates of growth in the world, required that this growth should be measured and evaluated and its success verified by world standards, i.e. on the world market at competitive world prices.

In contradiction to the old autarchic idea that economic development makes a country independent of the world market, in the sense that trade with other countries decreases, it soon became evident that economic development actually strengthened external trade and that national independence would have to be achieved in some other way, i.e. through balancing trade. For this it was necessary to have a point of reference, a single rate of exchange for the domestic currency, trade at world prices and convertibility.

In other words the illusion of political and national autarchy in a country of 20 million people with a *per capita* income of $500 had to be abandoned. The 1965 economic reform mapped out a fairly resolute policy of deliberate and conscious attempts to obtain a greater share of world trade, not only through

TABLE 9

*Exports, imports and balance of Yugoslav
foreign trade 1947–67*
(in million new dinars; $1 US = 12.50
new dinars)

Year	Exports	Imports	Balance of trade
1939	5,521*	4,757*	+764*
1947	2,046	2,076	−30
1948	3,712	3,831	−119
1949	2,484	3,685	−1,201
1950	1,929	2,883	−954
1951	2,234	4,797	−2,563
1952	3,082	4,664	−1,582
1953	2,325	4,941	−2,616
1954	3,005	4,242	−1,237
1955	3,207	5,512	−2,305
1956	4,042	5,927	−1,885
1957	4,939	8,266	−3,327
1958	5,517	8,563	−3,046
1959	5,958	8,590	−2,632
1960	7,077	10,330	−3,253
1961	7,111	11,379	−4,268
1962	8,631	11,097	−2,466
1963	9,879	13,208	−3,329
1964	11,164	16,540	−5,376
1965	13,644	16,099	−2,455
1966	15,251	19,693	−4,442
1967	15,661	21,345	−5,684

SOURCES: *Statistika spoljne trgovine Jugoslavije, 1966*
(Yugoslav foreign trade statistics, 1966) (Belgrade,
1967), p. 15; *Indeks* (Index), no. 2 (Belgrade, 1968);
Statistički godišnjak FNRJ. 1961.

* In current prices.

commercial operations but by efforts to integrate the Yugoslav
economy into the international division of labour.

This change of attitude was brought about by various influences:

(1) As a result of the increasing discrepancy between

TABLE 10

Structure of Yugoslav exports and imports by
commodity groups 1952–67
(in percentages)

Year	Exports			Imports		
	A	B	C	A	B	C
1952	87.9	0.8	11.3	52.0	37.7	10.3
1953	77.0	3.2	19.8	56.6	37.9	7.7
1954	68.9	4.8	26.3	60.1	31.5	8.4
1955	72.3	3.5	24.2	59.0	29.6	11.4
1956	53.9	3.1	43.0	51.0	14.0	35.0
1957	52.6	5.0	42.4	55.2	18.2	26.6
1958	44.4	8.1	47.5	52.1	23.6	24.3
1959	47.2	11.8	41.0	56.2	19.8	24.0
1960	45.5	9.7	44.8	56.6	28.6	14.8
1961	44.0	10.5	45.5	52.3	28.2	19.5
1962	43.5	17.6	38.9	54.6	25.2	20.2
1963	41.7	13.9	44.4	57.7	20.0	22.3
1964	42.1	11.7	46.2	62.5	21.6	15.9
1965	42.0	17.2	40.8	62.1	19.7	18.2
1966	43.0	18.3	38.7	57.5	21.8	20.7
1967	48.1	14.1	37.8	57.1	21.7	21.2

A = intermediate goods; B = capital goods; C = consumer goods.

SOURCE: *Statistika spoljne trgovine Jugoslavije*, for years concerned.

world prices, export subsidies reached a level which the state budget could no longer bear (300 milliard dinars) and began to hinder the implementation of the policy of decentralization and federalization at home.

(2) Multiple rates of exchange made it impossible to organize a rational exchange of goods and services with other countries, and for this reason in 1965 the parity of the domestic currency was fixed at 1,250 old dinars (12.50 new dinars) to the dollar.

(3) A trade deficit had been a constant feature of Yugoslav foreign trade ever since 1945 and to offset it exports had to be increased. This could only be achieved by liberalizing foreign

trade. Liberalization according to GATT principles led to a reduction in customs duties from an average rate of 23 per cent to 11 per cent. Liberalization of trade in its turn required currency liberalization, with the aim of reaching convertibility of the dinar abroad as soon as a reserve of 500 million dollars was attained.

Foreign indebtedness became a serious problem and by 1965 31 per cent of all foreign exchange went in repayment of principal and interest charges. The policy of contracting short-term and commercial loans to cover the foreign trade deficit could not be continued indefinitely.[1] In order to increase

TABLE 11

Inflow and outflow of foreign currency 1965 and 1966
(in million new dinars; $1 US = 12.50 new dinars)

	1965		1966	
I Inflow				
Total	16,828		19,406	
Exports of goods	13,022		14,362	
Freight and insurance	1,651		1,965	
Other invisible items	2,069		3,010	
emigrants' remittances		726		1,190
foreign tourism		1,014		1,459
maintenance of diplomatic missions		329		361
Miscellaneous	86		69	
II Outflow				
Total	18,681		20,920	
Imports of goods	16,252		17,830	
Freight and insurance	1,145		1,362	
Other invisible items	554		839	
Miscellaneous	730		889	
III Balance (I−II)	−1,853		−1,514	

SOURCE: *Statistički bilten Službe Društvenog Knjigovodstva* (Statistical bulletin, Social Accountancy Service), vol. 1 (Belgrade, 1968), p. 78.

[1] The State Secretary for Finance boasted in 1968 that all Yugoslav debtors were being promptly paid.

exports and to replace imported goods by home-produced, it became necessary to buy foreign licences, mainly for machines and chemical processes. From 1954 to 1965 Yugoslavia bought 358 such licences abroad and by 1968 had herself sold abroad 56 such licences.

TABLE 12

Financial transactions with the rest of the world
(in million new dinars; $1 US = 12.50 new dinars)

	1965		1966	
I Inflow				
Total	5,541		5,166	
Decrease in foreign exchange reserves				
Increase in clearing obligations			8	
Claims	5,290		4,931	
loans and credits		4,551		4,905
short-term credits		671		
reparations and special claims		30		15
special loans		38		11
Subsidies and advance credit payments	251		227	
II Outflow				
Total	3,688		3,652	
Increase in foreign exchange reserves	957		501	
Decrease in clearing obligations	334			
Repayments	2,249		2,822	
loans and credits		2,229		2,692
short-term credits				111
nationalized property		20		29
Miscellaneous	148		319	
III Balance (I − II)	1,853		1,514	

SOURCE: *Statistički bilten Službe Društvenog Knjigovodstva*, vol. I, p. 79.

An important role in the Yugoslav balance of payments is played by invisible trade, which also has great potential for growth. Especially important here is tourism, particularly on the Adriatic coast. Although it was a long time before it was accorded proper attention as part of the national economy, tourism now (1966) directly or indirectly, contributes almost 250 million dollars to the balance of payments. Remittances from emigrés and from workers in Western Europe bring in around 100 million dollars. There are also considerable earnings from transport services, in which the main role is played by the Yugoslav merchant fleet, which has a capacity of 1.1 million GRT.

An activity of growing importance is the operation of Yugoslav firms abroad. By 1967 the value of this work, undertaken not only in underdeveloped countries but also in Europe (West Germany and Czechoslovakia), had reached a million dollars.

One cause of difficulty in developing foreign trade is the lack of regional balance.

Table 14 shows the developments in individual years. Forced exports to the Soviet Union, prompted by the relatively high prices paid for Yugoslav goods there, are offset by substantially smaller imports from the same country, due to its rigid foreign trade policy and to the limited choice and poor quality of products, particularly consumer goods.

The principal problem facing Yugoslav foreign trade policy now is how to distribute the responsibilities assumed with integration into the structure of world trade among the various factors of production and trade, and especially between the two major trading groups the West and the East.

Comparative advantages in relation to the world market are expected in the following fields: non-ferrous mining and metallurgy (copper, lead and zinc, bauxite); manufacture of equipment (shipbuilding and production of durable metal consumer goods); agricultural products (maize, wheat, meat and some industrial crops); mechanical and chemical wood-processing; tourism; entrepôt trade; steel production; modern building materials; crude oil and natural gas; chemical fertilizers; plastics; non-metallic minerals; ready-made clothing (particularly knitwear and leather goods); industrial firms which have already established a reputation.

Many of the expected internal effects of the increase in foreign trade have already been outlined. It will also directly affect the large number of enterprises whose equipment is outdated, or which work below capacity, or which lack technical know-how.

TABLE 13

Yugoslav foreign trade with West and East 1962, 1966 and 1967
(in million new dinars)

	Exports			Imports			Balance		
	1962	1966	1967	1962	1966	1967	1962	1966	1967
EFTA	1,280	1,666	1,721	1,396	2,185	2,651	−116	−519	−930
Percentage of trade	14.9	11.8	10.3	12.6	11.1	12.4			
EEC	2,482	4,617	5,020	3,360	5,412	6,593	−878	−795	−1,573
Percentage of trade	28.8	30.2	30.2	30.4	27.5	31.0			
COMECON	2,087	5,575	5,670	2,352	6,152	5,532	−265	−577	138
Percentage of trade	24.3	36.6	34.0	21.2	31.2	25.9			

SOURCE: *Statistika spoljne trgovine Jugoslavije*, for revelant years.

TABLE 14

Yugoslav foreign trade by countries
(in percentages and in milliard new dinars; $1 US = 12.50
new dinars)

	1946		1961		1965		1967	
	Exp.	Imp.	Exp.	Imp.	Exp.	Imp.	Exp.	Imp.
Total – × milliard dinars	0.7	0.5	7.1	11.4	13.6	16.1	15.6	21.3
Percentage distribution								
Total	100	100	100	100	100	100	100	100
Europe	96.3	97.1	76.7	68.7	78.5	67.3	80.5	79.1
of which								
USSR	42.2	22.4	8.9	3.5	17.2	8.4	17.5	9.6
Italy	7.2	9.1	12.4	14.6	13.2	10.7	18.0	13.4
Germany – West	4.7	—	10.2	15.8	8.8	9.1	7.7	16.8
Germany – East	0.1	2.8	5.3	4.1	7.0	4.9	5.0	4.0
North America	—	2.4	7.0	20.0	6.5	15.2	6.8	7.5
of which								
USA	2.3	2.1	6.4	19.9	5.7	14.8	6.3	7.3
Asia	0.4	—	9.9	5.0	9.3	7.6	7.9	6.2
Africa	0.6	0.0	4.7	2.3	4.8	5.0	3.6	2.8

SOURCE: *Statistika spoljne trgovine Jugoslavije* for relevant years.

Yugoslavia's main interests link her with the European markets, and she has to find some way of adapting to the integration taking place there. She also faces the problem of finding the most advantageous way of dealing with the developing countries and establishing satisfactory trade links with America, the biggest technological and world power. Table 14 shows the relative importance of various countries for Yugoslav exports and imports for 1946, 1961, 1965 and 1967.

Both traditional and current trends favour foreign trade with European countries, and in fact 80 per cent of Yugoslav trade is with them. There are a number of permanent factors underlying this. First, there is Yugoslavia's geographical position and her trade routes by sea, air, river, rail and road. Second, the technical equipment of the country is largely based on European sources, the legal regulations and commercial conditions are also in the European tradition. As a result of the free circulation of labour within Europe, 400,000 Yugoslav workers are employed (1966) in the countries of Western Europe, 60,000 of them highly qualified. In the important new tourist industry, the majority of visitors come from Western Europe, as do the bulk of the earnings of the merchant fleet and from *entrepôt* trade.

These are all weighty arguments in favour of lasting arrangements with other European countries. Arguments against such arrangements are that the economic organization of Western Europe is exploited by international cartels, and that the political conditions are unacceptable for socialist Yugoslavia. There is a real fear of big-power policies and intentions. The economic argument is also voiced, that Yugoslavia will find it too difficult to reach European standards of production and productivity of labour, and that she would do better to direct her foreign trade towards the developing countries. There are many, however, who think that industry needs to think in terms of long-term adaptations over 20 or more years, as is the case in Greece and Turkey, and that excessively close links with less-developed countries will hold back technological advance, weakening the country's relative position on the world market.

Cooperation with European economic groups

Yugoslavia has good but non-formalized relations with EFTA. She first approached the Common Market in the second half of 1962 in an attempt to start negotiations, and has tried again several times since. Real possibilities for some kind of commercial negotiations began to open up in 1967. There are many who favour the long-term adaptation of the Yugoslav economy to Common Market requirements on the lines of other less developed countries, and this is implicit in the aims of the reform. Another possibility is for long-term cooperation arrangements between firms in Common Market countries and Yugoslav firms.

Yugoslavia has had an observer with COMECON since 1956, and since 1964 has had a special arrangement which favours her, in that she can participate in those COMECON forms of action which she finds advantageous.

As far as further cooperation here is concerned there are three trends of opinion, which might be called the ideological, the technological and the commercial. The ideologists, mostly

found among the dogmatists, see in COMECON an organization which will further international socialist cooperation and
the future of communism. The technological argument runs
roughly like this: it is easier for Yugoslavia to find employment
for the unused capacity of her factories through the centrally
planned economies of the Eastern countries, and for the future
economic development of socialist world trade contracts and
subcontracts between planned economies are necessary. Those
convinced by commercial arguments see the Eastern European
market as one on which Yugoslavia can make use of the
favourable prices which her products enjoy in these countries,
particularly her consumer goods, and believe that by trading
here she would avoid having to restructure her economy.

That there is, nevertheless, a certain reluctance to develop
trade with these countries any further can be explained by the
following political and economic reasons:

(1) Fear of a revival of the 'big brother' policy.

(2) The experience of those countries which are full members of COMECON and which are now trying to limit their
involvement.

(3) Fear that close links with this economic group would
militate against a link-up with the world market.

(4) Fear of the effect that trading with centrally planned
economies would have on the processes of decentralization and
democratization within Yugoslavia (especially because of buying and selling arrangements dominated by foreign trade state
monopolies on the macro- and micro-levels).

(5) Close links with COMECON and a move away from the
world market would prevent the adaptation of prices to international levels, and would not stimulate technological progress,
which always increases as a result of international competition,
while centrally planned economies are slower to accept technical change.

(6) Bilateral clearing payments are either a brake on economic development or, by creating anticipated demand in the
form of unsettled surpluses in the clearing balance, will develop
into a kind of forced import, even if this does not suit Yugoslav
economic interests.

In short, the opinion prevails that the policy of the reform,
which aims to strengthen Yugoslavia's position on the world

market, will not be served by close ties with autarchic systems, and that economic interests should guide trade with Eastern countries.

Relations with the developing countries

After long and expensive experience based on political and ideological optimism, relations with the developing countries have now reached a more realistic stage. Account is now being taken of the speed, level and potential of development of individual countries, and a realistic appraisal is being made of Yugoslav interests in, and possibilities for taking part in, this process.

In addition to the well-known difficulties of economic relations with these countries (for example high fiscal burdens, balance-of-payment difficulties, etc.), Yugoslavia has certain special advantages and disadvantages in this respect. The advantages are that demand from these countries can bring about an acceleration of Yugoslavia's own industrialization, in which the effect of the accelerator can be fully expressed (e.g. the particularly successful work of enterprises building ports, electric power stations, doing geological surveying, etc.). The requirements of these countries do not differ greatly from Yugoslavia's own home market requirements. Yugoslavia is a relatively more developed country in comparison with them, which means that her exports to them are not her traditional exports. An understanding of the needs of the developing countries is seen in Yugoslavia's policy of non-alignment (especially as reflected in her statements in UNCTAD I and II). However, this favourable political climate of opinion does not always coincide with adequate commercial organization and production efforts. In some of the less developed countries themselves this policy has sometimes led to unfounded expectations, based more on ideology than on economic criteria. The fact that Yugoslavia is a maritime nation with her own merchant fleet is also an advantage in trading with these countries.

There are, however, disadvantages. There is insufficient knowledge of foreign markets in Yugoslavia and insufficient experience in preparing goods for these markets, especially overseas ones. The costs of acquiring the necessary experience are very high. The sensitivity of these markets and the amount of foreign competition on them has often been neglected. In addition, Yugoslavia does not have sufficient crediting capacity, especially for exports of expensive machinery and equipment. Up to 1967 she extended export credits of 800 million dinars, a large sum by Yugoslav standards. This means that the market potential of the developing countries exceeds Yugoslavia's capacity to trade there.

Foreign investment in Yugoslavia

There has always been a greater flow of foreign capital into Yugoslavia than into other socialist countries. It has come mainly through government loans extended by other states or international organizations, but another source has been credits from foreign firms or banks for specific purposes. These are extended for the purchase of industrial equipment, licences and the financing of industrial cooperation arrangements. If they are loans then interest charges are paid on them. Licensing contracts are paid for in cash and industrial cooperation in goods.

This inflow of capital did not have sufficient effect. It all entered the country on the basis of government agreements or with a government guarantee regarding the credit-worthiness of debtors and the transfer of profits. This method of acquiring capital meant that the Yugoslav contracting parties (importers of capital) did not have to take great pains to use the capital in the best possible way, since this was the state's responsibility, or more precisely the responsibility of the National Bank, which to this end appropriated and centrally distributed all foreign currency; and that those supplying the capital were more or less uninterested in who got it and how it was used, since they had a state guarantee.

The results of this policy were as follows:

(1) The capital goods which were imported were not those which could be best used, but rather those for which a central guarantee could be provided. Such credits were mainly given for large-scale projects, for example, the purchase of complete new plants, and not for the modernization of existing industry or the import of single machines.

(2) This capital inflow was regulated more by the monetary

situation outside and inside Yugoslavia than it was by economic criteria.

(3) The system was out of step with the development of Yugoslavia's internal economic policy of decentralization and modernization.

(4) It was very expensive because there were no individual deals and the import of capital depended on central decisions, which were in their turn influenced by the general position of the country in the world economy. The whole chain of imports of capital depended on the strength of the weakest link (i.e. the greatest risk), which entailed the most unfavourable terms.

A changeover to a system of direct foreign capital investment is not only demanded by the policies of the reform, i.e. stabilization of the market, prices and money, which are preconditions, but also because of the level of commercial indebtedness and short-term obligations which have proved to be irrational and expensive.[1]

There are, however, more basic reasons. Yugoslavia has reached a point in her development where she is leaving the stage of an underdeveloped economy and assuming all the characteristics of a developed one. There is a great need to increase the volume of foreign trade and the structure of the country is becoming complex and sensitive, so that it can no longer tolerate the crude methods of central decision-making and criteria. There is now differentiation among enterprises, regions and industries. Technological progress is accelerating this differentiation. It is from this point of view that the need for investment by foreign companies must be considered.

The following advantages are seen in foreign investment. Direct investment means that the foreign investor has an immediate interest in the profitability of his investment; he is likely to introduce more up-to-date methods, know-how, equipment and marketing; he will take upon himself part of the responsibility for placing the products abroad, in order to earn his transferable foreign exchange and collect his profits, and this should increase exports; he will contribute to the rationaliza-

[1] For this reason a law was passed in 1966 making direct foreign investment in Yugoslav enterprises possible. *Zakon o proizvodno financijskom povezivanju Jugoslavenskih i inozemnih partnera* (Law concerning production and financial links between Yugoslav and foreign partners) (Belgrade, 1966).

tion of operation in enterprises in which he is co-investor (especially in methods of management and the organization of production). This should obviate many of the bottlenecks plaguing Yugoslav industry at present, and accelerate the modernization of the whole of the Yugoslav economy.

From the point of view of the theoretical economist, the fields of foreign investment which are most likely to meet the above criteria are: where there is already a demand both at home and abroad, which cannot be met because of insufficient capital available in Yugoslavia. An obvious example here is tourism on the Adriatic; where supply, or potential supply, exists but there is not enough capital to increase the exploitation of natural sources. Examples here are production of bauxite and aluminium, and oil extraction from the Adriatic; where production exists and there is demand for it which cannot be met because output is too small, or not steady enough to capture the market or, even more serious, to retain it once captured, i.e. furniture exports; where both production and the market exist, but the goods are too expensive or out-of-date, and there is not sufficient capital to be found in Yugoslavia for the modernization necessary to reduce production costs. Examples here are metal-using and machine-building industries. A reduction in the number of different kinds of products, combined with modernization, is impossible if conditioned by the gradual development of the home trade network only; where production could be increased to include new products and techniques.

Some branches of the economy are specifically forbidden by law from using imported capital, namely: banks, insurance, internal transport, domestic retail trade, utilities and public services.

Direct investment of foreign capital is carried out on the basis of *sui generis* contracts. Until now (1967) no joint-stock companies, partnerships nor mixed firms (part Yugoslav, part foreign) have been formed. So far, commerce with foreign firms has been carried out on the basis of purchasing contracts, acquisition of industrial property (patents, trade marks, etc.), and agency contracts in which each side had its own interests and bore its own risks.

The new arrangement is for joint contracts based on specified

common interests and liability. This is possible because Yugoslav enterprises are economically and legally independent, are
responsible for their own business decisions which they take
according to market prices, can engage and dismiss workers,
and adopt their own plans (which are of an indicative character and not legally binding as far as business operations are
concerned).

Investment agreements must meet three main conditions:
social ownership of the means of production, workers' management and the requirement of registration. In order to register a
joint investment contract, certain conditions must be met. The
most important of these are: that foreign capital should not, as a
rule, exceed 50 per cent of the value of assets of the domestic
affiliate (exceptions are, in principle, allowed); that the contract must conform to certain conditions under which some
international cooperation is carried out; that it must not place
the domestic economy or enterprise in a disadvantageous position, and that it must bring about technical progress assessed
according to realistic criteria. These conditions are entered into
the register. Experience will show to what extent they can be
forecast and adhered to.

Enterprises are managed by their workers' councils, while the
operation of capital brought in by the foreign investor is regulated by contract. The contract may also provide for the setting
up of a business committee and may lay down its powers and
responsibilities. Foreign investors are liable for the obligations of
affiliated enterprises only up to the amount of the capital invested, and are not liable for other obligations contracted by the
Yugoslav affiliates.

The domestic affiliate is liable for the share of capital invested
by the foreign affiliate according to the provisions of private
law. The state on its part has retained its sovereignty in decision-
making, but is bound by the provisions and principles of international law.

For the time being little can be said about contracts signed
under this law. Both foreign and Yugoslav companies seem to
be waiting to see what forms the first ventures will take. This is
quite understandable in the present situation, while the future is
still uncertain. It may well be, however, that this new aspect of
the Yugoslav economic system will have important results both

internally and externally, for, as some other socialist states are in a similar stage of development, it may suggest new paths for peaceful cooperation in the promotion of technological progress and the creation of stronger ties of partnership in international trade.

9
Policy towards underdeveloped areas

One of the most striking characteristics of Yugoslavia is the great variety and diversity of her natural, economic, and cultural levels of development. Here ecology and history, geography and sociology combine with the effects of technology and finance to produce a very diversified picture. Some of these diversities are of a more or less permanent character, such as endowment with natural resources, while others are of more temporary significance. Some of the variations between regions are man-made and others have been reduced by man.

The fact is that today in Yugoslavia differences in developmental level are such that the variation in gross social product per head between the most advanced republic and the least advanced is in a ratio of 3:1. If we compare districts the ratio rises to 10:1.

Conclusions should not be drawn too hastily from this situation. Obviously a policy is needed to cope with problems created by differences in levels of development and variations in economic conditions. Superficial observation sometimes seems to lead to the conclusion that the solution lies in a more egalitarian policy run from the centre in order to redistribute income and resources. But for twenty years there was such an intensive policy towards underdeveloped areas. The results of this central redistributive policy have not been very promising, since the gap between developed and developing areas in Yugoslavia measured in conventional terms, i.e. by gross social product *per capita*, actually increased during the period.

In this chapter we shall first examine the motivation behind the policy of aid towards underdeveloped areas, and then we shall examine the definition of an underdeveloped area; then we shall consider the machinery by which developmental aid is distributed and the principles and priorities which are applied.

Finally we shall discuss the different kinds of aid which have been given and look at some recent problems of developmental policy in Yugoslavia.

Motivation

Development policy has become a major issue not only in economics, but also in inter-national and inter-republic relations in Yugoslavia.

We can distinguish four main kinds of motivation which may guide development policy towards underdeveloped areas: humanitarian, national, socialist and economic.

The *humanitarian* motive arises from feelings of moral solidarity among human beings and a desire to help those less fortunate in life. In Yugoslavia this moral and humanitarian obligation also has an important political element. Some of the underdeveloped parts of the country bore the brunt of the liberation struggle during the Second World War and their development efforts were therefore felt to deserve special attention. The political overtones of this humanitarian and moral approach in fact developed into legal obligations. The Constitution of 1963 laid down the principle that it was a duty to help the underdeveloped areas and included a special provision to that effect.

The *national* motive of solidarity does not find expression in a multinational state in the same way as it does in a nationally homogeneous one. This is especially so in Yugoslavia because the levels of development of the different nations vary so much. A development policy cannot be operated from a single centre. Therefore the principle of the national solidarity of each of the constituent nations is complemented by the principle of the 'Brotherhood and Unity' of all the nations of Yugoslavia. As Yugoslavia is a federation of five nations and the republics have an important voice in planning their own and Yugoslavia's social and economic development, federal aid had to be given to the republics according to federal principles. All nations have the right to appeal to the Council of Nationalities, in which all republics are equally represented, for a discussion of development problems.[1]

[1] Indeed, the first occasion on which the Council of Nationalities was called together was at the initiative of the Republic of Bosnia and Hercegovina, which wanted the problem of the distribution of federal aid to different republics discussed.

In *socialist* motivation, the attitude towards helping under-developed areas is greatly influenced by the desire to build socialism in Yugoslavia. Thus there is the same long-term objective of socialist development policy for all parts of the country, and this creates special bonds of socialist solidarity. The main principle of socialist policy is to promote economic growth by distributing income according to the principle: to each according to his work. It was therefore necessary to find a way in which the socialist principle of income distribution could be reconciled with development aid, which is by definition a unilateral transfer over and above this principle. The policy of building socialism was in this context interpreted to mean that the federation should redistribute the national income in such a way that all parts of the country could progress towards socialism on an equal footing, and so that the less-developed regions could achieve a higher rate of growth than the more-developed parts.[1]

There is an *economic* motivation for giving aid to under-developed areas, because it is in the interests of the developed parts of the country. Encouraging the development of the less-developed areas will eventually benefit the development of the more-advanced regions. This is often represented as a choice between short-term and long-term gains, i.e. the developed parts have to decide whether to sacrifice their short-term interests and help to develop the other areas, which will benefit them in the long run by expanding the market, developing natural resources, creating employment, etc. We shall see that there are various interpretations of the economic motivation for development aid.[2]

In the course of time, when it was seen that development policy had to be a long-term affair, the emotional and political approaches were increasingly replaced by rational and economic attitudes. The development of the underdeveloped areas in spite of the considerable sums spent, did not occur either quickly enough for their problems to be satisfactorily solved or as

---

[1] In this policy of accelerating the growth of the less-developed areas, the example of the Soviet Union had a significant demonstration effect.

[2] One should not ignore the influence of international politics on the granting of aid to underdeveloped countries, countries with which the leaders of Yugoslavia had close political relations. There was a desire that Yugoslavia should act as a model in this respect.

rapidly as some people had over-optimistically expected. The underdeveloped areas demanded an ever-larger volume of investment credits, at certain periods reaching 25 per cent of all investment, and this put a brake on the further development of the developed areas and led to inflationary pressures.

Definition of an underdeveloped area

In the First Five-Year Plan the whole of Yugoslavia was regarded as an underdeveloped country. Indeed the plan's first general objective was to overcome the economic backwardness of Yugoslavia as a whole. In addition, special attention was given to the less developed republics, of which Bosnia and Hercegovina came first, followed by Macedonia, Montenegro and the autonomous territory of Kosmet. As all the country's resources were centrally controlled and allocated in a very authoritarian way, there was no real need for a more specific definition of the areas which should be considered undeveloped. The decision was left to *ad hoc* considerations.

Under the new system the process of decentralization meant that these territories had to be more specifically defined, and two trends of thought appeared. The first held that large regions should be designated underdeveloped areas, with detailed specification, i.e. entire republics, which meant in effect including all the republics except Croatia and Slovenia. The second proposal was to define small areas, i.e. districts, as underdeveloped areas. This view was strong in Croatia, which was very unequally developed, and where some districts would thus have qualified for privileged treatment as underdeveloped. The Second Five-Year Plan (1957–61) contained a compromise solution, by which specific districts were declared underdeveloped and therefore entitled to federal aid. However, as these districts were subordinate to the republics in political, administrative, financial and planning matters, it was decided that federal aid to underdeveloped districts should be given to the republics for further allocation to the underdeveloped districts. The underdeveloped areas included the southern districts of Croatia, the whole of Bosnia except for the three most north-eastern districts, the whole of Montenegro and Macedonia, Kosmet and several districts of south-eastern Serbia. There were continuous attempts, through discussion, to find an appropriate definition for these areas. Finally a number of degrees of underdevelopment were agreed upon, but no concrete criteria were worked out. As a result, decisions continued to be made on mainly political grounds, which caused some tension. For a time, the republic of Bosnia and Hercegovina was no longer considered underdeveloped, and the federal plan decreed that special attention should be given to the province of Kosmet as the most poorly developed area.

In the period of the reform the definition of underdeveloped areas was fixed by law, so as to avoid arbitrariness and continual political bargaining. The Federal Constitution of 1963 provided that a special federal law should decide which were the underdeveloped areas, in order to provide a basis for a responsible long-term development policy. A law was passed in 1966 which defined the republics of Bosnia and Hercegovina, Macedonia, Montenegro and the autonomous province of Kosmet as insufficiently developed areas. These areas accounted for 33 per cent of the population and 40 per cent of the area of Yugoslavia. It was left to the developed republics to decide which of their areas they considered underdeveloped. These were not entitled to federal aid.[1]

The problem of definition of undeveloped areas has also arisen within the undeveloped areas themselves.[2]

Not only has the gap between developed and underdeveloped republics widened over the last 20 years, in spite of the central redistribution of national product, but so also has the gap between the more and less developed parts within the backward areas. Moreover, the difference has increased more in the underdeveloped than in the developed areas. Thus the problem of

[1] For instance, in Croatia a republic law was passed defining the underdeveloped areas and here communes were taken as units. These are given aid by the republic fund for underdeveloped areas and the matter is considered to be a republic affair.

[2] In the Republic of Bosnia and Hercegovina, for instance, there was a controversy as to whether certain areas of the republic should be singled out and entitled to specific aid, and the others not. The disagreement was between the administration of the republic, which considered it unnecessary to define such areas specifically, and which was clearly influenced by a number of members (staff) who came from the obviously undeveloped regions, and the republic parliament, which held that legal definition would prevent dissatisfaction with subjective and *ad hoc* decisions, and which wanted to maintain its own control. It was the latter view which finally prevailed.

development cannot be considered only as a spatial one; there are discrepancies not only between regions, but also between classes and sectors.

The relative level of *per capita* income is not a sufficiently reliable indicator of underdevelopment. It has to be used in conjunction with absolute figures for the different levels of development. It is one thing if a 3:1 difference exists at income levels of 300 and 100 dollars per head, and quite another if the same 3:1 ratio occurs between incomes of 900 and 300 dollars per head. From the point of view of development it is more difficult to raise income from 100 to 300 dollars *per capita* than from 300 to 1,000 dollars *per capita*, mainly because heavy initial investment is needed in the infrastructure, which will cause the capital–output ratio to fall at first. Moreover, the amount of investment cannot be indiscriminately increased since there are technological, economic and social limits to the amount of investment which can be absorbed.

If maximizing investment is the only criterion of developmental policy, it will automatically lead to lower marginal utility of investment projects, lower profitability (diminishing returns), and to relatively useless investment for investment's sake (e.g. in industries producing for stocks, etc.).

Development policy

In the period of administrative socialism the motives outlined on pp. 182–3 above were accepted in principle, but individual decisions were made in a subjective and arbitrary way. Little assessment or analysis was carried out of the distinction between financial subsidies to administrative budgets in the underdeveloped areas and economic investment and development projects for growth purposes. Also, in the central distribution of developmental aid, little distinction was made between grants (which did not have to be reimbursed) and credits (which did). The policy of central distribution finally led to a situation where everybody wanted to be classified as underdeveloped, and to rely on central income redistribution rather than his own work and efforts.

Under the new economic system, the great step forward was

made in 1957 with the Second Five-Year Plan. The following principles were adopted:

(1) That the development of the underdeveloped areas must principally be the concern of the people of those areas themselves.

(2) That it must also be the continuous concern of all organs of state authority; not only of the Federal Government, but also of republics, districts and communes.

(3) That the granting of aid for the development of such areas must not hinder the progress of the already developed areas. Thus the policy of overall levelling, according to which the developed areas were not permitted to develop further until the others had caught up with them (and in fact were likely to slide backwards), was rejected.[1]

Another principle which was established was that in their requests for loans from the General Investment Fund the underdeveloped republics, Macedonia, Montenegro and the autonomous province of Kosmet, had priority over other areas as long as their choice of projects was guided by the principle of profitability. In general, priority was to be given to agriculture, transport (particularly the main trunk roads), forestry and exploitation of natural resources.[2]

In 1958 a further step was taken in the specification of priorities. In order to reduce political pressure for short term fiscal aid, the principle was established that in investment priority should be given to the building up of an infrastructure suited for the further development of the area, and financial subsidies to local administrative budgets should take second place.

Further changes in development policy took place when the Third Five-Year Plan (1961–5) was accepted. The principle agreed upon was that the basic aim should be the industrialization of the underdeveloped areas, i.e. creation of industrial nuclei which would radiate development. The industries should be those likely to mobilize the increase in national income most quickly, to create the highest rate of employment and to change

[1] See Tito's speech at the Central Committee of the League of Communists of Yugoslavia in November 1959, pp. 13–14.
[2] *Društveni plan privrednog razvoja Jugoslavije 1957–1961* (Social plan of economic development of Yugoslavia) (Belgrade, 1957), pp. 209–12.

the social structure of the area. Attention was also given to building up the economic and social infrastructure. A new element in this policy was the creation of a special federal fund for the development of underdeveloped areas, which was intended mainly to give credits for the development of manufacturing industries. It was also to give preferential loans and to provide itself with the participation and the guarantee for investment which the socio-political communities (communes, districts and republics) generally had to give the General Investment Fund for loans in other areas. The following criteria were agreed upon: number of inhabitants; level of development; economic strength; whether the republic in which the area was situated had its own means for helping its underdeveloped areas; whether the republic itself was developed or underdeveloped and to what extent. Certain specific development criteria could also be taken into consideration.

In this plan the role of the republics was stressed. They acted as intermediaries for the funds which the Federal Fund for Development allocated to the underdeveloped areas, i.e. credits were granted to the republics, which then distributed them to specific projects within the general policy framework. The social plan of 1965 emphasized that priority for credits from the General Investment Fund to the underdeveloped areas should be given to those projects which would increase the volume of production and productivity most quickly from the point of view of the Yugoslav economy as a whole. Difficulties in fulfilling the programmes should also be taken into consideration, by giving the underdeveloped areas aid in the form of experts and know-how.

In the federal plan for the year 1965 it was decided that the resources of the fund for underdeveloped areas should be used primarily for finishing projects already started. This was partly in order to check the impatience of the developers, who, instead of concentrating their energies on implementing already accepted projects, preferred to make new requests for further projects, often neglecting the old ones.

The 1966–70 Five-Year Plan[1] introduced significant changes in policy objectives. First, in order to underline their impor-

---

[1] *Društveni plan razvoja Jugoslavije od 1966–1970 godine* (Social plan of development of Yugoslavia from 1966–1970) (Belgrade and Zagreb, 1966), pp. 73–9.

tance, the description of the areas was changed from 'under-developed' to 'insufficiently developed' areas. Two conditions were set. The first was that they should achieve a certain level of development, and the second that the objectives, plans and trends of development should be determined by the social plans of the republics and provinces. The most rapid development was foreseen for the autonomous province of Kosovo and Metohija. The aim was that by 1970 the insufficiently developed areas should achieve a level of development which would be 90 per cent of the 1965 level in the developed parts of the country. Thus a seven-year lag in development was accepted as admissible. As for economic objectives, it was emphasized that the insufficiently developed areas should experience almost the same degree of qualitative development as Yugoslavia as a whole underwent during the Second Five-Year Plan (1957–61), i.e. special attention should be given to transport and communications; national resources should begin to be exploited; new kinds of industrial production should be started; and the structure of the areas should approach that of a developed country. Accumulation of savings in these areas should increase to the extent that tertiary services could be developed. The problem of over-population was underlined, in spite of the rapid rate of development planned. Therefore in agriculture labour intensive crops are advocated, cooperation in agriculture is to be stimulated, and handicrafts and cottage industries are recommended. Migration towards more-developed areas should be carried out in an organized way.

Aid allocation

The question of who should collect funds for aid and who should distribute them has been answered in many ways during the course of the last twenty years. According to the First Five-Year Plan the agent for redistribution was the overall state budget, which collected and redistributed all resources, including those for developing the underdeveloped areas. But this distribution was too much influenced by the day-to-day economic and political situation, because it was done on an annual basis. It was therefore not very well suited for a long-term policy of development. In order to avoid this under the new system resources for investment were separated from the state budget in 1957 and put into a General Investment Fund which allocated credits and grants for underdeveloped areas under more favourable conditions than the budget. Soon, however, it was discovered that the general character of this fund was such that not enough attention was given to aid to underdeveloped areas, and a special fund was therefore created for them in 1963. The money for this fund was allocated by the federal social plan to the republic, which further allocated it to specific projects. Thus the problem of financing the underdeveloped areas was decentralized, although decisions were still made through administrative channels.

The Constitution of 1963 heralded a new era of the reform, and provided that 'the economically underdeveloped republics and areas should be given material and other resources by the Social Community to allow their speedier economic development and the creation of a material foundation for social services' (Federal Constitution, Article 27). The constitution decreed that the special federal fund set up for aid to these areas should have its own permanent financial resources, and would provide special credit services, as well as giving aid to those republics which were not able to finance their social and other services alone.

In this connection two laws were passed. The first imposed a contribution amounting to 1.85 per cent of the social product of enterprises in the socialist sector, to be paid into the fund for insufficiently developed areas. The controlling board of the fund, consisting of one representative of each of the republics and six members elected by the Federal Parliament, proposed a special federal law to allocate the funds for the period 1966–70. The criteria for distribution were as follows: income per head of the population; volume and structure of saving in the area; proportion of production capacity employed and efficiency of use of investment (the means of social reproduction); and other circumstances of importance. Altogether 820 milliard dinars were to be allocated as follows: Bosnia 31 per cent, Kosmet 30 per cent, Macedonia 26 per cent and Montenegro 13 per cent.

The second law stipulated that additional funds should be allocated by the federal budget to socio-political communities which do not have sufficient means of their own to provide indispensable social services. The criteria are applied according to the fiscal income of the republics. The federal budget provides the difference between the funds collected by the community and the average *per capita* expenditure in Yugoslavia, or the *per capita* expenditure of the republic which is closest to the average. This is Serbia, whose income, taken as 100, provides a yardstick, by which Bosnia gets 11 per cent, Macedonia 1 per cent and Kosmet 19 per cent per inhabitant of the sum spent in Serbia.[1]

It has also been found that financial aid in the form of investment funds is not enough, because there are other limitations, such as lack of projects which have been properly worked out, shortage of experts, etc. Therefore the nature of aid is being extended from financial to technical assistance of many types.

In July 1967 the board of the fund decided that in future 2 per cent of the total allocated sum should be spent on improvement of productivity and technical aid.

It is thus expected that the fund will act as a catalyst which will activate other agents. Therefore it is planned that, of the total sum invested in the insufficiently developed areas up to 1970, the fund will provide 800 milliard dinars, while the Federal Government will allocate another 500 milliard dinars out of its budget, the socialist business enterprises of the areas will provide 1,200 milliard, and 500 milliard dinars will come from banks and business organizations in other parts of Yugoslavia and abroad.

[1] This compares with the expenditure on social services in Slovenia, which is 87 per cent, Croatia which is 28 per cent, and Montenegro, which is 22 per cent above the level in Serbia.

Concepts of economic development in Yugoslavia

We have already mentioned in an earlier chapter that the general aim of economic development in Yugoslavia after 1945 was to build socialism and communism as quickly as possible. Since 1948 an important additional principle has been that each country should follow its own road to socialism, and this was accepted by other European socialist countries in 1955. In Yugoslavia this newly-conceived objective had to be achieved in a country where natural resources were distributed very unevenly and as a result, levels of economic development and the structure of class relations varied between regions; and a diverse historical and cultural inheritance had contributed to the forming of the natural consciousness of a state made up of five nations and several nationalities.

It is not surprising that in the implementation of the general principle various concepts of development have crystallized over the last twenty years, all claiming to fall within the framework of the socialist theory of development. The more experience was gained and the longer the process of development lasted, the greater was the diversity of concepts and the more different the theories that appeared, as opportunities for different paths of development emerged. This is in a sense a logical outcome of economic growth. Some of these concepts developed in a sequence, one after another, as a result of economic development and political events. Others, however, existed simultaneously with each other. Some were formalized in official statements, others were discussed in scientific papers and still others were just 'in the air'.

The autarchic concept of development

This theory follows a classical pattern of argument. The

country must be developed as a closed economic unit, in which the objective of economic policy is to produce only for the domestic needs of the population and to consume only what can be produced domestically. Therefore, it is said, production forces should be developed only as far as is necessary to meet the established needs of the domestic population and these needs should be satisfied only to the extent made possible by the production forces within the country. The purpose of economic policy is to achieve an equilibrium between these two magnitudes.

We can distinguish in Yugoslavia three variants of this autarchic concept of development: the primitive or romantic, the nationalistic and the socialist.

Primitive autarchy sets as the limit to national consumption the level of production based on home-produced natural resources. It follows the principle: 'We cannot consume what we have not produced', and this slogan is still often heard in Yugoslav political statements. It is interpreted to mean that account should be taken only of domestic physical production and consumption. Thus it does not take into account the foreign trade effect, which transforms domestic physical products by money exchange into foreign made products.

This slogan comes up against the problem of the distribution of gross national product, particularly when the rate of investment is too high and personal consumption is thereby reduced to a low level, and when budgetary expenditure is too heavy a burden on the productive sector. It ignores the fact that the modern economy, producing goods with different gestation periods, has to take account of the credit mechanism, which irons out the differences between the rhythm of acquiring income and the rhythm of spending it, and between the rhythm of production and that of consumption. It gives economically unjustified preference to 'our products', 'our men' and 'our way of life', which is basically a traditional concept. In particular this concept of development opposes the demonstration effect and tries to reduce it. Primitive autarchy does not take into account that the demonstration effect can be a stimulating factor in the development process.[1] The struggle is in particular

[1] Quite recently (1967) a prominent Yugoslav economist criticized the increase in the consumption of new consumer goods of foreign origin, which he interpreted as

directed against new products, which are considered to be dangerous. Any increase in their consumption is taken as a sign of the degeneration of socialism or the corruption of the consumer – especially of youth by Western influences.

The primitive concept of autarchy is based on the idea that the development of the country should rely on its own physical resources. Consumption must be restrained and there is a certain pride in economic asceticism, with the result that the poverty of underdevelopment is mistaken for a virtue of socialism. Production of consumer goods should be kept to a minimum and the import of such goods is considered to be a sin against the development of socialism. In fact this concept is looking towards past patterns of life, even when its upholders are preaching about the future. By contrast, there are some people who think that it is rather dangerous for socialism to identify demand for new consumer goods simply with Western influences.

The *nationalistic* concept of autarchic development is also based on a model of a closed economy and grants a monopoly position to domestic production and domestic capital.[1] It is felt that under capitalism, domestic capital ought to be owned by 'our' capitalist class and develop for its benefit, while under socialism it should be held by 'our' socialist state, which should reap the benefit from its growth. Accumulation of domestic capital for the purpose of growth has to be provided in both cases by imposing on the domestic population. In some circles the arrival of socialism has not weakened the belief in development by nationalistic autarchy. On the contrary it has in a way strengthened it, because it is no longer a question of the private interests of a national capitalist class but of the socialized interest of the nation. Clearly this type of autarchy in a multinational state is likely to develop specific forms and to create tensions. The questions arise: What, in this context, is a nation? How far

an obstacle to development. He was not ready to take into consideration that increased production of consumer goods is a stimulant to development, inducing people to want to consume more and to work harder in order to earn more, and is an incentive for those who produce them to increase their production. Even in 1967 criticism could be heard in the Federal Parliament of imports of certain new products into the country. There is a lag in the spreading of consumption habits between some advanced and other more closed communities in Yugoslavia.

[1] In the case of Yugoslavia this concept fell on fertile ground, because of the old nationalistic policy of pre-First World War Serbia and of pre-Second World War Yugoslavia, which we have already described (pp. 6–10, Ch. 1).

does national solidarity apply in economics? What is the position of different nations within a federation of nations?

The nationalistic development concept of autarchy also aims at strengthening 'the nation'. It does not take into account either intra-national differences and international solidarity among nations or changes in their relative positions in the course of development. It attempts to achieve a certain unity between the volume of production and of consumption, which, it is believed, ought to balance each other within the frontiers of the country. If they do not balance, then either higher prices must be paid by domestic consumers to the domestic producers, or consumption must be subsidized through redistribution of the national income by the state. Thus balanced growth is achieved by restricting consumption, and the scales are kept in the hands of the central government. This is particularly complicated in a country where different areas and nations are at different levels of economic development, and where levels of productivity, standards of consumption and rates of saving therefore vary. Here the equilibrating role of the centralist state and the policy of balancing growth are bound to meet with almost insurmountable obstacles. Whenever people talk about the role which the State or the Nation or Society must assume in order to attain a better distribution of goods, income or wealth, they are speaking to some extent from a position of national autarchy. Their standards stop short at the frontier of the nation, the state or the society. The availability of a restricted range of products is the price which has to be paid for pride in national autarchy. The question of to what extent this policy can increase exploitation of natural resources and create employment for the domestic population is not a matter of national solidarity but a problem of technology and economics.

The third variant of the policy of autarchy is *socialist* autarchy, which was applied in Yugoslavia from 1947–51, and even up to 1965. Some of the principles of that period are still retained, either deliberately or through inertia. This concept is based on Stalin's idea of the besieged fortress: the development of a socialist country surrounded by capitalist states and not strong enough economically to resist foreign competition. Autarchy therefore has a dual function here: outwardly, deliberately to sever the developing socialist system from connections with the outside world, because of fear of competition in the international division of labour and the feeling that comparison is to the disadvantage of the socialist economy; inwardly, to erect a barrier which will transform the flows between the planned system of the socialist domestic economy and the world market, so as to allow the domestic flow of goods and services to take its own course, according to decisions in the political system.

Thus socialist autarchy means the political redistribution of purchasing power abroad and of gains and losses from trade within the country. It does not provide an appropriate yardstick for the measurement of economic growth, which is measured in prices decided on the basis of political (= extra-economic) criteria. It cannot answer the question as to who gains and who loses in exchange with foreign countries, or even among importers or exporters within the country,[1] questions which in the course of development increasingly begin to affect the development policy itself. It leads to an ever-increasing political redistribution of the gross national product by the state, which to an ever greater extent blurs the issues of 'socially necessary labour'.

The application of this concept results in higher costs of production compared with foreign countries, prices higher than on the world market, the production of poorer quality goods, less choice for the consumer, a lower technological level of production of machinery, and consequently a smaller share of the national income going into people's pockets as personal income.

The motivations of such an autarchic development policy are to be found in the strategic field of national defence, in a policy aimed at national independence, and in the maximization of national growth.

The technocratic concept

The technocratic concept of development aims at the rational optimization of development. This optimization is to be achieved, from the point of view of Yugoslavia as a whole, by

[1] The history of the discussion of price formation within the socialist common market (CMEA) and the interminable controversy regarding the role of the plan and the market in socialist countries are the outward signs of these dilemmas.

treating the country as a homogeneous environment, a field of action where progress is made in the name of science implemented by authoritarian means. Vulgarization and misrepresentation of cybernetics are the favourite excuse for the arbitrariness that usually ensues. The road to optimum development must follow norms of behaviour and objectives set by the small number of initiates who have mastered scientific methods. The way in which this development is to be achieved has to be decided by a single centre, according to the most 'rational scientific criteria'. Those few who 'know better' what is good for the country and its population often show little concern for other factors of development. Yet this apparently reasonable and objective concept has developed several variants and raised many questions.

First of all it is not always quite clear what the criteria of the purely scientific approach are. The scientific authority which determines the criteria of optimization may present its own subjective opinions and ideas as objective scientific results. This has already happened in the past in some countries. A second question that arises is why the rationale should be limited to determining an optimum within one country, thus aiming for a nationalistic solution of the problem of optimum development and selling nationalism in the disguise of scientific development. A third objection is that human beings do not follow technological ends exclusively in their actions, because they have their own wills and self-respect, their own level of social conscience which has to be respected. They also have desires and propensities which are already formed and for whose fulfilment they strive. It is not always clear that the technocratic search for the optimum takes into account this complex of human wants and social requirements, particularly when people are not asked what they want. Modern technology does not require solutions which are formulated and carried into effect by a single centre. On the contrary, it makes it possible for initiative and action from many sources to take into account the optimum result for the whole community.

The economistic concept of development

A third group of concepts of economic development found in

Yugoslavia can be called economistic, i.e. economic model-making carried to the extreme and determining development according to Yugoslav economic factors alone. These concepts are found in the form of maximization of production, maximization of consumption and achievement of equal rates of development.[1]

The first economistic concept of development is inspired by the overall maximization of possibilities of development. According to this concept, Yugoslavia should develop all kinds of production, wherever and however this can best be done; it should open every possible mine, build factories of every kind, raise every kind of crop and livestock wherever technically possible and economically favourable. This sounds justified when people talk of overall development of production to the maximum in a country. It was the leading developmental theory of the First Five-Year Plan. But questions were soon raised about limited means, priorities in time, about who was to come first and who would have to wait, and who was to decide on the order of priorities and the distribution of the means of development. A policy based on this theory raises great hopes and creates conflicts which cannot be solved to the general satisfaction. In the late fifties in Yugoslavia, when it became impossible to satisfy the demands from all quarters for development, a policy was initiated: to everybody a little of everything. This method of decentralization without specialization is the least economical and the most expensive policy of development, except for centralization without liberalization. The consequence was the creation of enterprises which were too small, too diversified and non-economic.

The second concept is that of the development of Yugoslavia from the point of view of optimizing consumption, i.e. limiting the development of production forces to the level which will meet the maximum requirements of internal consumption within Yugoslavia. The limit here is set according to the socially recognized needs of the economy. Thus the economy has to expand the production of products until their costs reach the level of marginal cost, at which a product is still worth pro-

---

[1] These theories have appeared in a similar form in the discussion among socialist countries in CMEA about which principle of development should be applied within the international socialist division of labour.

ducing. This policy was advocated by the supporters of the concept of a welfare state, and caused some difficulties when the attempt was made to apply it. The conflict between the various investment criteria, the problem of choice between a closed or an open economy, and in particular the difficulties in the development of underdeveloped areas, were largely consequences of the search for balanced growth according to the optimum internal consumption concept.

The third concept of economistic development is the theory of the development of all parts of Yugoslavia by maximizing the rate of growth 'justly'. Those sectors should be developed first which can provide maximum saving, i.e. which have the smallest capital–output ratio, and then saving should be centrally distributed to all, including the slow accumulating sectors. The role of the state should be to redistribute the social income so as to take away from those which grow faster and give to those which grow more slowly.

This theory of development was dominant after 1966, and placed the problem of political income redistribution in the province of economic policy. Redistribution of the gross social product by a centre which takes away from one group of the population and gives to another is against the socialist principle 'to each according to his work', a principle established as the guiding rule in income distribution in 1958 and taken as the dominant principle by the reform.

Development by domination

The fourth group of monocentric concepts are the theories of domination, i.e. leadership in economic development, by some leading sector, leading nation or leading region.[1] Development must be actively led. This means that someone or something has to pull others 'forward' to do something which they would not otherwise do. This kind of development is not unknown in the history of socialist development. It is said, usually by those who aspire to become the leaders, that somebody has to lead

---

[1] The best known is the theory of institutionally defined, 'leading sectors' of economy. The predominant theory has been that of priority development for the socialist sector, which we have already discussed in the chapter on the formation of the socialist sector.

development, and if somebody has to lead those who have realized this are usually inclined to find it 'natural' that they are the most appropriate people to do it. In this way we come to concepts of poles of economic development. Which links in the chain should be pulled first, which clusters of production relations can pull the others forward most strongly?

In Yugoslavia there were three groups of such concepts: those of leading sectors, of leading regions and of a leading nation.

The theory of the *leading sector* was based on technological sectors (agriculture, industry, transportation, etc.). It allocated priority in investment as follows: industry first, and after it agriculture, transportation and, finally, housing. This theory of leading sectors was a legacy of Stalin's developmental policy, which created a rigid order of leading priorities in which industry was to lead the national economy, led itself by heavy industry, which in turn was led by its hard core, the machine industry. This was considered to be a general theory of socialist development valid for any country, large or small, at any level of development, in any ecological environment. A rigid theory of development by sectors was predominant in Yugoslavia up to 1955, but in practice it was still strong even up to 1965.

The concept of the leading sector was thus a concept of the leading industrial sector. But in the course of time there were three stages of industrialization, one of which was based on requirements contrary to, and in conflict with, the requirements of the previous ones. As a result of this development policy a fairly large industrial sector was developed, working at low capacity and, because of preferential treatment, at a low level of productivity. Therefore, instead of industry as an overall leading sector, the reform introduced a selective growth policy for various sectors.

Another concept of domination in the spatial sense is the theory of the *leading region*. Here again there are two main concepts in Yugoslavia: the Danubian and the Adriatic. The first sees the leading pole of development at the affluents around the big rivers of the Danubian plain, holding that economic flows should follow the flow of the rivers downstream. The leading region should be where the rivers such as the Sava, Tisa, Tamiš and Morava flow into the Danube. This region is open to the Danube and here, according to the theory, the most important industrial zone ought to be developed (Belgrade, Pančevo, Smederevo, etc.), with electrical power stations, oil refineries, steel mills, chemical and fertilizer plants, etc. Belgrade, at the confluence of the Danube and Sava, should be the leading economic pole of the country. This continental theory of river confluence is hampered by the rather restricted possibilities for river transport in Yugoslavia, particularly in so far as it is based on the Danube, which, although an international water-way, does not flow into an open sea and is therefore vulnerable and subject to various limitations.[1]

The Adriatic concept of development is that the Yugoslav economy as a whole should be attracted to the Adriatic and not towards the north. This maritime concept is aimed at linking the country to the whole world, East, West and underdeveloped areas, as Yugoslavia chooses. Some people have said that this concept is pro-Western, but in answer to this it should be mentioned that the East may have an interest in it as well. When the Soviet economic mission visited Yugoslavia in the 1960s they explored possibilities in the development of shipping, ship-building and aluminium, all located on the Adriatic coast. It is not therefore solely a Western concept but is a developmental concept which takes a global point of view, by using the possibilities of the open sea.

Another concept of development, originating in Slovenia, is that the leading area should be the most developed area in the country, which by its fast development can accumulate resources for investment in the development of other areas, which should follow the lead of the most industrially advanced parts. This investment should not be done by extra-economic, politi-

[1] It is easy to show the risks which are attendant on this concept of development by some historical examples. The old Kingdom of Serbia waged a customs war with the Austrian Empire for five years before the First World War, when nine-tenths of Serbian exports travelled up the Danube into Austro-Hungary, which was in a position to open or close the gates on the Danube at will. Serbia, which was small, had already realized that this reliance on the Danube did not give much choice in development.

Another difficult situation developed after 1933, during Hitler's economic penetration towards South-East Europe, which again was based on the Danube and represented a very great threat to Yugoslavia.

For a third time in the same generation, the reliance on the Danube in 1946–8, during the Soviet economic penetration, put Yugoslavia in a precarious position which ended with the Soviet economic blockade. This again showed how dangerous dependence on the Danube is for the Yugoslav economy.

cal and administrative decisions of secretariats and ministers, but on business lines by enterprises and banks.

The opposite concept is that of the political centre retaining economic control and compensating for economic backwardness by political influence. In this concept the political redistribution of the national income becomes the main instrument of development, in order to create leading sectors in less developed areas and to compensate politically for what people do not achieve economically. This is a form of exploitation born in a socialist system, but explained by a policy of equal stomachs. It is said that equality of consumption should be the measurement of development. Thus the political centre should be the main agent of development, and the aim should be equalization of consumption by political means, on the basis of standards set and means manipulated by the centre.

The next concept of development is that of the leading nation as a state builder, the 'big brother' concept.[1] Development in the country should be led by the nation with the largest population, in this case the Serbian nation. Since the Serbs make up 42 per cent of the population they should have the role of leading nation in Yugoslavia, and Serbia should be the leading pole of development. This theory, particularly dear to the central bureaucracy in Belgrade, proclaimed that the Serbs should have 'equal rights but greater duties', i.e. duties towards the community greater than the others, because they are the largest nation.[2] This greater duty is to lead, i.e. to make decisions on behalf of the others.[3]

[1] A similar concept developed in the USSR and some other socialist countries, was known as the 'big nation' concept.

[2] Ranković said at the Third Plenary Meeting of the Central Committee of the League of Communists of Yugoslavia before his downfall in March 1966, 'Serbia is the greatest Republic and the Serbian nation the most numerous nation in the socialist commonwealth of nations and nationalities of Yugoslavia. Therefore it is quite justified that this puts on this nation also a higher degree of responsibility for a correct development of inter-nation relationships.' In other words the Serbs should be responsible both for themselves and for others, i.e. the leading nation has to oversee the behaviour of the others. According to this concept one nation should have more responsibility than the others for the policy of the state, including the policy of development through the redistribution of national income.

[3] In the past a similar theory was used by King Alexander's dictatorship, with the goal of 'creating one nation' in Yugoslavia round Serbia as the centre of power. After the war the aim was to speed up the development of socialism with Serbia

Bicentral concepts of development

Bicentral or bipolar concepts of development in Yugoslavia start from the standpoint that the country has two poles of development which correspond to the two large industrial zones. One is in the west, centred round Zagreb and the other in the east, with its centre round Belgrade.[1] In the case of Yugoslavia the multinational character of the state must be taken into consideration. The western zone is economically the more developed and industrially the more powerful. The eastern zone, including the capital of Yugoslavia, is politically stronger.[2] Decisions about development policy should therefore, according to this concept, be made in two centres. In fact economic power is concentrated round these two centres and much economic integration of industrial enterprises takes place in the two areas.

as the pole of development and, as Serbia was not strong enough to lead economically, political means were to be used to strengthen her so that economic leadership could be developed. The historical roots of this theory are as follows: the old pre-1918 Kingdom of Serbia had not developed a strong capitalist class; the ruling class lived to a very large extent on the state, and even the businessmen and industrialists did the bulk of their business for state contracts. The state was the main support of this élite, which therefore felt that the state should be preserved. Its members put themselves in the position of defenders of the state, the only people who were presumed to be trustworthy in this function. This psychological and political concept survived capitalism.

In the areas which were under the multinational Austro-Hungarian monarchy the situation was different. National development with the Croats, the Slovenes and the Serbs from these areas took place on different lines. All that they had achieved in their national life they had achieved against the will of the state, by relying on their own forces. Even the capitalist class had its own economic roots; it did not live off the state. History taught these people that what they had had been created by their reliance on their own strength and not on the state apparatus. Therefore they did not consider the state to be the source of their development. They existed as nations even when the state was against them. This is another historical survival which has outlived capitalism as far as the Croats, Slovenes, Montenegrins and Macedonins are concerned, the last having come off even worse than the first two, regarding the role of the state in development.

It is not surprising that there is a difference of opinion and tension between these two concepts.

[1] As an analogy to such bicentral systems of development the example of Italy is mentioned, where Rome is the political centre and Milan the economic one. Similar relationships exist between Moscow and Leningrad, Madrid and Barcelona; Ankara and Istanbul, Amsterdam and The Hague, etc.

[2] Such a theory was given political expression in the bifocal theory which was already dominant in the National Council of the Slovenes, Croats and Serbs in 1918, when the unification of Yugoslavia was discussed in the provisional parliament in Zagreb, which at one time proposed to make a state treaty of union between Croatia and the Kingdom of Serbia.

For example, in oil there is INA in the west against the Petrol Union in Belgrade. There are also the radio industry in Niš as against the integrated radio industries of Zagreb, Banja Luka and Ljubljana, the two concentrations of steel producers, etc.

The organization of many economic activities in Yugoslavia is centred round these two foci. This tendency is strengthened by the fact that it is not a matter of complementary but of competitive sectors. Both areas are developing oil wells and oil refineries, steel mills and fertilizer plants, chemical factories and power stations. When investment activity in Bosnia and Herce-govina was reduced, the bicentral character of these two in-dustrial zones became even more emphasized. Lack of com-munications between the Adriatic ports of Central Dalmatia and Bosnia and the eastern parts of the country increases this polarization.

This situation is to some extent counteracted by the existence of the special industrial zone of Slovenia and of the development of Macedonia as a specific industrial area.

Oligocentric theories of development

These theories centre development round the administrative division of Yugoslavia into six republics (and two autonomous provinces in Serbia), most of which are based on national groupings, i.e. a Serbian, a Croatian, a Macedonian, a Slovene and a Montenegrin republic. Each of these nations develops according to its own interests, led by its own political centre, and they also serve their common interests by using compara-tive advantages. The theory is in essence that each republic should have a double interest in its development policy: that each should develop its own territory and that each should in-fluence the development of Yugoslavia as a whole.

The result is a development policy for Yugoslavia as a whole which is based on the conflict and cooperation of joint interests and on bargaining. For this policy to work tensions and con-flicts have to be solved by agreement and negotiation about what joint policy should be adopted in the interests of all. The aim is not to isolate each republic within its own political fron-tiers, so that it takes account only of its own interests, but just the opposite, to have the most open policy possible, so that each republic takes into account the behaviour of the others. Each should have its own concepts of economic development for itself, for the other republics, and for the community of all the republics in the country. Thus in answer to the critical question 'a single system or a bargaining system?', asked by 'worried patriots' who obviously fear the latter, the answer is 'What are the alternatives: the dictates of one or agreement by all?'

To those who have a special interest in monocentrism this concept appears as disorganization or even anarchy. For others it appears to offer a higher degree of social integration of economic interests, which will be stronger than any dictates imposed from the centre. Thus the development policy is conceived in six or more mutually interdependent centres and formulated by joint cooperation.

The practical application of this policy is seen in the 1967 amendments to the Constitution of 1963. According to Amendment Three there is a Chamber of Nationalities, which is composed of delegations from the parliaments of the six republics, each consisting of ten members, and five representatives from each of the autonomous provinces of Vojvodina and Kosmet.

Polycentric concepts of development

Polycentric theories, as they have appeared so far, fall into two different groups; one is the general idea of development by workers' self-management as a technological organization; the other is the development of the Yugoslav communal system as a territorial organization.

The system of development policy based on workers' self-management in business organizations is a polycentric system because the decisions in this system are made by the autonomous plans of each of the working organizations, including self-financing of growth. This is a system of technological polycentricity, because the workers' collectives in larger organizations are formed according to the connections between workers in the production process. Self-managed units (working organizations) are linked together on horizontal and vertical lines. Other links between them, instead of an administrative hierarchy, are through the banking system on one hand and professional organizations and chambers of commerce on the other.

The chambers of commerce have the task of representing their members before the authorities, and also undertake actions of common interest, but not operational action on the business level. The banking system is envisaged as the instrument by which capital is supplied for development.

The communal system in development policy operates so that every commune is responsible for its own development. It works on a territorial principle, which means that the primary decision in development is with each of the communes, and further that federations of several communes together undertake actions of common interest. This system is being developed in the re-organization of the local administration by the abolition of the district as the administrative supervising unit and the transfer of jurisdiction to the communes. Even among those who believe that decisions concerning development are so numerous, and interests so varied, that it is necessary for small units to make such decisions themselves, the problem still arises of how to integrate the actions of these many communal centres. A large number of small and varied poly-centres cannot influence decisions with regard to the whole social community. There are two conflicting opinions about how to meet this problem. One conclusion drawn is that the central departments of the state, i.e. the Federal Government, should represent the integration of interests of communes. This argument has been used by some people in support of the claim that the republics should be abolished, because they are obstacles to the rational organization of the communes. Thus there would be a large number of comparatively small communes, unable to have much influence on the centre of power, which would be the federation.

A second concept is that the communes should develop so as to reduce the domination both of the Federal Government and of the governments of the republics. The decisions of the numerous centres should be combined so that they are co-ordinated first in the republics, and these larger and more influential centres of development should then act in an oligo-centric–polycentric combination in making the decisions at the federation level. It is easier to think simply in terms of decision-making from one point, especially for those used to the primitive approach of centralism, than to conceive of a social matrix of decision-making, where each cell of the matrix is dependent on all other cells. This requires a greater degree of socialization and a more complex attitude. It means great interdependence of interests and a large number of agents. But there are many who believe that the complexity of the modern economy and the interdependence of the socio-economic process will lead inevitably to such a polycentric system of decision-making.

Open theories of Yugoslav economic development

These theories conceive development as taking place within the framework of a larger system of regional or world economic relations. Their advocates consider that the development problems of a country transcend national frontiers and that the basic problems of Yugoslav development cannot be solved in isolation. All concepts of a closed autarchy seem as out-of-date and out-of-place for socialist countries as they are for non-socialist. The basis of such theories is therefore the international division of labour.

Each of the concepts of development in Yugoslavia hitherto presented, taken by itself, can be conceived as a closed model of development. However, they may, in fact, often be combined with open concepts of development. The resulting policies would have varying degrees of openness and integration in the international division of labour. They would all, however, have in common the fact that they must take into account both the economics of Yugoslavia and the flows within the system of world economic or regional relations. They all allow for the fact that the economic problems of Yugoslavia cannot be solved within the frontiers of the country.

These development policies have to be implemented in an open economy, with an understanding of the ever more-intensive link with the world market as an expression of modern economic development. The time has passed when nationalistic autarchies were formed. Instead ever stronger inter-territorial links are being forged. The economic concept of 'the nation' is weakened but no super-nations are being created to replace the nations; rather there is an economic interconnectedness strengthened by large-scale movements of integration.

Appendix

Yugoslavia's three economic systems

A SYNOPTIC TABLE

	Administrative socialism (1946–51)	New economic system (1952–65)	Reform (1965–)
State administration	Centralized	Decentralized	Polycentric
Economic management	Monopoly of Party-state economic machinery	Economic operation freed from state administration	Economic operation freed from state administration and political decisions (depoliticization)
Planning	Global	Parametric	Matrices
Political growth policy	Arbitrary	Maximization	Optimalization
Capital coefficient	Growing	At turning-point	Falling
Priorities in industrialization	Heavy industry infra-structure Unskilled labour	Light and consumer industries (all decentralized) Skilled labour	Selective industrialization with comparative advantages Scientific research Highly-skilled labour

Agrarian policy	Compulsory deliveries to state Forced collectivization Depressed agricultural prices Cost-of-living parity	Free market sales Decollectivization Socially-owned estates Price parity	Gradual formation of socialist sector (vertical integration) Lack of manpower in agriculture (rural exodus) Technical progress Income parity
Market	Marginal	Administered (imperfect competition)	Liberalized
Prices	Planned	Administrative domestic market prices	World prices
Monetary policy	Money neutral	Inflation	Deflation
Enterprises	State planning administrative control	Autonomous planning Autonomy in current transactions, not in investment Linked territorially	Free to make decisions in current production and investment Linked on market
	Linked administratively		
Position of workers	Under control of state bureaucracy	Workers' self-management Managers appointed	Increased workers' self-management Free selection of managers

	Administrative socialism (1946–51)	New economic system (1952–65)	Reform (1965–)
Taxes	Turnover tax Planned profits Income tax	Turnover tax levied on production Interest charges on fixed assets Taxation of enterprise income Taxation of salaries	Sales tax Gradual abolition of interest on fixed assets Income tax Tariffs
Investment (source)	Central state funds	Autonomous investment funds	Self-financing Bank credits
Investment decisions (distribution of investment)	Central state plans (macro and micro)	Micro: business organizations Macro: political redistribution	Micro: induced decisions by business enterprises Macro: social plans and banking system
Consumption	Residuol Priority of production over consumption	Consumer selection Priority of production over consumption	Consumer selection Priority of consumption over production
Foreign trade	State monopoly Adjustable rate of exchange Bilateral clearing	Commercialization Multiple rate of exchange Bilateral clearing and hard currency markets	Integration into world trade Single rate of exchange Convertibility

Postscript

The economic system since 1965

The economic reform of 1965

The reasons for the reform

The first attempts at economic reform, the 'new economic system' of 1961, were neither sufficiently comprehensive nor sufficiently radical: they were limited to a revision of the way the income of enterprises was distributed and to some reform of the fiscal, foreign trade, foreign exchange and banking systems. The reform was conceived on the principle of increasing the influence of the law of value, or in other words of the market, in the expectation that market forces would promote growth. The aggregate targets of the 1957–61 plan had been achieved in four years instead of five, fostering the optimistic belief that the economy could be planned in the same way in the 1961–5 period. Even in 1961 there were signs of a drastic deceleration in economic activity accompanied by a steep rise in prices and very considerable illiquidity. The reform recognized that the market mechanism can operate effectively only by making enterprises bear the risk of their decisions. This need arose from the restriction which had previously been set on how enterprises could dispose of their assets. Each self-managed enterprise had its own funds for fixed capital (*osnovna sredstva*) and for working capital (*obrtna sredstva*), the second of which could only be used for working capital, although the first could finance both fixed and working capital. At the beginning of 1961 these two funds were merged into the Business Fund (*poslovni fond*) at the discretion of the enterprise, but it was not free to distribute its net (or residual) income (*dohodak*) as it liked. After the payment of taxes net income had to be divided into a part which went to pay personal incomes (*osobni dohodak*) to those working in the enterprise and a part which constituted the funds of the enterprise; the elements of this income distribution were strictly controlled by legal regulations.

Enterprises paid the following direct taxes:

(1) On net income, a flat rate of 15 per cent, the tax-base being total revenue (*ukupni prihod*) less material costs including repayment of investment loans, and depreciation.

(2) On 'surplus revenue' (*izvanredni prihod*) *either* a flat rate of 25 per cent, the tax-base being after-tax income less personal remuneration and a 6 per cent charge on the total fixed and working assets which the enterprise had at its disposal in the fiscal year, *or* the residual after deducting from after-tax income the sum of personal remuneration augmented by 30 per cent. Of these two alternatives the higher assessment was levied.

(3) A tax payable to Republic and Commune Social Investment Funds, initially 20 and later 30 per cent of the sum paid into the Enterprise Business and the Enterprise Welfare Fund (*fond zajedničke potrošnje*).

(4) A Common Reserve Fund (*fond zajedničke rezerve*) was established into which enterprises paid 3–5 per cent of the aggregate paid into the Enterprise Business and the Enterprise Welfare Fund; this money was to cover operational losses and to expand and modernize production.

A charge at a uniform rate of 6 per cent was levied on the Business Fund which financed the Federal Investment Fund, mainly used to provide investment credits.

Between 1960 and 1965 a single-tier turnover tax (*porez na promet*) was paid on the value of production. There were a large number of different tariff rates, used by the government as an instrument of price policy. In addition, at the beginning of 1961 a multi-tier turnover tax was introduced at a rate of 0.5 (later 1.0) per cent, payable on inter-enterprise trading but not on retail purchases, that is, when the buyer (or user of the service) was a private citizen.

Until 1959 customs duties on imports were paid only by private citizens and not by enterprises; in place of duty enterprises paid premiums on the prices of imported goods according to certain fixed coefficients, but in 1960 they became subject to the tariff. This extension of liability was linked to Yugoslav associate membership of GATT in 1959, altered to temporary membership in 1962 and to full membership in 1966.

As an exception to the 1952 rule that all enterprises be administered under self-management, banks remained state-owned organizations until 1965: the bank's founders, viz. public bodies at the federation, republic or commune level had full power of decision and carried out the credit policy of the National Bank.

The new economic system failed to produce the expected results: economic activity fluctuated, prices continued to increase substantially and many enterprises remained illiquid; the balance of payments deficit was serious.

TABLE 15

Percentage growth of social product and price increases, 1961–4

	Social product		Prices
	1960 prices	Current prices	
1961	5	16	11
1962	4	12	8
1963	12	21	9
1964	13	32	19

SOURCE: *Jugoslavija 1945–1964, Statistički pregled,* pp. 80-1.

The economic reform in enterprises

In 1965 the economic reform was introduced. Its aim was to leave enterprises a greater proportion of their net income, thus in effect strengthening workers' self-management by leaving them more funds to distribute according to their own decisions. Between 1961 and 1964, 54 per cent of the incomes (net) of enterprises went to the state and only 46 per cent was retained for payment of wages and salaries and allocation to enterprise funds. As from 1964 there was a gradual reduction in taxes on net income and on surplus revenue, and in payments to social investment funds. After 1965 enterprises no longer paid any taxes on either net income or profits. This was expected to increase the amount left to the enterprises to 70 per cent.

The economic reform also changed the turnover tax system,

replacing the single-tier turnover tax on production with a turnover tax on retail sales (sales-tax).

All restrictions on the distribution of the enterprises' net income between personal incomes and enterprise funds were also removed. The principle that personal incomes should be allowed to increase parallel with increased productivity of labour was adopted.[1] For the whole economy this was an acceptable principle, but it raised many problems when looked at from the point of view of individual enterprises. The differences in the capital–labour ratios between individual enterprises resulted in differences in their net incomes, causing considerable inter-enterprise variation in personal incomes for the same kind of work. This differential was sometimes as great as 1:3 or 1:4.

TABLE 16

Percentage composition of enterprises' working capital by source, 1964–7 (socialist sector)

	1964	1965	1966	1967
1 Own working capital	18.7	18.4	22.2	10.0
2 Bank credits	49.3	42.2	37.2	36.5
3 Liabilities to suppliers	25.2	25.3	27.2	47.5
4 Other liabilities	6.8	14.1	13.4	6.0
Total	100.0	100.0	100.0	100.0

SOURCE: Social Accountancy Service, annual balance sheets of enterprises.

Some authors referred to this differential as a dividend due to technical progress.[2] These differentials resulted in strong pressure for increased personal incomes in enterprises where the productivity of labour was low, so as to bring them up to the level of incomes earned in enterprises with high productivity of labour.

Since enterprises were diverting larger sums for personal incomes this necessarily reduced their own investment, and they became increasingly dependent on bank credits. It had been

[1] Branko Horvat, *Privredni sistem i ekonomska politika Jugoslavije* (The economic system and economic policy in Yugoslavia) (Belgrade, 1970), pp. 63–4.

[2] *Ibid.*, p. 63.

expected that as a result of the abolition of direct taxes the
larger sums left to enterprises would be used for increasing fixed
and working capital. But in fact enterprises largely used them
for increasing personal incomes. In the expectation that there
would be more investment from enterprises' own resources the
banks introduced a restrictive credit policy at the beginning of
1964. Since the enterprises were not allocating a sufficiently
large share of their net income to their funds, and the amount of
credits diminished, serious financial illiquidity resulted. Enterprises could not meet their liabilities and the result was a criti-
cally high level of inter-enterprise indebtedness, with an
increase in stocks and a slow-down in production.

Changes in the economic system

The growth of gross national product, which in 1959–64 (in
1966 prices) had been 7.6 per cent per annum, and in 1954–9 as
high as 10 per cent,[1] was planned for the 1966–70 period at a
rate of 7.5–8.5 per cent, with industrial production increasing at
an average rate of about 9–10 per cent per annum.[2] However,
the substantial increase in prices, the financial illiquidity of
enterprises and the adverse balance of payments slowed down
economic development so that in the 1964–9 period the social
product grew at an annual average rate of only about 4.5 per
cent and industrial production by only 5.5 per cent.

TABLE 17

*Percentage growth of gross national product and price
changes, 1966–9*

Year	Gross national product 1966 prices	In current prices	Price increase
1966	7	25	18
1967	1	4	3
1968	4	8	4
1969	1	18	17

[1] *Samoupravljanje i društveno-ekonomski razvitak Jugoslavije 1950–1970* (Self-management and socio-economic development in Yugoslavia 1950–1970), Savezni
zavod za statistiku (Federal Statistical Office) (Belgrade, 1971), pp. 105–7.
[2] *Društveni plan razvoja Jugoslavije od 1966. do 1970. godine* (Social plan of development of Yugoslavia from 1966–1970) (Belgrade and Zagreb, 1966).

When Yugoslavia adopted the system of centralized planning and administrative direction of the economy in 1947 she rejected the law of value; in other words, market prices were no longer formed by supply and demand on the market but according to social usefulness, as set out in the plan which was arbitrarily drawn up by government agencies. This led to great price distortions and when there was a return to a market economy it was difficult to establish correct relationships between prices and also to gain any foothold in the world market. The reform envisaged that the general level of prices would rise by about 24 per cent in 1965, but the increase was expected to vary between different activities, so as to achieve a proper price equilibrium. Table 18 shows what rise in prices was expected and what actually occurred.

TABLE 18

Planned and actual price increases during the 1965 reform
(in percentages over average for 1964)

	Increase in prices 1965		Estimated increase up to 1970
	planned	actual	
Industry and mining	14	15	48
Agriculture	32	43	95
Building and construction	22	21	108
Services	45	30	145

SOURCE: Krešo Džeba and Milan Beslać, *Privredna reforma* (The economic reform) (Zagreb, 1965), pp. 132–41; *Indeks*, Savezni zavod za statistiku, No. 3 (Belgrade, 1971), p. 5.

Within industry prices in manufacturing were planned to increase by about 8 per cent and prices of raw materials by about 24 per cent.

These price changes were intended to alter both the surplus value[1] and the rate of capital formation[2] in individual branches

[1] Surplus value (*višak vrijednosti*) is obtained by deducting material costs, depreciation, wages and salaries (i.e. personal incomes) and contributions to the enterprise welfare fund from its total revenue (*ukupni prihod*).
[2] The rate of capital formation is the ratio of surplus value to the total amount of assets employed.

of the economy. An approximate calculation shows the following planned changes in rates of capital formation.[1]

Because the actual increases in prices differed from the planned ones, capital formation in individual economic branches did not change as anticipated by the economic reform and new imbalances in investment capacity were added to those inherited from the past.

TABLE 19

Rates of capital formation in 1964

Economic activity	Rate of capital formation	
	at old prices	at planned price relationships
Coal	7.7	17.5
Oil and oil products	11.3	9.5
Ferrous metals	7.4	8.2
Lead, zinc and precious metals	19.0	36.7
Metal-working	12.9	3.1
Shipbuilding	16.0	1.2
Building materials	17.8	13.3
Chemical industry	12.0	10.6
Pharmaceuticals	72.2	16.7
Textile industry	31.0	5.3
Leather and footwear	29.2	10.1
Construction	27.6	25.1
Rail transport	3.5	5.0
Postal services and communications	14.1	20.7

There were important changes in the tax system. As already mentioned, at the beginning of 1965 all direct taxes paid by enterprises were abolished; the only one retained was the charge (*naknada*) paid by enterprises for the use of social capital assets. The average rate of interest on this business fund, which was paid by enterprises (fixed and working capital) was reduced from 6 per cent to 4 per cent, but in 1966 an upward

[1] Džeba-Beslać, *Privredna reforma*, pp. 138–9.

revaluation of fixed capital was carried out so that there was hardly any difference in the actual sum paid by enterprises. An important change in the taxation of private citizens was laid down in the Basic Law on Contributions and Taxes paid by Citizens, on the basis of which republics and communes passed their own regulations. According to Yugoslav legal definition there are two kinds of taxes. Contributions (*doprinosi*) are paid on income from personal work and taxes (*porezi*), on income from property rights and the labour of others. Federal, republican and communal authorities can all demand contributions of every kind, although in practice they do not do so. The federation and republics determine the contributions on personal income from employment and from agriculture. The communes can demand both of these and many other forms of contribution. Practically all tax liabilities are assessed by the communes and rates vary between republics and also between communes in the same republic. The favourable aspect of this varied tax system is that in taxing private citizens more account can be taken of the level of economic development of districts, their historical background and the needs of the population, etc.

The turnover tax was also altered in 1965. A single-tier turnover tax at a uniform rate (except for certain products and services) payable on retail trade replaced the single-tier turnover tax with a large number of varied rates levied on production. Thus what had been a turnover tax on production now became a sales tax. The Basic Turnover Tax Law expressly stated that the aim of the tax was threefold: to balance production and consumption; to adjust price relationships; and to accumulate funds to meet the needs of the socio-political communities.[1]

Since turnover tax was levied at a uniform rate (at the beginning the rate was 20 per cent of the retail price, of which 12 per cent went to the federation, 2 per cent to republics and 6 per cent to communes) it could not in fact bring about a balance between production and consumption in a macro-economic sense. Still less could it regulate prices and thus it retained only a fiscal character as the largest source of government revenue. A federal sales tax was also levied at special rates on coffee,

---

[1] 'Socio-political community' (*društveno-politička zajednica*) is a term which includes the federation, republic, autonomous provinces and communes.

alcoholic beverages (other than wines and brandies), alcohol, tobacco products, cars, objects made of precious metals, jewellery, medicines, perfumes, cosmetics, liquid fuels and lubricants, matches, decorative articles, playing cards, cigarette paper, building materials and table salt. In addition taxation at special rates was levied on services in connection with visible and invisible trade with foreign countries, and on bills of exchange.

Of special importance was the Basic Law on Financing of Socio-Political Communities, which came into force at the beginning of 1965. This law limited the role of budgets to that of financing government administration, including defence, while the financing of other public and social services, such as education, health and social security, was separated from the budgetary account and made the responsibility of the newly-established 'communities of interest' with special funds.[1] For example, to finance education there is an Educational Community with its fund whose main source of revenue is part of the 'contribution' levied on personal incomes of employees.[2] Table 20 shows the relationship between budgets and other funds in 1969:

TABLE 20

Percentage composition of tax revenue and expenditure, 1969

Revenue	
Budget of socio-political communities	44.6
Communities of education	10.5
Social security	26.5
Labour exchange and child care	3.7
Interest on Business Fund of enterprises	6.6
Other	8.1
Total	100.0

[1] *Interesne zajednice* or 'communities of interest' are representatives of the common interests of private citizens in the main public and social services such as elementary and secondary education, further education, hospitals, health services, social security and welfare.

[2] This contribution from personal incomes of employees (*doprinos iz osobnog dohotka gradana u radnom odnosu*) is a tax deducted at source in the enterprise on the basis of the wages and salaries bill.

TABLE 20—*contd*

Expenditure

Current cost of and investment in non-economic activities	46.0
National defence	14.0
Economic investment subsidies, and allocation to under-developed areas	16.0
Social security and social welfare benefits to households	24.0
Total	100.0

SOURCE: *Samoupravljanje i društveno-ekonomski razvitak Jugoslavije 1950–1970*, p. 178.

According to this law the federation provides supplementary financial resources for republics, in which the joint republican and communal budgetary *per capita* revenue is lower than the average Yugoslav *per capita* revenue. Supplementary financial resources from the federation are paid into the budgets of Bosnia-Hercegovina, Macedonia, and Montenegro and Kosmet. There are similar republican laws concerning the financing of socio-political communities, which provide for the payment of supplementary funds from the republican budgets into the budgets of communes where the budgetary *per capita* revenue is below a certain fixed amount.

In 1969 the joint expenditure on budgets and other funds amounted to 42.6 per cent of the national income, although budgetary expenditures alone were only 19 per cent of the national income. The funds at the disposal of the communities of interest are managed by citizens, which is a further step in the withering away of the state and the strengthening of self-management in the public services.

A new (1965) Bank and Credit Law was of special importance, and had far-reaching consequences both in theory and in practice. Previously the founder-members of banks had been socio-political communities. Banks did have boards of management on which there were some members who represented enterprises, but these boards had only an insignificant effect on the business and credit policy of the bank. The bank manager and the members of the boards of management were all nominees of the socio-political community that had founded the bank. This was changed by the new Bank and Credit Law. Banks were divided into investment, commercial and savings banks. Banks can now be founded by both business enterprises and socio-political communities. There must be at least 25 founder members, but savings banks can be founded by a single socio-political community, e.g. a commune. The founder members of an investment bank must invest in the bank at least 150 million new dinars (then approximately £4.2 m) and the founder members of commercial banks at least 10 million new dinars plus deposits of at least 20 million new dinars.

The main managing body of banks is now the assembly in which the founder members have the right to vote. Thus the self-management system is not fully applied in banks as in other enterprises. A bank does in fact have a workers' council, but it has no influence on business and credit policy. The voting rights of the founder members are in proportion to their investment, but no member can have more than 10 per cent of the votes. Special restrictions apply when socio-political communities are among the founder members. If two such communities are involved each has a number of votes commensurate with its deposits, but never more than 10 per cent of the total. If three or more such communities found a bank, then they can all together have no more than 20 per cent of all votes. Within this 20 per cent each socio-political community has votes proportionate to its deposit. The workers' council may, but need not, have up to 10 per cent of the votes in the bank assembly. Whether it does or not depends on the bank regulations which are introduced by the bank assembly. From this it will be seen that enterprises can found banks alone without socio-political communities, but that socio-political communities cannot do so without economic organizations. It is a consequence of the law that enterprises must always have a majority of votes (at least 70 per cent) in the bank assembly. The bank assemblies decide on business policy, draw up annual financial statements, the executive committee select from their own numbers and elect the manager. The executive committee considers and draws up proposals which are submitted for decision to the bank assembly, and is also responsible for carrying out the decisions of the assembly. The manager is automatically a member of the

executive committee, and if provided by the regulations, one
member of the executive committee can be a representative of
the staff of the bank. Banks also have a credit committee formed
from those employed in the bank and nominated by the bank
assembly. This committee is responsible for dealing with demands for credit. The bank manager is president of the credit
committee. Some are of the opinion that the credit committee
should be formed not only from those working in the bank, but
also from representatives of other enterprises, business firms,
etc., but this has not yet been accepted.

When the annual financial statement is drawn up, the income
of the bank, according to the decision of the assembly, is distributed in three parts. The first part goes to the working collective of the bank, which then redistributes it to cover operating
expenses, depreciation, legal and contractual obligations, personal incomes and the bank funds. The second part goes into the
credit fund of the bank in order to strengthen its credit potential. The third part is divided among the founders of the bank in
the form of interest on investment. Higher interest can be paid
to those economic organizations and socio-political communities whose time deposits exceed a period of three years.

Banks issue certificates to founder members to the value of
their investment. These certificates are registered securities.
A certificate can be transferred either with or without compensation to another enterprise, but if this is done the bank which
issued it must be notified. Certificates cannot be transferred
either to another bank or to another socio-political community.

The Bank and Credit Law was drawn up with the intention
that the enterprises should manage the banks and should regulate their credit policy. However, although enterprises must
have at least 70 per cent of the votes in a bank assembly, they
are in the main dissatisfied with the banks' credit policies and
consider that they are in an unequal position *vis-à-vis* the banks
and have no control over them. This is most probably because
the bank assemblies are composed of a large number of members representing very varied business interests and the varied
and often conflicting interests tend to cancel each other out.
Thus the members of the assembly who represent business
interests are not in a position to formulate a bank's credit policy,

but are forced to accept the proposals of banking experts. They also feel in an inferior position since they do not sufficiently understand banking or monetary and credit policy, and are thus not equal partners. Last but not least, the enterprises are in most cases very much in debt to the banks and being in the position of debtors cannot direct what credit policy the banks should follow.

A special problem is posed by the distribution of a bank's income. The banks are in fact joint-stock companies, and the certificates are in fact registered shares. That part of the income which is paid to the founder members in the form of interest is in fact a dividend. The Bank and Credit Act of 1965 was the first to come into contradiction with the principle that income can only be received as a result of work performed. For the first time it was made possible for income to be received as a result of investment. This theoretical and practical innovation had far-reaching consequences. It opened up the possibility for existing enterprises to found new ones and to participate in the distribution of their income. This had previously been impossible. Before 1967 if an existing enterprise founded a new one, from the moment the new enterprise elected its own managing bodies and began to do business the founder enterprise lost all right to influence the running of the new business and also all right, on the basis of investment, to share in its income. Later it was made possible for enterprises which had taken part in founding new enterprises to share in the distribution of income. But what they received in this way had to be paid into their business fund and did not become part of total revenue. It could thus only be used to increase fixed or working capital and not to increase the personal income of workers. Naturally this state of affairs did not provide any great incentive for enterprises to divert part of their incomes for the starting of new enterprises. In 1968, after it had first been made possible in the case of banks for one enterprise to take part in the management of another and to share in the income distribution of another on the basis of money invested, a law was passed which made it possible for any enterprise to participate in the income distribution of another in which it had invested money. Constitutional Amendment XV, adopted by 1968, allowed far greater flexibility in the workers' management system and made it possible for enterprises which had taken part in the founding of another enterprise to take part in its management as well.

The result of this is that today there are two kinds of enterprise in Yugoslavia. One kind is those enterprises which were founded by socio-political communities and in which only the workers of the enterprise manage the business and distribute the income. Secondly, there are those which were founded by other enterprises. In this second kind the founder enterprise, as well as the workers of the new enterprise, has the right to take part in the management and the income distribution. Too little time has elapsed yet to see whether this development in management and income distribution is desirable, or where it is likely to lead.

The 1965 Bank and Credit Law also had to provide a different system of financing investment. Up to 1965 the socio-political communities had decided on investment and credit policy, and granted enterprises credits from their investment funds. The assets of these funds were amassed through the use of fiscal instruments, i.e. interest on the business fund, part of the tax on the net income of enterprises, part of the tax on surplus revenue, contributions to social investment funds, etc. Although each socio-political community had its own investment fund these funds did not have their own administration; instead, credits from them were placed through the banks. During 1964 the Social Investment Funds were abolished, and the Bank and Credit Law laid down that the socio-political communities must place the assets of what had been their social investment funds in the credit funds of banks, though leaving them free to choose in which bank they would deposit these funds. In this way the enterprises were able to influence the use of the assets of the former social investment funds in the same way as they could influence the use of all other bank assets. This situation lasted only one year. At the beginning of 1966 the Bank and Credit Law was amended and the socio-political communities were permitted to withdraw the assets of their former investment funds from the credit funds of banks and use them in one of three ways: invest them in the banks as time deposits with the proviso that they could extend investment credits to enterprises through the banks; lend these assets to the banks at an agreed interest with the proviso that the banks should use

them as investment credits; invest the assets in the credit
funds of banks so that the banks could use the assets to extend
investment credits to enterprises. The original intention of the
new law, that the enterprises and not the socio-political
communities should be in a position to decide not only on
short-term credits but also on long-term investment credits,
was not realized. The socio-political communities, which
had very considerable financial resources in their investment
funds, especially the federation and the republics, withdrew
these resources from the credit funds of the banks and were once
again in a position to decide, through the banks, to which enterprises and for what kind of investment credits should be granted.
The sources of investment before and after the economic reform
are shown in Table 21.

TABLE 21

Sources of investment in fixed and working capital,
before and after the 1965 reform
(socialist sector)

	1953–64	1970
1 Investment credits from the funds of socio-political communities	57.6	5.2
2 Budget resources	10.5	10.3
3 Bank resources	0.9	51.1
4 Enterprise resources	31.0	33.4
Total	100.0	100.0

The amendment to the new law put the socio-political
communities in a position to use the financial resources of what
had been their investment funds outside the budget and thus free
from any public control. This provoked outspoken criticism,
especially the use of the non-budgetary funds of the federation,
so that in 1970 it was agreed that non-budgetary funds should
be abolished.

Yugoslavia is making every attempt to develop her links with
other countries as much as possible. There are two reasons for
this. First, she must import raw materials for her industries

and also equipment for further industrial development. Second, as a medium-developed country, she must export, the home market being too small. Like most developing countries Yugoslavia imports more than she exports. But at the same time she sells more services abroad than she buys. She has therefore a visible balance of payments deficit and an invisible balance of payments surplus. In the total balance of payments there is a deficit.

TABLE 22

Balance of payments before and after the 1965 economic reform
(million dinars)

	1964 Debit	Credit	Balance	1970 Debit	Credit	Balance
Visible trade	9,020	6,499	−2,521	35,868	21,338	−14,530
Other current account	1,185	1,936	+751	5,960	14,130	+8,170
of which						
revenue from tourism		514	+514		3,432	+3,432
transport and communications	612	783	+171	2,087	3,356	+1,269
remittances from workers abroad		432	+432		6,260	+6,260
other	573	207	−366	3,873	982	−2,891
Total	10,205	8,435	−1,770	41,838	35,368	−6,460

The fact that Yugoslavia has a persistent deficit in her balance of payments is the main reason why the dinar cannot be made convertible. Payments to socialist and a large number of developing countries are made through clearing arrangements. Payments to developed countries are made in convertible currencies. In 1964 the percentage of imports (by value) paid for through clearing arrangements was 41.2 and in 1970 it was 27.2. In the same years 50.0 and 41.7 per cent respectively of Yugoslav exports were sold through clearing arrangements.

A very important aim of the reform was to make the dinar convertible. To achieve this the following conditions had to be met: payments had to be balanced; a realistic rate for the dinar as against gold and other currencies had to be introduced; a foreign currency reserve had to be amassed. The most important of these three, balancing payments, was not achieved, nor does it seem likely to be in the near future. Thus, in spite of the continual insistence of politicians and economists, it is unlikely that the dinar will become a convertible currency in the near future.

The foreign exchange system is closely linked with that of foreign trade and this has for a long time been under sharp attack from exporters. According to present currency regulations the majority of exporters retain only 7 per cent of the foreign currency they earn. There are also some branches that can retain a larger percentage of currency earned abroad; for example, civil engineering firms which carry out work abroad have control over 100 per cent of foreign currency earned. This percentage can be raised by up to 100 per cent if more than 51 per cent of total enterprise receipts are in hard currency (the status of a 'preponderant exporter') or an enterprise agrees to maintain a constant ratio of imports to exports and a predetermined level of foreign exchange earnings. Tourist enterprises retain 20 per cent, the vehicle industry 12 per cent and exporters of machinery and equipment 10 per cent. Foreign currency over and above the percentage which, according to existing regulations, exporters are allowed to retain, must be sold to authorized banks at the official rate (£1 = 36 new dinars). Importers can buy foreign currency from the authorized banks at the official rate, but the amount that they can purchase depends on the kind of goods they import. There are no restrictions on the import of most raw materials, and importers can buy from the banks as much foreign currency for dinars as they need to pay for imports of goods which can be freely imported. The import of some goods, however, is restricted. Certain enterprises get a set sum of foreign currency, i.e. a limited amount, with which to pay for goods bought in this category. For some goods there are currency or commodity import quotas. All enterprises, whether they are foreign currency earners or not, can buy foreign currency at the official rate of exchange to the value of a certain percentage of their dinar depreciation allowances in order to pay for imported equipment.

Exporters demand that an enterprise's income in foreign currency be treated in the same way as its dinar income. They demand that those who earn foreign currency should have control over the entire sum that they have earned. They would agree to sell a certain pre-arranged percentage of this to the National Bank and other authorized banks at the official rate. The exporters consider that the right of all enterprises to get a percentage of the dinar value of their depreciation allowances in foreign currency in order to pay for equipment should be terminated. They complain of the overvalued rate of the dinar in comparison with other currencies. The result of this is that exporters receive too small a sum in dinars for the currency they have earned while importers are able to buy foreign currency cheaply and often import goods which are produced in Yugoslavia, thus competing with home producers.

From the beginning of 1952 to the middle of 1965 the official rate for the dinar was set at 3 new dinars to the dollar. On the basis of this official rate various premiums were computed. At the beginning of 1961 a uniform premium rate of 7.5 new dinars to the dollar was introduced, and in the year of the reform (1965) the dinar was devalued and the rate became 12.5 new dinars to the dollar. In January 1971 there was a new devaluation to 15.0 new dinars to the US dollar. In December 1971 there was a further devaluation and the dinar now stands at $1 = 17.0 new dinars (or £1 = 44 dinars).

Until 1967 it was not possible to invest foreign capital in Yugoslavian enterprises. This became possible in 1967 and in 1968 foreign agencies were also permitted. Foreign partners investing in Yugoslav enterprises could not 'own' more than 49 per cent of the assets of the enterprise. They had to reinvest a minimum of 20 per cent of their profits in the same or another Yugoslav enterprise or in one of the Yugoslav banks. They paid a profit tax at a flat rate of 35 per cent on all their profits. If foreign partners reinvested in enterprises or works more than the minimum of 20 per cent, or invested in one of the underdeveloped parts of the country, they got in the first case a progressive reduction in tax rate and in the second especially favourable tax relief (for example in Montenegro the tax rate on profits that are reinvested may only be 7 per cent). Foreign partners could repatriate the rest of their profit only if the sum did not exceed either the quantity of foreign exchange retained[1] by the joint enterprise or one-third of the total foreign currency earned by the joint enterprise.

Yugoslav expectations from investment by foreign firms are: the import of new technology and methods; the introduction of modern business organization; use of sales network of foreign partners for sales of goods produced in joint ventures. Contracts concerning joint ventures between Yugoslav and foreign partners must be registered with the Federal Secretariat for Economic Affairs, but the relationship between the Yugoslav enterprise and its foreign partner is regulated by the agreement that they have entered into and there is no state interference in this.[2]

It is obvious today that the economic reform of 1965 did not produce the results expected of it. In spite of the fact that the income of enterprises is no longer taxed, business conditions have not improved. On the contrary, as a result of the insufficiency of their own capital enterprises are illiquid and in debt to the banks. It seems likely that, as in 1962, there will have to be a multilateral settlement of all debts and credits of the enterprises, that a considerable amount of short-term credits will have to be converted into medium-term and long-term credits, and that long-term credits will have to have more favourable repayment terms. Enterprises have not achieved the influence on bank credit policy that was expected. No satisfactory solution of the division of net income between the enterprise and the government has yet been found, nor of the distribution of income left to enterprises between the personal incomes of employees and the enterprise funds.

Very little advance has been made in respect of workers' management of economic affairs and in reaching agreements based on workers' self-management of personal incomes, investment, and joint placing of goods abroad.

Economic growth has been considerably slower than was expected, which has resulted in a great exodus of workers to economically more advanced countries of Western Europe. It is estimated that at present about half a million workers from

---

[1] See p. 227.
[2] Dr. M. Sukijasović, *Foreign Investment in Yugoslavia*, The Institute of International Politics and Economics (Belgrade, 1970).

Yugoslavia are employed abroad.[1] It seems that some of these workers, especially skilled workers, did not go abroad because there was no work available in the country, but because the pay abroad was higher. In any case it is obvious that a satisfactory way must be found of increasing the gross national product.

There has not been the necessary restructuring of the economy. Inefficient enterprises and those with no future have not closed down. Enterprises which have a future for development but are in temporary difficulties have not received assistance. Growth-inducing enterprises, which if expanded would be able to advance the fortunes of whole industrial branches, have not been given adequate credit to allow them to develop to the full.

TABLE 23

Gross investment in fixed assets, as percentage of gross national product, 1962–9

year		year	
1962	35	1966	25
1963	35	1967	29
1964	33	1968	31
1965	27		

SOURCES: *Jugoslavija 1945–1964, Statistički pregled*, Savezni zavod za statistiku (Federal Statistical Office) (Belgrade, 1965), p. 83; and *Statistički godišnjak*, Savezni zavod za statistiku (Belgrade, 1967, 1968, 1969).

Inflation has not been halted. Prices have continued to rise in an uncontrolled way, but there are various opinions as to the causes of inflation and how it might be slowed. There appear to be two principal causes. The first is over-investment. In Yugoslavia for years about 30 per cent of the gross national product went as gross investment in fixed assets. There was not enough capital to cover such investments and part necessarily had to be financed by increased issue of money.

[1] Census of Population, 1971. However, there are also other estimates which give much higher figures, e.g. *Samoupravljanje*, 15/12/1970 states that *c.* 850,000 workers are employed abroad.

Another source of inflation is excessive personal incomes paid out of the enterprise's income. Seventy-eight per cent of the income retained by enterprises was paid out in wages and salaries in 1961 and 81 per cent in 1968.

There has been no improvement in the balance of payments deficit. On the contrary, it shows a tendency to become larger in spite of increased receipts from invisibles such as tourism, transport and remittances from workers and emigrants abroad. Because of the low elasticity of demand for imports and exports the devaluation of 1971 did not have the desired effect on the adverse balance of payments. The dinar did not become convertible, nor is there any likelihood of it so becoming in the near future.

The economic, social and political importance of the constitutional amendments

Because of the relative failure of the economic reform and the slim chances of finding any solution promising faster development, full employment and relatively stable prices within the present economic and political system, at the end of 1969 and the beginning of 1970 moves began towards piecemeal changes in the economic and political system. It very soon became obvious that something far more radical was needed. Thus at the end of 1970 and the beginning of 1971 came the proposed constitutional amendments 20–40 (amendments 1–19 having been passed in 1967 and 1968).

The amendments took into account the following facts:

(1) Yugoslavia is a multinational state in which the nations can live in harmony, cooperate and develop only in conditions of complete national equality, and only if the largest among them have their own republics.

(2) That the cornerstone of socialist society is Man, freely able to develop all his abilities, and the cornerstone of a socialist economy is the free association of workers in enterprises which are nothing other than the organization of associated labour of various kinds and intensity.

(3) That a socialist economy of the Yugoslav type must be organized on a polycentric basis with the republics in a position to develop a high degree of inter-relationship in the formation of

economic policy, thus bringing into being a unitary, or in the
opinion of some, a common market.

Although post-war Yugoslavia was always a federation, the
republics played a restricted role. This can be seen from the
fact that in 1969 the share of the federation in total budget
expenditure was 50 per cent, the share of the republics 20 per
cent and the share of the communes 30 per cent. The centralized
direction of the economy provoked resistance in the republics
and to a certain extent diminished their efforts to achieve
optimal results with the very limited resources at their disposal.
More effort was expended on trying to get as much as possible
from the central funds than in using the available means in the
best possible way. Strengthening the position of the republics
in the organization of the economy is likely to result in a cultural and economic upsurge, a better organization of economic
life, greater readiness to make sacrifices and increased working
élan. There are, of course, many economic problems for which
the constitutional amendments do not provide detailed answers,
but what they do provide is a framework within which such
answers can be sought. They regulate the position of individual
citizens and relations between the republics and the federation.

The amendments give a more important place to the private
sector than was hitherto the case. There are special regulations
concerning the pooling of labour and capital by private citizens. Those who do this will be able to dispose freely only of
that part of their income which was gained by use of their
personal property and labour. What remains over and above
this, after the deduction of personal incomes of workers, will go
to social ownership and be managed according to the principles
of workers' management. Until now the maximum size of
private agricultural holdings has been 10 hectares (24.7 acres),
but in hilly areas this may now be increased.

The amendments define enterprises as the basic organization
of associated labour, in which the working people, on the
basis of work and their use of the socially owned means of
production, earn income and decide how it shall be used, always bearing in mind that enterprise income is part of gross
national product.

Workers have the right to organize every section of an enterprise as a unit of associated labour where the results of associated

labour can be separately assessed through exchange of goods or services. When distributing that part of the enterprise income that is to be spent on personal incomes it is expected that workers, in agreement with the workers' management organizations of other enterprises, with the trade unions and the socio-political communities, will come to a *social agreement* (*društveni dogovor*) on the principles and measures for distribution of income. If any enterprise should not abide by such agreements when they have been reached, or if agreement is not reached and the income distribution of an enterprise disrupts the normal functioning of the economy, then legal measures can be taken to see that agreements are respected, or to provide proper measures if no agreement has been reached. Temporary laws may be passed restricting the amount of income which can be distributed by the workers' management bodies, or making it obligatory for enterprises to make an agreed part of their income available to finance certain special investments.

Enterprises can associate in founding new enterprises and in participating in the distribution of the income of these new enterprises. The amendments also allow private persons to invest in enterprises and receive bonds on which interest will be paid either at a fixed rate or at a rate depending on the business success of the enterprise. The question as to whether the income of an enterprise shall be taxed, or whether, as until now, only workers' income at source shall be taxed, has been left open.

There is very little in the amendments about the social plan, but a great deal about how to organize and retain a unitary market in Yugoslavia. All that is said about the social plan is that it is to be based on the *social agreement* of the working people of enterprises, on citizens' communities of interest and on agreement among republics and autonomous provinces concerning economic policy of common interest.

Much more attention is given to the unitary market, and there are a number of well argued cases for the use of the term 'common market' rather than 'unitary' (*jedinstveno*) market. The following are fundamental to any unitary market: free movement and association of labour and investment, free exchange of goods and services and of scientific achievements over the whole of Yugoslavia; a common national currency, a uniform monetary system and monetary policy, and a common basis of credit policy; a common policy and system for economic relations with other countries; freedom to found enterprises and for joint operations among enterprises over the whole country; the development of free competition on the market among enterprises and agreement between enterprises and socio-political communities with the aim of furthering production and the integration of associated labour; avoidance of situations giving unfair social and economic advantages, arising from monopoly positions; planned economic and social development. Restrictions can only be placed on the free circulation of goods and services throughout the whole country on the basis of federal law. Citizens must be free to seek employment anywhere in the country under labour conditions that apply in the part of the country where they take up employment. It is a punishable offence to violate the unity of the market.

The amendments provide what is largely a legal definition of a unitary market. The economic definition is shorter and may be briefly formulated as a situation in which equal economic units do business under equal conditions. If we take the legal definition of the unitary market then we see that it existed to a greater or lesser extent even before the amendments. It is difficult to say the same for economic unity. The Yugoslav market is not at present a unitary one and it is a matter of speculation whether the legal regulations will alter the situation. There are, for example, variations in the system of both direct and indirect taxation in the various republics. There are also variations, sometimes even considerable, in the tax systems of different communes within the same republic. Finally, the possibilities of obtaining credits for both fixed and working capital are not the same for enterprises engaged in the same work or for enterprises in different parts of the country. All this suggests that it might be more accurate to speak of a common market rather than of a unitary market.

The changes envisaged for the National Bank are far-reaching though not completely new. Until 1961 the National Bank was organized on a federative principle. There was a main centre in Belgrade and national banks in the main towns of the republics, with a certain amount of freedom in decision making and credit policy. In 1961 this position was reversed and the

National Bank became centrally organized. According to the amendments the activities of the National Bank will from now on be controlled by a board of governors consisting of the governor of the National Bank of Yugoslavia and the governors of the national banks of the republics and autonomous provinces. According to some views there is no need for a governor of the National Bank of Yugoslavia, and this function should rotate among the governors of the republic and provincial banks.

The amendments do not contain anything new in respect of the founding or management of business banks. It is most likely that the banking systems of individual republics will be organized either on the basis of republican regulations or on the basis of agreement between the republics and the business banks, or among the banks themselves. The banking system is inextricably bound up with the economic system as a whole. In capitalist countries the banks are companies which are financial intermediaries. In socialist countries with central planning and where the economy is run on administrative lines the banks are state institutions which handle credits according to the plan. In Yugoslavia's socialist, plan-market economy, which is based on workers' self-management, a special kind of bank needs to be organized. When the system of workers' self-management is finally built up then banks are likely to become an economic service organized on the basis of agreements among enterprises or according to industrial branches or economic activities. It is just because there is at present no institution which can draw together and provide an organizational centre for enterprises carrying out the same or similar work that enterprises in the same economic branch or activity do not cooperate more closely, and that there is little standardization of production or agreement on the use of capacity, investment decisions or levels of income. The chambers of commerce are not suitable to fulfil this function because any form of joint production or cooperation can be effective only if financially backed by the partners. For this reason the banks would seem to be the proper institutions to become the backbone of an autonomously organized economy within specific branches and finally of the autonomy of the whole economy. The credit plans of business banks would, in effect, be the economic plans of various branches of the economy.

The amendments envisage a further decentralization of the tax system, which was already considerably decentralized. They propose that the republics and autonomous provinces should establish the system, and decide on the sources and kinds of taxes and contributions paid by private citizens and enterprises. In order to achieve uniformity and stability of the Yugoslav market the republics and autonomous provinces will discuss and agree on adjustments to basic tax and contribution policy. It is proposed that in order to prevent disturbances of the market or to overcome them if they should occur, the federation will: propose that socio-political communities reduce or increase the taxes and contributions that they have laid down; propose that socio-political communities do not spend a certain proportion of their income for a limited period; provide the initiative for agreement between republics and autonomous provinces concerning the principles of their policies.

The amendments propose that sales tax should be regulated by the federation, even though the income from this tax will go to republics and communes. In the opinion of some the republics should come to a mutual agreement on taxation policy so that this will be basically the same throughout the country.

The federal budget will in future finance only military expenditure, federal administration, economically under-developed republics and autonomous provinces, and a reserve fund which will be formed in accordance with the rights and duties of the federation. The federal budget will come from customs duties, stamp duties and from quotas paid by the republics and autonomous provinces out of the sum accruing from the sales tax. There are some differences of approach here. In the opinion of some the federation should not have its own budgetary resources but should be entirely financed by quotas from the republics and provinces. Others again consider that the federation should have its own sources and that in addition to those mentioned above the sales tax should go to the federation. The federation will no longer be authorized to build up funds nor to contract loans, either in Yugoslavia or abroad, except according to the constitution or with prior agreement of the republic and province assemblies. It can float bonds only for financing economic development in the less developed republics and provinces.

The passing of the constitutional amendments will strengthen the inner cohesion of Yugoslavia. These amendments will, to a great extent, only legalize the existing position. In Yugoslavia for years each republic has in fact organized its own economic life. Now, instead of strength being wasted in sterile competition to grab as much as possible from the central chest, the same energy can be used to find creative and effective ways of making use of one's own resources. Instead of the fiction that the Yugoslav economy is a uniform one, the amendments create conditions for effective and closely linked cooperation among republican economies.

It now only remains to try to look briefly into the future. In the long run the vision of a Yugoslav economy based on workers' management is fairly clear. But how will the economy function in the interim period between the present time and a functioning model of socialism run by workers' self-management? One of the most important single elements will be the relation between the plan and the market. To put it broadly, it is obvious that planning ought to be strengthened, and it will be necessary to give planning a greater role in the immediate future. But it must be kept in mind that the best plans produce no useful effects if there are no instruments or measures available to ensure that they are carried out. The present position in Yugoslavia is that self-management, which has developed so successfully in enterprises and institutions, has not yet managed to gain control of the economy to the extent that administrative interference is no longer necessary for the even development of the economy. Up to 1963 a system of fiscal and credit instruments still existed which could exert an influence on enterprises and thus regulate economic development. There are now no fiscal instruments as far as enterprises are concerned, and only a very limited credit system. This restricts social guidance of the economy. It is unlikely that Yugoslavia can, in the long run, manage without an effective and flexible system of instruments and measures which can be applied to enterprises in order to influence developments in the economy. There are three possible models for such a policy:

(1) The income of enterprises may be taxed by a selective and flexible system. Both enterprises and socio-political communities would be able to found banks, but socio-political

communities would only have a voice in the formation of credit policy commensurate with their investment in the credit fund of the bank and would guide credit policy along the lines of the social plan.

(2) In order to strengthen the material basis of workers' management enterprises might continue not to pay any direct tax on their income. In that case the credit policy of the banks would be the main tool in guiding economic development. Who controls the credit policy will depend on the degree of autonomy of the economy. The lower the stage of autonomy the greater will be the role of the government in credit policy. In a fully developed system of workers' self-management and an autonomous economy the business banks will be the medium by which enterprises engaged in the same activities will, through bank credits, realize the aims of the plan.

(3) The capital, income, profit and turnover of enterprises may all be subject to a flexible tax system. The enterprises would be free to distribute what was left after taxation. Banks would be economic organizations like any other. The state would influence the economy through the tax system. One part of taxes would be placed in the banks, and another in funds for infrastructure and investment and to provide any necessary subsidies. The tax system would affect the degree of credit worthiness of enterprises and the effectiveness of credits to individual economic branches or groups.

Because of the possibility that, through changes in the amount of influence the banks can have on the realization of social plans, the quality of their influence may also change, and because the banks may develop from organizations through which an influence is exerted on enterprises and the economy into organizations through which the enterprises and the economy exert an influence, the second model seems to me the most acceptable. However, the laws of development inherent in self-management will influence the organization of banks, enterprises and the economy as a whole with a force which is stronger than the conjectures or wishes of individuals.

MARIJAN HANŽEKOVIĆ

Faculty of Economic Sciences
University of Zagreb

Bibliography of the writings of Rudolf Bićanić

This bibliographical survey is taken from *Zbornik Pravnog Fakulteta U Zagrebu* (Journal of the Zagreb Faculty of Law), vol. XIX, nos. 3–4 (1969), and is reproduced by permission of its compiler, Dr Stanko Pintarić.

BOOKS

IN YUGOSLAVIA

Kako živi narod. Život u pasivnim krajevima (How people live. Life in the under-developed regions). Vol. I, Zagreb, 1936; vol. II, Zagreb, 1939.

Ekonomska podloga hrvatskog pitanja (The economic basis of the Croatian question). First ed., Zagreb, 1938; 2nd ed., 1938.

Gospodarska politika (Economic policy). Zagreb, 1939.

Pogled iz svjetske perspektive i naša ekonomska orijentacija (A world view of our economic orientation). Zagreb, 1939.

Najnužnije narodne potrebe. Prehrana-narodne potrebe-seljačka tržišta-lokalni disparitet cijena. (The most essential national needs. Food supply, national needs, peasant market, local price disparities). With A. Mihletič and D. Štefek. Zagreb, 1940.

Hrvatska ekonomika na prijelazu iz feudalizma u kapitalizam (The economy of Croatia during the changeover from feudalism to capitalism). Vol. I, *Doba manufakture u Hrvatskoj i Slavoniji 1750–1860* (The period of manufacture in Croatia and Slavonia 1750–1860). The Yugoslav Academy, Zagreb, 1951.

Počeci kapitalizma u hrvatskoj ekonomici i politici (The beginnings of capitalism in Croatian economics and politics). Mala historijska knjižnica (Small Historical Library Series) no. 6. Zagreb, 1952.

Ekonomska politika (Economic policy). 2 vols., Zagreb, 1953.

Ekonomski razvitak Zagreba i zagrebačkog regiona (The economic development of Zagreb and the Zagreb region). Zagreb Town Planning Institute, 1953.

Predavanja iz ekonomike FNRJ (Lectures on the economics of FPRY). 1. Introduction; 2. People's property. Zagreb, 1953.

Trgovina, platežna bilanca i životna razina stanovništva kotara Krapina (Trade, balance of payments and living standard of the population of the Krapina District). Town Planning Institute of Croatia, Zagreb, 1956.

Ekonomska politika FNRJ (Economic policy FPRY). Vol. I, Zagreb, 1960; vol. II (b), Zagreb, 1961; vol. II (a and b), Zagreb, 1962.

ABROAD

Problems of planning East and West. Institute of Social Studies, The Hague, 1967.

Turning points in economic development. The Hague, 1972.

ARTICLES IN BOOKS AND PERIODICALS, BOOKLETS AND PAPERS

IN YUGOSLAVIA

'Ljudski rad kao objekat socijalne politike' (Work as the object of social policy). *Radnička zaštita*, no. 1, 1930.

'Neprekinuti tzv. engleski radni dan' (The so-called unbroken English workday). *Radnička zaštita*, no. 7, 1930.
'Da li postoji kod nas hiperprodukcija inteligencije?' (Do we have a hyperproduction of intelligentsia?). *Nova Europa*, no. 7, 1931.
'Industrijalizacija i vanjska trgovina Jugoslavije' (Industrialization and Yugoslav foreign trade). *Privreda*, no. 1, 1932.
'Kriza nacionalizma' (The crisis of nationalism). *Nova Europa*, no. 5, 1932.
'Naša trgovinska bilanca i njezino sezonsko kretanje' (Seasonal fluctuations in our balance of trade). *Financijski arhiv*, no. 6, 1932.
'Sezonski karakter našeg izvoza' (The seasonal character of our exports). *Privreda*, no. 3, 1932.
'Uvoz i njegovo sezonsko kretanje' (Imports and their seasonal movement). *Privreda*, nos. 7–8, 1932.
Podignimo cijene stoci (Raising the price of cattle). A report given at a meeting of The Economic Unity Association 2 Feb. 1936. Suggestions to peasant farmers on how to increase the price of cattle. Published as booklet, Zagreb, 1936.
'Strukturne promjene našeg uvoza u pravcu industrijalizacije' (Structural changes in imports in the direction of greater industrialization). *Privreda*, no. 12, 1936.
'Škare agrarno-industrijskih cijena' (Agrarian-industrial price scissors). *Ekonomist*, no. 2, 1936.
Što će biti sa pšenicom? (What will happen to the wheat?). Published as booklet, Zagreb, 1936.
'Trebaju li seljaštvu poljoprivredne komore?' (Do peasants need an agricultural chamber?). *Ekonomist*, nos. 7–8, 1936.
'Tržište i cijene pšenice' (The market and the price of wheat). *Ekonomist*, no. 6, 1936.
'Agrarna kriza u Hrvatskoj 1873–1895' (The agrarian crisis in Croatia 1873–1895). *Ekonomist*, nos. 3–5, 1937.
'Agrarna prenapučenost V' (Agrarian overpopulation). *Gospodarska struktura Banovine Hrvatske*, no. 3, 1940.
'Ekonomski faktor u porastu stanovništva' (The economic factor in population increase), *Liječnički vjesnik, god. 62*, no. 11, 1940.
'Jedan presjek kroz našu društvenu strukturu' (A cross section of our social structure). *Kolo Matice Hrvatske*. Zagreb, 1946.
'Ekonomska politika' (Economic policy). Shorthand notes of lectures. 3 vols., Zagreb, 1946/7.
'Naš petogodišnji plan treba da riješi i temeljne zadatke naše privrede' (Our Five-Year Plan ought to find solutions to the basic problems of our economy). *Zadrugar III*, no. 10, 1947.
Review of 'M. Dobb, *Study in the development of capitalism*'. *Historijski Zbornik*, vol. 1, 1948.
'Druga godina planske privrede u Poljskoj' (The second year of Poland's planned economy). *Djelo*, no. 4, 1948.
'Ekonomska struktura nove Poljske' (The economic structure of new Poland). *Današnja Poljska*, 1948.
'Industrijska revolucija u Hrvatskoj i 1848 godina' (The Industrial Revolution in Croatia and 1848), *Historijski Zbornik*, vol. 1, 1948.
'Narodna imovina u našem planskom gospodarstvu' (People's property in our planned economy). *Zbornik Pravnog fakulteta*, vol. 1, 1948.
'Oslobođenje kmetova u Hrvatskoj 1848' (The freeing of the serfs in Croatia 1848). *Djelo*, no. 3, 1948.
'Rezultati druge godine IV pjatiljetke u SSSR-u' (Results of the second year of the Fourth Five-Year Plan in SSSR). *Djelo*, no. 2, 1948.

Review of 'Vučo, M. *Privredna historija naroda FNRJ do prvog svjetskog rata*' (M. Vučo, The economic history of the peoples of Yugoslavia before the First World War). *Historijski Zbornik*, vol. II, 1949.

'Dva nova rada o periodizaciji ruske povijesti' (Two new works on the periods of Russian history). *Historijski Zbornik*, vol. III, 1950.

Review of 'Gorodeckij, S.*O predmetu i sadržaju ekonomskih nauka – O granama narodnog gospodarstva*' (S. Gorodecki, The subject and content of economic sciences – concerning the branches of the national economy). *Ekonomski pregled*, no. 1, 1950.

'Knjige o ekonomici FNRJ' (Books on the economics of Yugosalvia). *Ekonomski pregled*, no. 5, 1951.

'Mjesto ekonomike FNRJ u sistemu ekonomskih nauka' (The place of Yugoslav economics in the system of economic studies). *Zbornik Pravnog fakulteta*, vol. IV, 1951. *Yearbook*, pp. 23–54.

'Problematika manufakturne periode u sovjetskoj historiografiji' (The problem of periods of manufacture in Soviet history). *Historijski Zbornik*, vol. IV, 1951.

'Začetki kapitalističkih odnosov v Horvatsko-slovenskom kmečkom uporu leta 1572' (The beginning of capitalist relations in the Croatian and Slovenian peasant revolts of 1572). *Ekonomska revija*, nos. 5–6, 1951.

'Agrarni odnosi u Slavoniji' (Agrarian relationships in Slavonia). *Historijski Zbornik*, vol. V, 1952.

'Suština jednog naučnog spora' (The essence of a scholarly disagreement). *Kolo Matice Hrvatske*, no. 3, 1952.

'Ekonomska povijest među ekonomskim i historijskim naukama' (Economic history as an economic and historical subject). *Zgodovinski časopis*, nos. 6–7, 1952–3.

Agrarna prenaseljenost – akutan problem' (Agricultural overpopulation – an acute problem). *Ekonomska politika*, VIII, no. 6, 1953.

'Diskusija o problemu razvoja poljoprivrede' (A discussion of the problem of agricultural development). *Ekonomska politika*, IV, no. 18, 1953.

'Dohodak evropskog agrara' (The income from European agriculture). *Ekonomska politika*, IV, no. 16, 1953.

'Kako trošimo naš dohodak (Odnos visine dohotka i strukture potrošnje)' (How we spend our income (Relationship between incomes and expenditure)). *Robni promet*, nos. 11–12, year 4, 1953.

'Metodologija za obračun narodnog dohotka u 1953' (The method of calculating the national income in 1953). *Zbornik Pravnog fakulteta*, vol. V, 1953.

'Pogovor knjizi Lawrence Ezekiel – *Selo i grad*' (Preface to book by Lawrence Ezekiel – Town and country). Zagreb, 1953.

'Pojam sektora u ekonomici' (Sectors in economics). *Zbornik Pravnog fakulteta*, vol. V, 1953.

'Primjedbe na desetgodišnji program unapređenja poljoprivrede u Hrvatskoj' (Observations on the Croatian Ten-Year Plan for agricultural improvement). *Agronomski glasnik*, no. 10, 1953.

'Stanovništvo FNRJ po nacionalnoj pripadnosti' (The Yugoslav population according to nationality). *Hrvatsko kolo*, 1953.

Review of 'R. Stone, *The role of measurement in economics*'. *Zbornik Pravnog fakulteta*, vol. V, 1953.

Review of 'J. Tinbergen, *Econometrics*'. *Zbornik Pravnog fakulteta*, vol. V, 1953.

'U.N. special study on economic conditions and development in selfgoverning territories'. *Zbornik Pravnog fakulteta*, vol. V, 1953.

'Važnost Rijeke u ekonomskom životu Hrvatske' (The importance of Rijeka in the economic life of Croatia). *Rijeka, Zbornik Matice Hrvatske*, 1953.

'Nekoliko misli o Pravnom fakultetu' (Some reflections concerning the Faculty of
    Law). *Naša zakonitost*, nos. 8–9, 1954.
'Ocjena naturalnog dijela narodnog dohotka' (An appraisal of the in-kind part of
    the national income). *Statistička revija*, nos. 3–4, 1954.
Problemi vanjske trgovine (Foreign trade problems). Published as booklet, 1954.
Review of 'Sirotković, J. *Novi privredni sistem FNRJ*' (J. Sirotković, The new eco-
    nomic system of FPRY). *Zbornik Pravnog fakulteta*, vol. vi, 1954.
'Uloga ekonomista i ekonomska nastava' (The role of economists and economic
    studies). *Ekonomist*, nos. 5–6, 1954.
'Ekonomska historija i marksizam' (Economic history and Marxism). *Ekonomski
    pregled*, no. 5, 1955.
'Još jedna riječ o ekonomskoj povijesti' (Another word about economic history).
    Zgodovinski časopis. 1955.
'Nepoljoprivredna zanimanja u seljačkom gospodarstvu' (Non-agricultural occu-
    pations on peasant holdings), *Statistička revija*, no. 2, 1955.
'Pregled ekonomike poljoprivrede u svijetu' (A survey of world agricultural eco-
    nomics). *Poljoprivreda svijeta*, no. 2, 1955.
'Zanimanje našeg stanovništva' (How our population earns a living). *Ekonomist*,
    nos. 5–6, 1955.
'Dohodak seljačkog gospodarstva u FNRJ i NRH u razdoblju od 1953–1955 g.
    Analitički pregled' (The income of a peasant holding in FPRY and PR Croatia
    1953–1955, an analytical survey), *Ekonomski pregled*, nos. 8–9, 1956.
Review of 'Kostić C. *Seljaci-industrijski radnici*' (C. Kostić, Peasant workers).
    Zbornik Pravnog fakulteta, vol. viii, 1956.
'Osvrt na predmet Ekonomika FNRJ' (Concerning the study of Yugoslav eco-
    nomics). *Zbornik Pravnog fakulteta*, vol. viii, 1956.
'Svjetsko stanovništvo i svjetska proizvodnja' (World population and world pro-
    duction). *Zbornik Pravnog fakulteta*, vol. viii, 1956.
'Uzroci i posljedice razvoja stanovništva' (Causes and results of population
    development). *Zbornik Pravnog fakulteta*, vol. viii, 1956.
Review of 'Bobrowsky, C. *La Yugoslavie socialiste*'. *Zbornik Pravnog fakulteta*, vol. ix,
    1957.
'Distribucija osobnih dohodaka seljačkih obitelji u FNRJ 1955 g.' (Distribution of
    income in a peasant family in FPRY 1955). *Statistička revija*, no. 3, 1957.
'Dobit privredne organizacije' (The gains of economic organizations). *Privredni
    vjesnik*, vi, no. 1, 1957.
'Nekoliko misli o problematici lične potrošnje u FNRJ' (Some thoughts concerning
    the problem of personal spending in FPRY). *Progres*, 1957.
'Podruštvljenje društvenih funkcija seljačke obitelji' (The socialization of the
    functions of the peasant family). *Progres*, 1957.
'Primjedbe na zakonski nacrt o raspodjeli ukupnog prihoda privrednih organi-
    zacija' (Observations concerning the draft law on the distribution of the total
    income of economic organizations). *Informator*, 23.X.19.X. i 2.XI.1957.
'Produktivnost investicija i brzina ekonomskog rasta' (The productivity of invest-
    ment and the rate of economic growth). *Ekonomska politika*, no. 267, 1957.
'Razvoj industrije u Zagrebu' (Industrial development in Zagreb). *Iz starog i novog
    Zagreba*, vol. i, 1957.
'Redukcija obiteljskih funkcija seljačke obitelji u FNRJ' (Reduction of family
    functions in the peasant family in FPRY). *Statistička revija*. 1957.
'Rječna plovidba i veza s Jadranskim morem' (River transport and connections
    with the Adriatic). *Pomorska enciklopedija*. Zagreb, 1957.
'Što očekujemo od naše statističke službe' (What we expect from our statistical
    service). *Ekonomska politika, February* 1957.

Review of 'Vinski, I. *Investicije na području Hrvatske izmedju dva svjetska rata*' (I. Vinski, Investment in Croatia between the two World Wars). *Historijski zbornik.*
1957.
'Zagreb kao multifunkcionalan grad i zanimanja njegovog stanovništva' (Zagreb as a multifunctional city and the occupations of its inhabitants). *Iz starog i novog Zagreba*, vol. I, 1957.
'Ekonomski rast i ekonomski sektori' (Economic growth and economic sectors). *Ekonomski pregled*, nos. 11–12, 1959.
'Ekonomski rast, ekonomski razvoj i planiranje' (Economic growth, economic development and planning). *Ekonomist*, no. 1, 1959.
'Interakcija odluka društvenih planova i odluka privrednih organizacija u FNRJ 1954–1957' (Interaction between social plans and the decisions of economic organizations in FPRY 1954–1957), *Jugoslavensko Statističko društvo*, 1959.
'X. Kongres agrarnih ekonomista u Mysore 1959 g.' (The tenth congress of agricultural economists in Mysore 1959). *Agronomski glasnik*, 1959.
Nastajanje kapitalizma (The development of capitalism). Zagreb, 1959.
'O institucionalnim promjenama u poljoprivredi' (Institutional changes in agriculture). *Medjunarodni problemi*, no. 2, 1959.
'Tipovi mješovite seljačko-radničke obitelji s obzirom na raspodjelu dohotka' (Types of mixed peasant-worker families with reference to distribution of income). *Sociologija*, no. 1, 1959.
'Zagrebački velesajam – barometar privredne situacije' (Zagreb Fair – barometer of the economic situation). *Yugoslav Export*, vol. III, no. 32, 25 July, 1959.
'Impresije s IV. svjetskog sociološkog kongresa u Stresi 1959' (Impressions of the Fourth World Sociological Congress in Stresa 1959). *Zbornik Pravnog fakulteta.*
1960.
'Današnja Industrijska revolucija i naučni rad' (Today's industrial Revolution and the scholar). *Univerziteti danas.* 1960.
'Industrijski odnosi kao predmet sveučilišne nastave' (Industrial relations as a university subject). *Sveučiliš ni vjesnik.* 1960.
'Matematika u sovjetskoj ekonomici' (Mathematics in Soviet economics). *Ekonomska politika.* 1960.
'Osnovna sredstva privrednih organizacija u FNRJ po kotarevima' (Fixed capital of economic organizations in FPRY by districts). *Ekonomski pregled*, no. 6, 1960.
'Planiranje i sociologija' (Planning and sociology). *Ekonomski pregled*, nos. 11–12, 1960.
'Pola stoljeća narodnog bogatstva i narodnog dohotka FNRJ' (Half a century of national wealth and national income). *Historijski zbornik*, vol. xiii, 1960.
'Pravilnosti u promjenama kapitalnog koeficijenta' (Regularity in changes of the capital coefficient). Mimeographed paper in the Economic Seminar of the Law Faculty for their 27th meeting. November, 1960.
'Sinhronizacija industrijskih revolucija' (Synchronization of industrial revolutions). *Medunarodni problemi*, no. 3, 1960.
'Stići i prestići – kvalitet ili kvantitet' (To catch up or to overtake – quality or quantity). *Medunarodni problemi*, no. 3, 1960.
'Ekonomski razvoj FNRJ i petgodišnji planovi (Yugoslav economic development and the Five Year Plans). *Zbornik Pravnog fakulteta*, no. 2, 1961.
'Kapitalni koeficijent, tehnički napredak i teorija praga ekonomskog razvoja' (Capital coefficient, technical progress and the theory of the threshold of economic development). *Ekonomski pregled*, no. 3, 1961.
'Valutni tečajevi kao instrument ekonomskog razvoja' (Exchange rates as instruments of economic development). *Ekonomska fakulteta.* 1961.
'Izbor integracije' (Selective integration). *Medunarodni problemi*, no. 4, 1962.

244 BIBLIOGRAPHY

'Promjene u agraru i poljoprivredna statistika' (Changes in agriculture and agricultural statistics). Mimeographed paper in the Law Faculty library. 1962.
'Tržište i njegove dimenzije' (The market and its dimensions). *Ekonomski pregled*, no. 4, 1962.
'Centralističko, decentralističko i policentrično planiranje' (Centralized, decentralized and polycentric planning). *Ekonomist*, no. 2, 1963. And *Naše teme*, no. 11, 1963.
'Ekonomski razvoj i planiranje' (Economic development and planning). *Ekonomski pregled*, no. 1, 1963.
'Inflacioni dohodak, administrativne cijene i imperfektna konkurencija' (Inflatory income, administrative prices and imperfect competition). *Ekonomist*, XVI, no. 1, 1963, and *Ekonomski pregled*, nos. 3–5, 1963.
'O monocentraičnom i policentričnom planiranju' (On monocentric and polycentric planning). *Ekonomski pregled*, nos. 6–7, 1963.
'Agrarna prenapučenost' (Agrarian overpopulation). *Sociologija sela*, no. 2, 1964.
'Koje su granice primjeni dohodne cijene?' (What are the limits to the application of 'dohodna' price?) *Ekonomist*, no. 4, 1964.
'Međunarodna ekonomska integracija in zunanja trgovina' (International economic integration in internal trade). *Naše gospodarstvo*, no. 10, 1964.
'O planu i sistemu' (Plan and system). *Ekonomska politika*, 14 March 1964, p. 413.
'Porodica u transformaciji' (The family in transition). *Man*, Royal Anthropological Society, 1964.
'Pregled razvoja ekonomike i ekonomske politike Jugoslavije 1918–1940' (Survey of the development of the economy and of economic policy in Yugoslavia 1918–1940). *Historijski pregled*, 1964.
'Problemi planiranja na Istoku i Zapadu' (Problems of planning East and West). *Ekonomski pregled*, nos. 1–2, 1964.
'Tri koncepcije ruralnog planiranja' (Three concepts of rural planning). *Sociologija sela*, nos. 5–6, 1964.
'Urbanistički plan Zagreba' (Zagreb city plan). *Čovjek i prostor*, nos. 133–4, 1964.
'Nekoliko misli o planiranjù povodom teza o planiranjù Saveznog zavoda za privredno planiranje od Aprila 1965' (Some thoughts about planning and some observations on individual aspects of the planning 'Theses' of the Institute of Economics SRH). Mimeographed paper in Law Faculty library. 1965.
'O jadranskoj koncepciji ekonomskog razvoja Jugoslavije' (The Adriatic approach to the economic development of Yugoslavia). *Pomorstvo*, nos. 9–10, 1964, and *Izbor*, no. 3, 1965.
'O odgovornosti planera' (The responsibility of the planners). Meeting of the Society of Economists in Maribor, June 1965; and *Ekonomski tehnički pregled*, no. 4, 1965.
'Plan i privreda' (Plan and the economy). *Ekonomist*, no. 3, 1965.
'Policentrično planiranje i privredni sistem' (Polycentric planning and the economic system). *Ekonomski pregled*, vol. XIV, nos. 6–7, 1965, pp. 469–527.
'Problem regionalne integracije' (Problems of regional integration). *Ekonomski pregled*. 1965.
'Sovjetska planimetrika-ekonomska kibernetika' (Soviet planometrics – economic cybernetics). *Ekonomski pregled*, nos. 9–10, 1965.
'Vasilij Sergejevič Nemčinov – In memoriam' (In memoriam – Vasiliy Sergeyevitch Nemchinov). *Ekonomski pregled*, no. 1, 1965.
'Zaokreti u ekonomskom razvoju i agrarna politika' (Turning points in economic development and agricultural policy). *Ekonomski pregled*, nos. 11–12, 1965.
'Privredna reforma, stabilizacija i technički napredak' (Economic reform, stabilization and technical advance). *Ekonomist*, nos. 1–4, 1966.

'Da li su kompjutori centralizatori ili liberalizatori' (Computers: centralizers or liberators). *Automatika*, 1967.

'Ekonomske promjene u Hrvatskoj izazvane stvaranjem Jugoslavije 1918' (Economic changes in Croatia caused by the creation of Yugoslavia in 1918). *Prilozi za ekonomsku povijest Hrvatske*, vol. 1, 1967.

'Monocentrična cikličnost ili policentrična stabilnost' (Monocentric cycles and polycentric stability). *Ekonomist*, nos. 1–2, 1967.

'Odluke o društvenom planiranju' (Decision-making and social planning). *Informator*, 26. VIII. 1967.

'Planeri i političari' (Planners and politicians). *Zbornik Pravnog fakulteta*, vol. XVIII, no. 1, 1967.

'Poljoprivreda i stručnjaci za političke nauke' (Agriculture and the experts in political sciences). *Sociologija sela*, no. 17, 1967.

'Radna organizacija i rizika za društvene odluke' (Work organizations and the risks of social decisions). *Informator*, 2. IX. 1967.

'Reforma, planiranje i samoupravljanje' (The reform, planning and self-management). *Informator*, 26. VIII. 1967.

'Reforma, planiranje i samoupravljanje' (The reform, planning and self-management). *Teorija in praksa*, nos. 8–9/1967.

'U sistemu društvenog planiranja bitno je da svaka grupa u raspodjeli prima dohohak prema svom radu' (In the system of social planning it is essential that each group take part in the income distribution according to their work). *Informator*, 30 August 1967.

'Uspješnost planiranja ovisi o kvalitetu predviđanja' (The success of planning depends on the quality of forecasting). *Informator*, 23 August 1967.

'Proces podruštvljenja i socijalizam' (The process of socialization and socialism). *Praxis*, 1968.

'Statistika i reforma' (Statistics and the reform). *Ekonomska politika*, no. 827, 1968.

'Tipologija tržišta u SFRJ/Simpozijum o istraživanju tržišta/' (Typology of markets in SFRY) at Symposium for Market Research, 1968.

'Pregledi teorija o agrarnoj prenapučenosti' (A survey of the theory of agricultural overpopulation). *Sociologija sela*, nos. 23–4, 1969.

'Problematika jedinstva privrede u Jugoslaviji' (Problems of economic unity in Yugoslavia). *Zbornik Pravnog fakulteta*, 1970.

ABROAD

'Central European stability and Yugoslavia'. *Journal of Central European Affairs*, vol. 3, no. 1, 1943.

'Excess agricultural population'. *British Association for Advancement of Science, European Agriculture*, 1942. (Also in: Statement on agricultural reconstruction, Bulletin of the Commission to study the organisation of peace. New York 1943).

'Effects of War on Rural Yugoslavia', *Geographical Journal*, no. 1, 1944.

'Cooperation in Yugoslavia', *Yearbook of agricultural co-operation, 1943–1944*. 1946.

'Some problems of sectors in the social accounting of different economic systems', International Association for Research in Income and Wealth, mimeo, no. 4, 1953.

'National income distribution in Yugoslavia', International Association for Research in Income and Wealth, mimeo., 1955.

'La concurrence socialiste en Yugoslavie', *Economie appliqué*, no. 3, 1956.

'Occupational heterogeneity of peasant families in the period of accelerated industrialisation'. *Transactions of the Third World Congress of Sociologists*. 1956.

Review of 'Bobrowsky, C. *La Yugoslavie socialiste du plan quinquennal de 1947 au bilan de 1955'. Kyklos*, 1957.
'Economic growth under centralized and decentralized planning: Yugoslavia – a case study'. Appeared first in *Economic Development and Cultural Change*, no. 9, 1957; later in M. Haldar and R. Ghish (eds.), *Problems of Economic Growth*, New Delhi, 1960; and in Marshall I. Goldman (ed.), *Comparative Economic Systems, A Reader*, New York, 1964.
'Interaction of Macro- and Microeconomic Decisions in Yugoslavia', 1954–1957. Appeared first in mimeo. form, 1957; later in G. Grossman (ed.), *Value and Plan*, Univ. of California Press, 1960.
'Personal income distribution in peasant families in Yugoslavia'. *IARIW*, De Pietersberg. 1957.
'Lack of institutional flexibility in agriculture'. *Proceedings of the International Conference of Agricultural Economists*. Mysore, 1958.
'Economic growth by exonomic sectors'. International Association for Research in Income and Wealth, mimeo., Portorož, 1959.
'The relevance of considerations underlying the awareness of need for industrialisation'. Institute of Social Studies, The Hague, Mediterranean Social Science Research Project, 1959, mimeo.
'A dialogue on planning and freedom'. *Way – Forum*, no. 36, 1960.
'Centralism and planning: the Hungarian experience'. *Kyklos*, vol. 13, 1969.
'Economic growth, development and planning in socialist countries' in E. Nelson (ed.), *Economic Growth*, Univ. of Texas Press, 1960.
'Lack of institutional flexibility in agriculture'. *Proceedings of the Tenth International Conference of Agricultural Economists*, 1960.
'La role du profit dans l'économie socialiste en Yugoslavie', *Economie appliqué*, 1960.
'Die jugoslawische Agrarpolitik in den Jahren 1953–1959', *Zeitschrift für das gesamte Genossenschaftswesen*, 1961.
'Industrialization in Yugoslavia', Institute of Social Studies, The Hague, 1961, mimeo.
'On comparative advantages in agriculture', *Proceedings of the XI International Conference of Agricultural Economists*. 1961.
'The role of socialist business enterprise in Yugoslav economics', Institute of Social Studies, The Hague, 1961, mimeo.
'Produttività del Capitale e lo sviluppo economico'. *Mercurio*, no. 11, 1962.
'The Threshold of Economic Growth'. *Kyklos*, vol. 15, no. 1, 1962.
'A gazdaszagi noveledes kuszobe'. *A gazdaszagi fejledes feltetelei*. Budapest, 1963.
'A grammar for Greek planning'. *Kyklos*, vol. 4, 1963.
'Economic Development and Agriculture', *Proceedings of the XI International Conference of Agricultural Economists*. 1963.
'La soglia dello sviluppo economico', *Svimez*, no. 131, 1963.
Review of 'Michal, Jan M. *Central planning in Czechoslovakia, 1960'. Kyklos*, fasc. 3, 1963.
'On monocentric and polycentric planning'. Institute of social Studies, The Hague, 1963, mimeo.
'Problemas de planificación en Oriente y Occidente'. *Revista de Economia Latinoamericana*. 1963.
'Quelques aspects de la politique des revenus ouvriers en Yugoslavie'. *Economie appliqué*, no. 4, 1963.
'Research on turning points in economic and social development'. Mediterranean Social Science Research Council, 1963, mimeo.
Review of 'Caire, G.I. *Economie Yugoslav'. Kyklos*, no. 4, 1964.

'E la concezione Adriatica che deve prevalere nella nostra economia'. *La voce del popolo*, 1964.

'La planification rurale'. Institut Agronomique Mediterranéen, Montpellier, 1964, mimeo.

'Le passage du seuil de dévélopement économique: condition prealables et effets ultérieurs sur le plan social'. *Revue Internationale des Sciences Sociales*, no. 2. 1964.

Review of 'Nemichinov, V.B. *Ekonomiko matematicheskies metodi i modeli, Moscow, 1962*'. *Kyklos*, no. 3, 1964.

'Problems of socialist agriculture'. *Indian Journal of Agricultural Economics*, nos. 2–4, 1964.

'Przemiany spoleczne i progi razwoju ekonomicznego'. *Studia Sociologiezne*, no. 1, 1964.

'Social preconditions and effects of moving over the threshold of economic development'. *International Social Sciences Journal*, no. 2, 1964.

'Three Concepts of Agricultural Over-population'. *International Explorations of AER Policy*. Iowa Univ. Press, U.S.A., 1964.

'Towards a typology of planning'. Institute of Social Studies, The Hague, 1964, mimeo.

'Attitudes to the Zadruga. The liberation of the Serfs in 1848', in D. Warriner (ed.), *Contrasts in Emerging Societies*, 1965.

'La politica dei reditti dei lavori in Jugoslavia'. *Mercurio*, no. 7, 1965.

'Le planificateur et le politicien'. *Bulletin SEDEIS, Futuribles*, 1965.

'On comparative advantages in agriculture'. *Proceedings of the XII. Conference of the International Association of Agricultural Economists*. 1965.

'The planner and the politician'. *SEDEIS, Futuribles*, 1965, mimeo.

'Yugoslavia: agricultural planning, organization and methods'. Second FAO Course on Agricultural Development Planning. Rome, 1965.

'Comment ne pas developper un pays'. *Le Tiers Monde*, 1966.

'Economics of socialism in a developed country'. *Foreign Affairs*, July 1966. Repr. in *Comparative Economic Systems. Models and Cases*. Ed. M. Bornstein. New York, 1969.

'Turning points in economic development and agricultural policy'. International Economic Papers, I.E.A. 1966. Repr. in Ugo Papi, Charles Nunn (eds.) *Economic Problems of Agriculture in Industrial Societies*, 1969.

'Agriculture and the Political Scientist'. *International Journal of Agrarian Affairs*, 1967.

'Comment on farming as a way of life: Yugoslav peasant attitudes', in J. F. Karcz (ed.), *Soviet and East European Agriculture*. Univ. of California Press, 1967.

'Effects of the First World War on the economics of Yugoslavia. A lesson in disintegration and reintegration'. The Institute of contemporary History, London, 1967.

'Gli elaborati di dati nella programmazione policentrica'. (La scuola in azione. Metanapoli, San Donato, Milanese). Nov. 1967.

'Planer und Politiker'. *Der Staat*, vol. 6, pt. 1, 1967.

'Three Models of Planning in Yugoslavia', in G. Grossman (ed.), *Essays in Socialism and Planning Festschrift in Honor of Carl Landauer*. N.Y., 1970.

'Jugoslawische Stellung in der Weltwirtschaft und das Auslandskapital in Jugoslawien'. *Osteuropa Institut*, 1968.

'The Watershed', P. Lengyel (ed.) in *Approaches to the Science of Socio-economic Development*, 1971.

Index

Accumulation of capital, *see* Capital formation, Investment *and* Primitive accumulation

Administrative socialism (1946–51), 63–4, 67–8, 93, 102–3, 119–20, 122–4, 127–32, 184, 186, 208–10, 218; *see also* Planning, centralized and foreign trade, 145, 153–4, 156, 158; *see also* State monopoly

Agriculture, 30–1, 33, 78, 83, 97–8, 143, 187
  between the wars, 6–7, 11–17, 19
  collectivization, 31, 33, 35, 77, 143, 209
  exports, *see* Exports, of agricultural goods
  nationalization, 23, 24, 33, 35
  prices, 9, 12–14, 20, 54, 116
  wages, 10–11
  see also Peasants *and* Rural exodus

Agricultural and Cooperative Bank, 33
Alcohol distilling, 6, 15
Austria, 3, 6, 8, 165
Austro-Hungarian Empire, 1–4, 19, 20n., 201n., 202n.

Autarchic policy
  abandonment, 60, 150, 165; *see also* Open economy, change to
  between the wars, 3, 6–10, 15, 17–21; *see also* Nationalism
  under socialism, 49, 59, 98, 133, 146–8, 192–6; *see also* Economic independence, policy of

Backwardness, problem of, 60–2, 72, 117–18; *see also* Regional development

Bakarić, V., 48n., 67n., 70–1, 79n.
Balance of payments, 4, 168–9, 213, 215, 226–7, 231
Balance of trade, 162, 166–9, 171, 226
Banat, 15
Banks, 4, 18, 122–3, 125–7, 133, 139, 142, 178, 205–6, 213, 215, 235, 237–8
  nationalization of, 23–4
  Bank and Credit Law of 1965, 220–5
  see also Agricultural and Cooperative Bank, Foreign Trade Bank, National Bank, Post Office

Savings Bank, State Investment Bank, *and* State Mortgage Bank; *also* Credit restriction, Deflationary policy *and* Monetary policy

Belgrade, 4, 201–4, 234
Beslać, Milan, 216
Bićanić, R. (other publications of), 11, 41n., 43n., 107n., 239
Blockade, *see* Economic blockade
Bosnia, 1n., 2, 5, 13, 32n., 76, 86–7, 89, 137–8, 182, 184–5, 190–1, 204
Brioni meeting of 1955, 76
Bulgaria, 1n., 8, 165
Bureaucracy, 47, 50, 67–9, 103, 119, 124–5, 136, 141, 202, 209; *see also* Administrative socialism *and* Planning, centralized
Business Fund, 211–12

California, 15
Capital formation, fixed, 74–6, 85–8, 138, 216–17; *see also* Economic growth, Industrialization *and* Investment

Capital goods
  demand for, 141–2
  exports of, *see* Exports
  imports, *see* Imports
  prices, 78–9
  production, 74, 78, 80, 83, 85, 93

Capital investment, 36–7
  foreign, 37, 176–80, 228–9
Capital, productivity of, *see* Productivity
Capitalism, return to, 38
Carynthia, 1n.
Ceylon, 83n.
Chamber of Nationalities, 137, 205
Clothing, 20n., 56n.
Collectivization of agriculture, *see* Agriculture
COMECON, 171, 173, 174
Communism, building of, 117, 192
Communist Party, 22, 45, 63, 65, 67–9; *see also* League of Communists
Comparative advantage, 60, 81, 98–100, 121, 128, 140, 150–1, 170
Compensation (for nationalization), 26, 28, 32n.
Constitutional Court of Slovenia, 32n.

Constitutional Law of 1953, 29, 31, 44
Constitutions
1946, 28–9, 44, 145
1963, 32, 44, 70, 116, 153, 162, 182, 190; amendments to: (1967) 123, 205; (1968) 223; (1970 and 1971) 231–8
Consumer goods
demand for, 77, 134, 140
exports, see Exports
imports, see Imports
prices, 78–9
production, 78, 80, 83, 85, 93, 135
Consumption
personal, 12, 61, 72, 135, 139–40, 194, 198–9, 202, 210
public, 135–6
Convertibility of dinar, 60, 61, 165, 168, 210, 226–7, 231
Cooperatives, 28–31
Council of Nationalities, 182
Cracow, 5
Craftsmen, 34
Croatia, 1n., 2–6, 8–9, 11n., 12–16, 32n., 68n., 76, 82, 86–7, 89, 99, 112n., 137–8, 184, 185n., 191n., 203n.
Credit restriction, 36, 215
Currency import and export coefficients, 160–1
Currency regulations, 227–8; see also Convertibility of dinar
Customs duties, see Currency import and export coefficients and Import duties
Cybernetics, 197
Czechoslovakia, 6, 8

Dalmatia, 1n., 4, 13
Decentralization, 64–7, 122, 125–7, 155, 174, 177, 184, 198, 236
of industry, 76, 79, 89–90
Decentralized planning, see Planning, decentralized and New economic system
Defence, 18, 61, 73–4, 77, 94, 196
Deflationary policy
1923, 8, 14
post World War II, 114–15, 127, 139, 142, 209; see also Credit restriction
Democratization, 60, 67, 70, 174
Demographic investment rate, 136–7

Demographic pressure, 13, 73, 117; see also Rural exodus
Demonstration effect, 22, 183n., 193–4
Denmark, 15
Depoliticization, 67, 70
Depolo, B., 134n.
Depreciation allowances, 82, 130, 132, 136, 227
Devaluation of dinar, 228, 231
Development, see Economic development, Economic growth and Industrialization
Distribution
of Gross National Product, see Gross National Product
of Gross Social Product, see Gross Social Product
of income, see Income
Dubrovnik, 15
Džeba, Krešo, 216

Economic blockade, 30, 85, 103, 135, 147
Economic development, different concepts of, 21, 192–207
autarchic, 192–6
bicentral, 203–4
domination, 199–202
economistic, 197–9
oligocentric, 204–5
open, 207
polycentric, 205–7, 231–8
technocratic, 196–7
Economic development, regional, see Regional development
Economic growth, 116–44, 229–30
intensive and extensive, 131–2
maximization of, 120–1, 130, 138–42, 196, 198
motivation of policy, 117–19
optimization of, 121–2, 138–42, 196–7
see also Industrialization and Investment
Economic independence, policy of, 73, 91–4, 117–18, 196; see also Autarchic policy
Economic reform (1965), 2, 19, 50–2, 54–5, 60, 67, 70, 81, 119, 121–2, 126–30, 133, 135, 136, 185, 188–9, 208–10, 213–31
effects of, 229–31
and foreign trade, 145, 150, 156–9, 164–76

111–12, 115–16, 122, 131, 134, 141, 142–4, 173, 214
Profit, 37, 55–6, 81, 103, 155, 161
  profit maximization, 128
  profit sharing, 47, 56, 105–7, 129
  profitability, criterion of, 75, 122, 126, 128, 154
Property
  cooperative, 28–31; see also Collectivization
  private, 28–9, 31, 38–40
  relations, changes in, 22–40
  socialist, 32, 67
  state, 28–9, 31
Protection, see Autarchic policy, Export and Import duties

Railways, 24–5, 75, 131
Ranković, Alexander, 68n., 202n.
Raw materials
  exports, see Exports
  imports, see Imports
  prices, see Prices
  production, 78–9, 83
Real income, see Income, real
Real wages, see Wages, real
Reforms, see Economic reform and Land reform
Regional development, 3–4, 20, 85–6, 87, 89, 137–8
  motivation for, 182–4
  policies, 181–91
Reparations (after World War II), 27n.
Rijeka, 5
Romania, 8, 122n.
Rural exodus, 11, 90, 114, 141, 143

Salonika, 5
Sandjak, 2
Savić, M., 7n., 18–19
Saving-wage-bill-rate system, 103–5
Savings, 77, 103–5, 119, 138, 199
Second jobs, 102, 114, 143
Sequestration, 24–5, 30
Serbia, 1–4, 13, 16, 76, 82, 86–7, 89, 112n., 137–8, 184, 191, 194n., 201n., 202, 204
Serbian Radical Party, 1n., 19
Shipping, 24
Skupština, Savezna Narodna, 8on.
Slavonia, 4–5
Slovakia, 15
Slovenai, 2, 4, 32n., 76, 82, 86–7, 89,

112n., 137–8, 184, 191n., 201, 203n., 204
Social control of economic system, 63–71.
Social integration, 47
Social organization sector, 32
Socialism,
  administrative, see Administrative socialism and Planning, centralized
  building of, 22–40, 117–20, 128, 192
Socialist Alliance, 70
Socialist sector
  building of, 60–2, 120–1; see also Economic growth
  formation of, 22–40
Soviet Union, see Union of Soviet Socialist Republics
Stabilization of economy, 52, 55, 61, 62, 139
Stajić, S., 6on.
Stalin, 77, 94, 103, 135, 195, 200; see also Economic blockade
Standard of living, 8–10, 61–2, 77, 117; see also Wages, real
State budget, 18, 56, 75, 77, 103–4, 120, 123–4, 130, 136, 162, 164, 190–1, 219–20, 232, 236
State Investment Bank, 66, 123–4, 153
State monopoly of foreign trade
  between the wars, 18n., 25
  under administrative socialism, 145–6, 151–4, 156–7, 164, 210
State Mortgage Bank, 7, 18n., 25
State ownership, see Nationalization and Socialist sector
State sector, 23, 25, 31–2
Stipetić, V., 5n.
Stojadinović, M. (Minister of Finance in 1923), 14
Styria, 1n., 15
Sukijasović, L. M., 229n.
Switzerland, 15

Taxation, 14–15, 49, 56, 79, 105, 111, 129–30, 140, 210, 212–13, 217–19, 228, 233–4, 236–8
  turnover tax, 56, 129, 210, 212–14, 218
Technical progress, 40, 57, 61, 62, 81–2, 86, 88, 117–19, 141–2, 151, 159, 174, 177
Tito, Marshal, 69n., 187n.